of
Legal

BUSINESS LAW GUIDE TO SPAIN

BUSINESS LAW GUIDE to SPAIN

Fabregat & Bermejo

Madrid
Barcelona
Bilbao
Valencia
Marbella
*
New York

CCH Editions Limited

TAX, BUSINESS AND LAW PUBLISHERS

Published by CCH Editions Limited
Telford Road, Bicester, Oxfordshire OX6 0XD
Tel. (0869) 253300, Facsimile (0869) 245814.
DX: 40162 Bicester

USA Commerce Clearing House Inc., Chicago, Illinois.
CANADA CCH Canadian Limited, Toronto, Ontario.
AUSTRALIA CCH Australia Limited, North Ryde, NSW.
NEW ZEALAND Commerce Clearing House (NZ), Auckland.
SINGAPORE CCH Asia Limited.

This publication is designed to provide accurate and authoritative information in regard to the subject-matter covered. It is sold with the understanding that the publisher is not engaged in rendering legal or other professional services. If legal advice or other expert assistance is required, the services of a competent professional person should be sought.

British Library Cataloguing in Publication Data
Business law guide to Spain.
1. Spain. Commercial law
I. Fabregat & Bermejo.
344.6067

ISBN 0 86325 227 3

Typeset in the United Kingdom by Wessex Typesetters
(Division of The Eastern Press Ltd).
Printed in the United Kingdom by Hartnolls Ltd.

Preface

In this period of rapid and significant change in Spain, we have tried to meet the challenge of capturing not only the letter of Spanish law, but also its spirit. Spain is experiencing the exhilarating effects as well as the difficulties that accompany rapid economic growth. The 'boom' in foreign and domestic investment and the process of harmonising Spanish law with EEC regulations has modernised the legal framework for doing business in Spain.

The following chapters are intended to offer the reader a practical guide to the legal aspects of doing business in Spain by setting out the law and supplementing it with practical information based on knowledge and experience. Where possible we have used terminology familiar to both American and British readers.

I would like to take the opportunity to thank the lawyers and staff of the Madrid office who contributed to this book, and Patricia Racicot Manso in New York, who worked closely with them. I also gratefully acknowledge the collaboration of the London law firm, Blyth Dutton, in the production of the English version of this book.

F. Javier Fabregat
April 1990

About the Publisher

CCH Editions Limited is part of a world-wide group of companies that specialises in tax, business and law publishing. The group produces a wide range of books and reporting services for the accounting, business and legal professions. The Oxfordshire premises are the centre for all UK and European operations.

All CCH publications are designed to provide practical, authoritative references and useful guides, and are written by CCH's highly qualified and experienced editorial team and specialist outside authors.

CCH Editions Limited publish bound books and loose-leaf reporting services for the United Kingdom and other European countries, as well as distributing the publications of the overseas affiliate companies.

About the Authors*

The law firm of Fabregat & Bermejo is a law firm of over 50 lawyers, which specialises in all aspects of general commercial and international legal work, serving both Spanish and international clients.

In preparing the English version, the authors have looked to Jennifer Lees and the London law firm of Blyth Dutton to relieve them from the additional time demands required to adapt the material to English editorial language and style. Blyth Dutton is a firm specialising in company and commercial work, with strong emphasis on corporate finance and commercial property.

* General Editor: Patricia Racicot Manso, JD, New York.
Assistant Editor: Jennifer Lees, MA (Hons), Solicitor, London.

Contents

1 Democratic Framework of Spain

POLITICAL SYSTEM

¶101 The Constitution

The Spanish Constitution of 1978 is Spain's supreme body of law in both in form and substance. The Constitution sets out the economic model which Spain has adopted; that of a free market economy based on private enterprise. The Constitution also provides that the State has the power to implement economic policy, a power which may be exercised to a greater or lesser extent by the political party in power, provided that the fundamental principles of a free market economy are respected.

¶102 Political organisation

The form of government adopted by the Constitution is a parliamentary monarchy. The King is the official head of state and Spain is officially known as the Kingdom of Spain (*Reino de España*) or the State of Spain (*Estado de España*). The Constitution also creates and empowers the three branches of government – executive, legislative and judicial – each of which serves as a check on the others.

(1) Head of State

The Crown is the symbol of the State's unity. It is represented by Juan Carlos I de Borbon and his successors. The power of the King is limited by the Constitution, and his actions must be endorsed by the President of the Government or other competent minister.

(2) Executive branch

The Government is the political direction of the State. The central government is made up of the President (prime minister), the Vice-president(s), and the ministers. The cabinet of advisers to the President is called the Council of Ministers (*Consejo de Ministros*). The President leads and co-ordinates the action of the Government, answering directly for its actions. The President is usually the leader of the majority party in Parliament and sets out the party's political programme. He is proposed by the King and elected by his parliamentary peers.

The Constitution itself lays down the precepts that the Government should observe, stating that it should 'serve the public interest with objectivity and act in accordance with the principles of efficacy, hierarchy, decentralisation, deconcentration and co-ordination, submitting fully to the law'. Within the system set up by the Constitution, the actions taken by the Government are subject to the approval of the Parliament, not of the King.

(3) Legislative branch

The Parliament (*Parlamento* or *Cortes Generales*) is the legislative branch. It is divided into two chambers, the Congress of Deputies (*el Congreso de los Diputados*) and the Senate (*el Senado*), and it is the basic institution of the parliamentary monarchy.

Members of Parliament are elected through universal, free, equal, direct and secret suffrage. They serve for a term of four years, pursuant to a system of proportional representation according to the percentage of votes obtained by each political party. The main function of Parliament is to draft laws and to act as a check on the Government. The Constitution provides for Parliament to oust the President and his Government through a motion of censure or demonstrate its support of the Government through a vote of confidence. All members of Parliament enjoy complete parliamentary immunity.

(4) Judicial branch

The judiciary enjoys total independence in respect of the other branches of the State. Judges cannot be removed, suspended, transferred or retired for reasons other than those laid down by law. The judges and the courts exercise their powers in all proceedings according to the rules of jurisdiction and judicial procedure.

The judiciary is governed by the Chief Judiciary Council (*Consejo General del Poder Judicial*), presided over by the President of the Supreme Court. It is made up of 20 other members, each appointed for a term of five years, of which 12 come from different levels of the judiciary and four are appointed by each of the Congress of Deputies and the Senate.

(a) *Constitutional Court*. The Constitutional Court is the highest authority on the interpretation of the Constitution. It receives on appeal questions of unconstitutional laws or regulations and is the ultimate guarantor of the Constitution throughout the legal system. In addition to the protection afforded by the courts, the Constitutional Court can also be called upon to make exceptional reviews of matters brought to it where there has been a violation of fundamental rights and freedoms provided by the Constitution (*recursos de amparo*).

Finally, the Constitutional Court resolves jurisdictional conflicts between the State and the autonomous regions or among the autonomous regions. The central government may challenge in court the laws and decisions of the autonomous regions, which remain suspended until the Constitutional Court decides the issue.

(b) *Ombudsman*. The Public Defender (*Defensor del Pueblo*) is a position created by the Constitution on the Swedish model. The basic duty of the Ombudsman is to act as a check on the Government and its administration at all levels in defence of the rights of all citizens. The Ombudsman reports to Parliament annually. The Ombudsman may not intervene in judicial matters.

¶103 Political divisions

Spain is a regional unified State and is divided into 17 autonomous regions (*comunidades autónomas*). For historical reasons, some of them – namely Catalonia, the Basque Country, Galicia and Andalusia – maintain a high level of political autonomy. The others are not so much politically autonomous as administratively decentralised.

The Constitution vests certain powers, such as international relations and defence, exclusively in the State, allowing the autonomous regions to legislate in other matters. For example, economic development is an area in which the central government and the autonomous regions play a role, and in a subsequent chapter incentives offered at both levels are discussed.

Each autonomous region has its own government, with a president and cabinet, its own courts and its own legislative assembly (*asamblea legislativa*).

Local government (*administración local*) is comprised of municipalities governed by a mayor (*alcalde*) and councillors (*consejales*). Groups of municipalities form the provinces, governed by provincial delegations (*diputaciones provinciales*). There are 50 provinces in Spain.

LEGAL SYSTEM

¶104 The civil law system

The Spanish legal system is a civil law system, as opposed to the Anglo-Saxon common law system. Law is never created by court decisions (*jurisprudencia*), but by codified legislation and custom applied by the courts. Although Supreme Court decisions carry great weight in the application and interpretation of the law, they are only complementary to it.

All legal norms are interpreted in accordance with the Civil Code, taking into account the time, meaning of the language employed (*sentido propio*), context, historic and legislative antecedents, the social realities of the time and their spirit and purpose.

Equity must be taken into consideration as a factor when applying legal norms, but court judgments may only rely exclusively on it if expressly permitted by law.

Spain became a member of the European Economic Community (EEC) on 1 January 1986 by signing the Accession Agreement. This means that EEC law takes precedence over Spanish internal law and, although Spain has been allowed time to adapt its laws to EEC regulations, she is a full member of the EEC.

¶105 Sources of law

According to the preamble of the Spanish Civil Code, sources of Spanish law are legislation, custom, and general principles of law.

(1) Law

Laws are express legal rules which are normally published in the Official State Bulletin (*Boletín Oficial del Estado* or BOE) 20 days before coming into force. They can only be repealed expressly by subsequent legislation and to the extent that the old law is incompatible with the new law. Laws may not be applied retroactively, unless it is expressly provided otherwise. In any event, the Constitution guarantees that any penalties or other unfavourable or restrictive provisions affecting individual rights may not be applied retroactively.

The Spanish legal system is hierarchical, which means laws have a different rank and order, and provisions of law with a lower status which conflict with those of higher status are invalid.

(a) *Organic laws*. Apart from the Constitution, the highest form of law is found in the organic laws (*leyes orgánicas*), which relate to fundamental civil rights and liberties, the approval of the charter of the autonomous regions, the electoral system, and other matters expressly laid down by the Constitution. An absolute majority of Congress is necessary for the approval, amendment or substitution of an organic law.

(b) *Ordinary laws* (*leyes ordinarias*). These laws are debated and approved by Parliament in accordance with the internal procedural rules of the Congress of Deputies and Senate.

(c) *Decree-laws* (*decretos-leyes*). These laws have the same status as ordinary laws and are provisional laws issued by the executive branch in special or urgent cases. They must be ratified by the Congress of Deputies within 20 days.

(d) *Legislative decrees* (*decretos legislativos*). The Spanish Parliament may delegate to the Government the power to issue executive orders on particular matters, which have the status of law. This is done by means of a basic law (*ley de bases*) if it involves drafting articled texts, or by means of an ordinary law if it is to consolidate a number of legal texts into one. Executive orders issued under this delegated authority are called legislative decrees and have the status of an ordinary law.

(e) *Decrees, orders and resolutions*. Of lower status are all other executive orders and regulations issued by the ministries and subordinate administrative agencies (public administration), called decrees (*decretos*), ministerial orders (*órdenes ministeriales*) and resolutions (*resoluciones*).

(f) *International treaties*. International agreements are not directly applicable internally in Spain until they are ratified by Parliament and published in the BOE.

(g) *Autonomous regions*. The autonomous regions may also legislate within their jurisdiction. Through the legislative assembly and autonomous governments, they may pass laws having a similar status as those passed by central government, although applicable only within the respective region. The autonomous regions do not have organic laws.

(2) Custom

Custom is only applied if no applicable law exists, provided that it is not immoral or contrary to public order. Its existence must be proved.

(3) General principles of law

The general principles of law apply in default of applicable law or custom, although their main function is to offer guidance on the application of law. These principles include:

- *freedom to contract*. Parties may enter into private agreements, covenants and conditions freely, as long as they are not contrary to law or public order and are not immoral;
- *good faith* (*buena fe*). This means that one may not abuse the law or exercise it in an anti-social manner. If, in the exercise of a legal right, one commits an act or omission that intentionally exceeds the bounds of

normality and thereby causes injury to another, then the injured party has the right to compensation (*indemnización*);

- *freedom of form*. This means that only in exceptional cases, such as mortgages and powers of attorney, is a specific form required in private contracts.

¶106 Notaries

No discussion of the Spanish legal system would be complete without the mention of the role of the notary. The function of the notary in Spain is very different from that of the English or American notary public. The Spanish notary's main function is to make public deeds which record particular legal acts, such as the transfer of real estate and the grant of powers of attorney.

Most legal transactions in Spain require the intervention of a notary, since a deed must be notarised in order to be used as evidence in court or to be submitted for registration at official registries. The notary interprets the will of the parties, puts it into legal form, drafts the appropriate documents and attests to their authenticity. He retains the original copies of such documents and produces copies of extracts to those requesting them.

Admission to the profession is regulated by the State. Notaries must be law graduates (*licenciados en derecho*) and they must pass a highly competitive examination, held annually, in order to be awarded one of the limited number of posts available. Appointments are made within a specific area, and a notary may not practise outside the district to which he is assigned.

¶107 Registries

Spain operates a registry system, whereby certain acts must be notarised and registered at a Public Registry in order to have legal effect. The Registry issues a public certificate of registration which is prima facie evidence and prevails over all unregistered documents relating to the same act or transaction.

(1) Public registries

There are three public registries in Spain:

(a) The Land Registry (*Registro de la Propiedad*) is where rights over real property are registered. Each sale of real property, and any mortgages, liens or other encumbrances relating thereto, must be duly registered. There is a Land Registry in most major provincial capitals or municipalities.

(b) The Commercial Registry (*Registro Mercantil*) is where legally significant information relating to companies and businesses must be registered. There is a central Commercial Registry in Madrid and others in most provincial capitals.

(c) The Civil Registry (*Registro Civil*) is where personal particulars of Spanish nationals are registered, e.g. births, deaths and marriages. Most major municipalities keep a civil registry.

Registrars of public registries must be law graduates and must have passed a special examination. A registrar may not hold any other public office in the province or municipality where he works, and upon taking up office he must place a bond to cover any liability he may incur in the course of his duties.

Registrars are responsible to the Ministry of Justice, and under the direct supervision of the General Directorate of Registries and Notarial Matters (*Dirección General de Registros y el Notariado*), to which registrars must submit an annual report of their activities.

(2) Administrative registries

Administrative registries are kept by central government ministries, both in Madrid and in other provincial capitals, as necessary. There are many different kinds of registries, examples being:

(a) the Industrial Property Registry, where trade marks, patents, trade names, and titles of establishment are registered;

(b) the Intellectual Property Registry, where all intellectual property rights and rights over original literary, artistic and scientific works are registered; and

(c) the Foreign Investments Registry, where details of all foreign investments are registered. This registry is kept by the General Directorate of Foreign Transactions (*Dirección General de Transacciones Exteriores* or DGTE), under the auspices of the Ministry of Economy and Finance.

2 Exchange Control and Foreign Investment

EXCHANGE CONTROL SYSTEM

¶201 Source of law

Any company or individual intending to do business in Spain must be familiar with the Spanish laws and regulations regarding exchange control and foreign investment. These consist of a set of administrative controls imposed by the Spanish government, which are designed to regulate transactions of any nature between residents and non-residents which, directly or indirectly, involve payments made into or out of Spain. Spain has been undergoing a gradual process of deregulation, largely due to its recent entry into the EEC, and, although this process is expected to continue, it is not anticipated that Spanish exchange control regulations will be abolished in the near future, at least with respect to non-EEC countries.

The most important legislation in this area is found in the 1979 Exchange Control Law, the 1980 Royal Decree concerning exchange control regulations, and the 1983 Law concerning monetary offences. By looking at how these laws are applied, together with EEC regulations which are geared towards the free flow of capital, a clear picture of the current exchange control system emerges.

¶202 Residents and non-residents

The concepts of residency and non-residency are of particular importance to the Spanish exchange control system. However, it should be noted that the following definitions of 'resident' and 'non-resident' apply only within the context of exchange control, and those terms may have a different meaning in other areas of the law.

(1) Residents

For exchange control purposes, residents are individuals who have their domicile or main residence in Spain. This includes foreign individuals legally resident in Spain, which means persons in possession of a residence permit or other public document authorising residence, issued by the Ministry of the Interior. Spanish citizens are presumed to be residents, unless proven otherwise. Spanish citizens residing abroad are deemed to be residents in respect of assets and income earned in Spain prior to taking up residence outside Spain.

A company incorporated in Spain and whose registered office is in Spain is deemed to be resident for exchange control purposes. A company whose registered office is abroad is deemed to be non-resident, although its branches or representative offices set up in Spain pursuant to Spanish law are deemed to be resident. This means that the assets of such a foreign company with branches or offices set up in Spain may receive both resident and non-resident treatment for exchange control purposes, since part of its assets are allocated to that branch or office. Unless a branch or representative office is established in Spain pursuant to Spanish law, it will be deemed to be non-resident and be subject to all administrative requirements applicable to non-resident companies.

(2) Non-residents

For exchange control purposes, Spanish individuals residing abroad are deemed to be non-resident. Spanish individuals residing in Spain are deemed to be non-residents with regard to their assets acquired outside Spain while residing abroad, but not in respect of income earned on such assets. Foreign individuals residing in Spain are treated as non-residents in respect of their assets and income earned outside Spain prior to taking up residence in Spain.

Branches and representative offices abroad of Spanish companies are deemed to be non-resident.

¶203 Implementation of the controls

Most transactions involving payments into or out of Spain are subject to some kind of control, even though in many cases this may be a formality. Depending on the nature of a particular transaction, it will need prior authorisation or prior verification from one of the following agencies. The terms 'prior authorisation' and 'prior verification' are defined in (2) below.

(1) Government agencies

Exchange control regulations apply both to the transaction itself and to payments arising from the transaction. The two stages are treated separately. An example illustrating this would be a company making a capital investment by setting up an office or branch in Spain. Both the original investment and the funds subsequently used to maintain it are subject to the same kind of control.

The Ministry of Economy and Finance supervises and regulates the exchange control system through the General Directorate of Foreign Transactions (DGTE or *Dirección General de Transacciones Exteriores*), the Bank of Spain and authorised banks (*entidades delegadas*).

(a) *DGTE.* The DGTE's main function is to authorise transactions effected by Spanish residents from which payments in pesetas or foreign currency arise. This includes credit facilities linked to imports and exports. Financial loans or credit facilities are supervised by the Bank of Spain. The DGTE also supervises deposits made in pesetas in bank accounts held in Spain by foreigners.

(b) *Bank of Spain.* The Bank of Spain is Spain's central bank. Its main functions are to centralise foreign and domestic currency reserves, make external payments, authorise commercial loans, authorise the opening of foreign bank accounts, accept and grant foreign currency loans, and publish the official daily exchange rates.

(c) *Authorised banks.* Some exchange control functions are delegated to the international departments of authorised banks, savings banks, and certain other lending institutions operating in Spain. Authorised banks have the authority to sell or buy foreign currency within certain limits laid down by exchange control regulations. They may also maintain accounts for non-residents, through which payments in and out of Spain can be made.

(2) Types of controls

(a) Prior authorisation

The basic presumption is that transactions between residents and non-residents involving payments into and out of Spain are subject to prior authorisation. Many types of transactions, however, have been exempted, with the result that almost all non-commercial transactions and a substantial number of financial and commercial transactions do not need prior authorisation. In order to obtain prior authorisation an application in the form of a report should be made to the DGTE, giving information such as the identity of the buyer and the seller, the subject matter of the transaction, the consideration to be paid, method of payment, and any other information which might be useful to the DGTE to process the application. The DGTE must grant or refuse the application, or request additional information within 60 days of the filing of the application.

(b) Prior verification

Even if payments are exempted from prior authorisation, they are usually subject to prior verification. The applicant may go personally to the DGTE or to an authorised bank. The application should be made on Form TE-13L, giving basic information concerning the transaction and the parties. Once the application is made, the DGTE has 30 days in which to grant verification, refuse it, or request additional information. If, after 30 days have elapsed, the applicant has received no notification from the DGTE, the transaction is deemed to have been approved.

Verification is mainly required for statistical purposes and as a check that certain minimum requirements are met. If such requirements are met, verification is usually a formality.

(c) Exemptions

Certain payments into and out of Spain are exempted from any kind of control because of their insignificant effect on the Spanish economy. This would include normal day-to-day living expenses paid in cash, payments made by residents to non-residents for services rendered, and rental payments of less than 500,000 pesetas per annum.

¶204 Enforcement

The Exchange Control Commission has authority, through its various administrative bodies, to detect and investigate monetary offences and administrative violations. It also co-ordinates other agencies involved in exchange control and offers assistance to the judiciary.

(1) Monetary offences

Certain transactions constitute a monetary offence if the act or omission involves more than two million pesetas and is performed without the necessary administrative authorisation or with unlawfully-obtained authorisation. Below are some typical examples of monetary offences:

(a) exporting or importing pesetas, foreign currency, or any payment order, deposit or transfer instrument in pesetas or foreign currency;

(b) the purchase by residents of real or personal property outside Spain or bearer securities issued abroad, the granting or taking out of loans or credit facilities by a resident from a non-resident, or guaranteeing any obligation of a resident to a non-resident;

(c) payments between residents and non-residents or between residents acting on behalf of non-residents, unless exempted from prior authorisation;

(d) residents holding foreign currency for over 15 days from the date of receipt in Spain or upon return to Spain;

(e) obtaining foreign currency fraudulently or unlawfully, or using legally-acquired foreign currency for an unauthorised purpose; or

(f) negligent acts of directors, managers or employees of banks facilitating any of the above offences.

The Spanish National Court deals with most monetary offences, except those which are turned over to the central criminal courts. Depending on the amount of money involved, penalties for monetary offences are usually short-term imprisonment and a fine. Long-term imprisonment may be imposed if offences are committed by directors or officers of companies, or by institutions particularly well-placed to commit such offences, such as multi-national companies, banks, and companies involved in international trade.

(2) Administrative violations

Administrative violations are classified as major or minor, depending on the amount involved and whether a prior authorisation was either not obtained or there is non-compliance with other provisions of law.

(a) Major violations

These include violations which meet the same criteria as monetary offences but involve less than two million pesetas, and negligent acts or omissions of directors, managers or employees of banks who facilitate a major or minor administrative violation. In addition, persons entering into any of the following transactions without prior authorisation commit a major administrative violation which may be subject to a fine amounting to half the amount of the transaction or, in some cases, the seizure of the pesetas or foreign currency involved:

(i) residents who export Spanish fixed- or variable rate bearer securities, or non-residents who purchase bearer securities with other than foreign assets;

(ii) residents who purchase or otherwise acquire tangible or intangible goods or rights outside Spain, involving less than two million pesetas, or who transfer such assets or rights, except by reason of death or pursuant to the regulations governing Spanish investments abroad;

(iii) non-residents who acquire tangible or intangible goods or rights owned by residents in Spain, except by reason of death or pursuant to the regulations governing foreign investments in Spain;

(iv) non-residents who guarantee the obligations of a resident, or residents who guarantee obligations arising between non-residents or between residents and non-residents;

(v) residents who possess bonds or payment orders outside Spain in pesetas or foreign currency.

(b) Minor violations

A minor administrative violation is any act or omission which does not comply with exchange control regulations and which is neither a monetary offence nor a major administrative violation. The penalty is a fine of at least 10,000 pesetas or half the amount of the transaction or, in some cases, the seizure of the pesetas or foreign currency involved.

¶205 Bank accounts and foreign currency

(1) Bank accounts held by residents

Spanish residents may only hold an account in ordinary pesetas, which means that the money in their account may not be taken out of Spain or converted into foreign currency. In order to do that they must hold convertible pesetas, for which prior authorisation is needed.

Non-residents who become residents may hold convertible pesetas as part of their assets abroad (see 2(a) below).

(2) Bank accounts held by non-residents

There are two types of bank accounts which may be opened by non-residents in banks in Spain: convertible peseta accounts and ordinary peseta accounts.

(a) Convertible peseta accounts

In a convertible peseta account, pesetas may be freely converted into foreign currency. These accounts may be used to receive funds from abroad which can be used without restriction by the account-holder or his nominee. As a general rule, only non-residents may open this type of bank account; residents require prior authorisation from the DGTE to do so. Upon acquiring Spanish residency, non-residents may retain their convertible peseta accounts as a part of their assets abroad, and the account-holder is deemed to be a non-resident in respect of those accounts. Nevertheless, the DGTE must be informed within one year of the change of residency status.

A non-resident can deposit into this kind of account monies received from residents which are transferable abroad (either because they are authorised or exempted under exchange control laws), pesetas or foreign currency exchanged in Spain, transfers from other authorised Spanish banks or the Bank of Spain, and accrued interest on the convertible peseta account itself.

A non-resident may also use this type of account to withdraw, authorise or extend payments to residents, in pesetas or foreign currency exchanged in Spain, of sums to be transferred to other authorised Spanish banks or the Bank of Spain.

(b) Ordinary peseta accounts for foreigners

This type of ordinary peseta account may only be held by non-residents; if residency status is changed to that of a resident, the account is automatically converted into an ordinary account for residents. An overdraft balance is not permitted and earned interest is treated in the same way as for resident accounts, without any special restrictions. As a general rule, money held in ordinary peseta accounts is not convertible. Only the interest on the sums realised from foreign investments temporarily held in the account and other interest accruing on the account may be transferred abroad.

Deposits may be made without giving proof of the origin of the funds. However, this does not exempt the account-holder from other exchange control regulations in respect of such funds. He may deposit pesetas obtained in compliance with exchange control regulations. This would include rental payments from residents to non-residents in respect of real property in Spain of up to 500,000 pesetas per annum, transfers from convertible or ordinary peseta accounts, or interest on the sums realised from foreign investments made with foreign capital which have been placed in the account on a temporary basis.

Withdrawals from this type of account may be made to pay for normal living expenses in Spain, to transfer sums to other foreign accounts in ordinary pesetas, and to make payments related to foreign investments in Spain.

(3) Foreign currency

Spanish banks may only take foreign currency deposits for accounts held by non-residents opened with the prior authorisation of the Bank of Spain. Interest rates on these accounts are not controlled. Spanish banks may otherwise deal in foreign currency on a temporary basis in relation to export payments, transfers from abroad, foreign investments in Spain, or as otherwise permitted by law.

Currently the European Currency Unit (ECU) and 19 foreign currencies are quoted on the Spanish market:

- French Franc
- British Pound
- US Dollar
- Canadian Dollar
- West German Mark

- Swiss Franc
- Belgian Franc
- Dutch Guilder
- Portuguese Escudo
- Swedish Krona
- Norwegian Krone
- Danish Krone
- Italian Lira
- Austrian Schilling
- Finish Markka
- Japanese Yen
- Irish Pound
- Australian Dollar
- Greek Drachma.

Any currency not included in the above list must be indirectly converted through a quoted currency.

Spanish residents must sell any foreign currency brought into Spain within 15 days at the official exchange rate, or obtain special permission from the DGTE to keep it. The main exception to this rule is foreign currency acquired during a period of non-residency.

TRANSACTIONS

¶206 Imports and exports

(1) Imports

The general rule is that prior verification is needed for imports, unless prior authorisation is expressly required. The terms of the transaction and the circumstances of the lender and the borrower determine whether a transaction requires prior authorisation or prior verification.

(a) *Prior authorisation.* The following transactions require prior authorisation from the DGTE: credit facilities or loans for terms of less than one year, if not on standard terms; credit facilities or loans granted by a non-EEC foreign supplier for terms of between one and five years, or if other than standard terms apply; credit facilities or loans for terms of over five years; credit facilities or loans granted by a finance company not resident in the EEC.

(b) *Prior verification.* This is required from the DGTE for credit facilities or loans granted by a finance company resident in the EEC. Prior verification from an authorised bank is required for credit facilities or loans given by a foreign supplier for terms of one to five years if that supplier is an EEC resident.

(2) Exports

Exports from Spain and related payments generally require prior verification only, unless otherwise stated. The resident exporter in Spain must convert payments received from abroad into pesetas. They must be received by authorised Spanish banks on behalf of the Spanish resident and be fully documented, with all relevant data (amount, currency, etc.) contained in the export documents.

(a) *Prior authorisation.* The following transactions require prior authorisation from the DGTE: credit facilities or loans for terms of less than one year, if not on standard terms; credit facilities or loans to a non-EEC resident by a Spanish finance company; and any credit facilities or loans granted for a term of over five years.

(b) *Prior verification.* This is required from the DGTE for credit facilities or loans for terms of less than one year, if on standard terms; credit facilities or loans for terms of between one and five years granted to a non-EEC resident, or not on standard terms; and any loan made by a Spanish finance company to an EEC resident. Prior verification is required from an authorised bank for credit facilities or loans for terms of between one and five years granted to an EEC resident, if on standard terms.

¶207 Invisible transactions

The term 'invisible transactions' is commonly used to denote those transactions that do not involve tangible goods, such as services or an exchange of money. In general, invisible transactions affected by exchange control are services performed by residents for non-residents or vice versa, and the transfer of monies in and out of Spain in payment therefor.

(1) EEC regulations

As a general rule, if a transaction is deregulated under EEC regulations, member States are obliged to deregulate payments and related transfers. The EEC has a non-discrimination policy with regard to employment, salaries and working conditions in member States. Employment-related transactions are completely deregulated, but member States may impose their own restrictions on related payments or transfers. EEC citizens have an unfettered right to engage in activities such as the setting up, incorporation, and management of companies, agencies or branches throughout the EEC. There is a residual category of invisible transactions not covered by any of the above which are deregulated, but allow individual member States to specify the degree of verification necessary.

(2) Spanish regulations

Within the limits of EEC regulations, Spanish exchange control regulations classify invisible transactions as:

(a) *deregulated*, i.e. those transactions, related payments and transfers which require prior verification by the DGTE; and

(b) *regulated*, i.e. those transactions, related payments and transfers which require prior authorisation by the DGTE.

As a general rule, transfers of less than one million pesetas into and out of Spain may be made if the transferor undertakes to furnish the supporting documents to the Spanish bank effecting the transaction within three months of the transfer being made.

For travel purposes, up to 100,000 pesetas and the equivalent of 350,000 pesetas in foreign currency may be taken out of Spain by residents without authorisation. Prior authorisation by the DGTE is required to purchase larger amounts of foreign currency. Prior verification by the DGTE is required before Spanish banks can make transfers of money abroad for travelling purposes. There is, however, no limit on the use of credit cards. The Government has the right to ask for proof of travel expenses claimed, and therefore it is advisable to keep relevant receipts for at least three years. If such proof cannot be shown, expenses are estimated at 30,000 pesetas per day.

On the other hand, non-residents may bring an unlimited amount of pesetas and foreign currency into Spain. If the money is declared at customs when entering Spain, it may also be taken out of Spain again in its entirety. If not, only 500,000 pesetas worth of currency can be taken out of Spain. Any excess will be retained by customs and turned over to the Government.

Travel agencies, airline and shipping companies holding a special government licence enjoy special treatment, giving them maximum flexibility.

¶208 Technology

Technical assistance may be defined as services rendered in connection with the distribution of goods and services, performed within a given period of time. These may consist of expert advice, the preparation of technical plans and designs, manufacturing supervision, market studies or personnel training. This broad definition also includes the transfer of technology, the transfer of patented and/or secret technical knowledge, and the acquisition of patents, designs, trade marks and copyrights.

(1) Payments

Transactions involving technical assistance are deregulated within the EEC. There are no restrictions on payments related to such transactions between citizens or residents of member States.

Under Spanish law, transactions involving the transfer of technology and foreign technical assistance must have prior verification. This is obtained by applying to the DGTE on form TE-30, giving the main details of the transaction and the parties, together with copies of the documentation evidencing the transaction and a translation into Spanish of that documentation. It is the responsibility of the Spanish company receiving the technical assistance to apply for verification. Verification is usually a formality, but every five years a new application must be submitted. Once verified, payments connected with such transactions may be made through authorised Spanish banks within six months from the date the payments become due in compliance with the DGTE procedure set forth above (TE-30, etc.).

Examples of technology transactions are:

(a) transfers by a resident to a non-resident of rights to patents, utility models, know-how and software; transfers by a non-resident to a resident of trade marks and other industrial property rights; and franchising contracts in which the non-resident is the franchisor;

(b) services rendered by a non-resident to a resident company, such as engineering, development of technical projects, access to databases, provision of technical or financial documentation or information service, or other forms of technical assistance, involving payments of over ten million pesetas; and

(c) payments made by a resident in connection with research and development performed by international consortiums, corporations, or associations in which the resident has a shareholding or other interest, or by a foreign corporation with a resident branch.

(2) Sharing the costs of a foreign parent company

If a resident company lends its expertise to the research and development projects of its foreign parent company, those 'payments' or contributions made by way of technical assistance must be differentiated from the sharing of costs and general expenses by the parent and the subsidiary, which must be reflected in the intra company account (see Chapter 5).

(3) Copyright

Payments of copyright royalties of up to five million pesetas by residents to non-residents require prior verification by an authorised Spanish bank. Larger royalty payments require prior verification by the DGTE.

(4) Construction contracts performed by non-residents

Prior verification by the DGTE is required for payments due under public bid contracts awarded to a foreign contractor for the construction or maintenance of public works, such as buildings, highways, bridges and ports, as well as under construction contracts for factories or plants.

¶209 Loans and guarantees

Financial operations abroad are subject to regulation within both Spain and the EEC. Regulation of these transactions tends to be much more restrictive than that governing the movement of merchandise, individuals, services or foreign investments.

(1) Loans by non-residents to residents

The general rule is that prior authorisation by the Bank of Spain is required for these types of loans; however, there has been a gradual movement away from this. Since 1987, certain kinds of foreign loans have been deregulated, and a rule of silent acquiescence was adopted, depending on the term and the amount of the loan. Loans with a term of over one year and involving less than 1.5 billion pesetas require prior verification by the Bank of Spain, unless the borrower is a Spanish branch of a non-resident lender. Loans which do not meet the conditions mentioned above are not deregulated and require prior authorisation from the Bank of Spain. However, if, within 15 working days from the date of receipt of an application for authorisation, the Bank of Spain does not refuse the application or otherwise notify the applicant, the authorisation is deemed to be granted.

(2) Foreign currency loans to residents

Authorised Spanish banks may make foreign currency loans to residents, subject to the conditions set out above.

(3) Indirect loans

If a resident converts the payment of a debt owed to a non-resident into a loan repayable in instalments, prior authorisation from the DGTE is required in order to convert that debt into a loan.

(4) Loans to Spanish branches of foreign companies
Strictly speaking, a transfer of funds from a parent company to its branch in Spain is not a loan because the branch does not have an independent legal existence. Under Spanish law these 'loans' are treated as advances, subject to repayment by the branch or office.

(5) Mortgage loans
The general rules for loans by non-residents to residents apply to mortgages. The creation of a mortgage as security does not require prior authorisation by the DGTE if the Bank of Spain has already authorised the underlying loan transaction.

(6) Guarantees
Failure to pay the underlying obligation covered by a guarantee may give rise to payments into or out of Spain made by the guarantor.

Under EEC law, each underlying transaction is considered separately in order to determine the degree to which a related guarantee is deregulated. Under Spanish law, guarantees given by non-residents in transactions arising between residents and non-residents are deregulated to the extent that the underlying transaction is deregulated or authorised. If the guarantee is given by a non-resident in connection with an agreement between residents, obligations arising from the guarantee require prior verification for amounts of up to 100 million pesetas per borrower–resident. Prior authorisation is required for amounts exceeding this limit.

Guarantees given by residents in connection with an agreement between a non-resident creditor and a resident debtor will need prior verification, as long as the underlying transaction is deregulated or authorised. If the guarantee given by a resident relates to a transaction between a resident creditor and a non-resident debtor, the guarantee will be subject to prior authorisation. If the underlying transaction is between non-residents, the guarantee given by a resident will require prior verification only if the underlying creditor–debtor relationship is between Spanish affiliates outside Spain and the Spanish parent company is the guarantor.

FOREIGN INVESTMENT IN SPAIN

¶210 Private investments

Internal legislation for foreign investments came into force in 1986 to harmonise with EEC regulations. The legislation applies to investments made by foreign individuals or corporations in the private sector, regardless of residence. This includes resident and non-resident foreign individuals, non-resident Spanish individuals, Spanish corporations with foreign-held capital, and subsidiaries and branch offices in Spain of non-resident companies.

Special authorisation by the Council of Ministers is required for all investments made in Spain by foreign governments and by state-controlled foreign entities of whatever type.

Foreign capital may be invested in Spain in the form of capital goods, technical assistance, patents and foreign manufacturing licences, foreign currency (either in its equivalent in pesetas at the official exchange rate or in convertible pesetas from a foreigner's bank account in Spain), or as otherwise permitted by law.

As a general rule foreigners investing in Spain with domestic capital must apply to the DGTE for prior authorisation, unless the investment is made by a Spanish company with foreign-held share capital, or by a branch or subsidiary of a foreign company with ordinary pesetas from a Spanish bank account.

¶211 Direct investments

(1) Definition

Direct investments are investments made in Spain for a business purpose and with the intention of creating or maintaining a lasting direct economic relationship between the supplier of the funds (the investor) and the individual or business receiving them. Spanish law uses the phrase 'effective control or influence' in its definition.

The following are deemed to be direct investments:

(a) An interest held by a foreign investor in a Spanish company at a level enabling the foreign investor effectively to influence or control the management of the Spanish company. This would include both the incorporation of a new company in Spain and the total or partial acquisition of shares or other interest in a company incorporated in Spain. One or more foreign investors will be deemed to have effective influence or control of the company if their holdings equal or exceed 20 per cent of the company's share capital.

(b) The establishment, acquisition, or enlargement of branches or subsidiaries of foreign corporations, or the expansion of business in Spain by non-resident individuals.

(c) The granting of loans for a term over five years with the intention of maintaining a lasting economic relationship. This applies only if the borrower is a Spanish company and the lender is a non-resident or the subsidiary or branch in Spain of a non-resident.

(d) The reinvestment of profits obtained by the foreign investor with a view to maintaining a lasting economic relationship.

(2) Administrative controls

It should be noted that all foreign investments in Spain are also subject to exchange controls (for payments), as well as to administrative controls. Administrative controls relate to the form of investment made and are distinct and separate from exchange controls.

There are currently three different types of administrative controls applied to direct foreign investments in Spain:

(a) *Notice 'a posteriori'*. This form of administrative control applies to acquisitions of an interest in a Spanish corporation, whether by forming a new company or by acquiring shares or other forms of interest in a Spanish company, as long as the interest acquired amounts to less than 50 per cent of its capital. Increasing the capital of a Spanish company by way of reinvestment of non-distributed dividends is included in this category.

Indirect foreign holdings in a Spanish company may also be affected, depending on the percentage of foreign capital in the Spanish company making the investment. If 50 per cent or more of the share capital of a Spanish company making an investment is foreign-owned, then that Spanish company will be deemed to be a foreign company. If less than 50 per cent of its share capital is foreign-owned, then a formula is applied in order to calculate what proportion of the share capital of the Spanish company in which it is investing will be deemed to be foreign.

Notice should be given to the DGTE using form TE-1.

(b) *Prior verification*. This form of control applies to investments subject to notice *a posteriori*, if the investment results in more than 50 per cent of the Spanish company being foreign-owned; the creation, acquisition or enlargement of branches or subsidiaries of foreign companies or the expansion of a business in Spain by non-resident individuals; the grant of loans to Spanish companies for a term of more than five years with the intention of maintaining a lasting economic relationship, except for loans from a Spanish lender, even if under a foreigner's control; and the reinvestment of non-distributed dividends, thereby increasing the capital of a branch or subsidiary of a foreign company.

Application should be made to the DGTE.

(c) *Prior authorisation*. Prior authorisation from the Council of Ministers is required for direct investments relating to gambling, television, radio, air transportation, or national security. Applications should be made initially to the DGTE in the form of a report, giving the information listed in ¶203 above.

As mentioned previously, authorisation from the Council of Ministers are also required for all investments made in Spain by foreign governments, foreign entities or public corporations, and state-controlled foreign entities.

It should be noted that the DGTE may suspend any proposed foreign investment if it considers that it may have a detrimental effect on the Spanish economy. The ultimate decision in respect of investments not greater than one billion pesetas lies with the Ministry of Finance and, for larger investments, with the Council of Ministers.

(3) Transfer of investment capital

Foreign investors are entitled to transfer abroad investment capital, profits derived therefrom and legally distributed dividends, including all profits from the sale of subscription rights if the original investment was required to have been made with foreign capital. The transfer abroad of capital, profits and earnings requires notice *a posteriori* or prior verification by the DGTE, as the case may be.

¶212 Portfolio investments

Portfolio investments can be distinguished from direct investments in that they do not establish effective control or influence, nor do they establish a direct and lasting economic relationship under the criteria used by Spain and the EEC for direct investments. EEC Directive 86/566 deregulates almost all portfolio investments.

Spanish law imposes effectively no restrictions on the acquisition of shares, whether or not quoted on the Spanish stock exchanges, or on subscription rights or securities traded on stock exchanges, other than an anonymous notice to the Investments Registry.

Portfolio investments, other than the acquisition of shares, include the acquisition of public funds, private securities with fixed interest rates, shares in investment funds, bills, notes or any other type of negotiable instrument quoted on the stock exchanges. These are completely deregulated and transferable, as long as the original investment was made with foreign capital. The conditions covering transferability of direct investments also apply to portfolio investments (see ¶211).

¶213 Real property investments

Owing to the great interest in this type of foreign investment in Spain, a separate chapter is dedicated to real property investments. In general, for the purpose of Spanish exchange control laws, such investments are completely deregulated, with the following notable exceptions:

(a) Real property investments made in Spain by non-resident Spaniards, resident foreigners, and offices and branches in Spain of foreign companies or non-resident individuals are completely deregulated (with some limitations as to the type of property subject to investment). This deregulation only affects the form of the investment and not the means used to effect it. The acquisition of premises by foreign companies is subject to prior verification by the DGTE. The transaction must be put in a notarised public deed and recorded in the Foreign Investments Registry.

(b) The purchase of property located in strategic areas of Spain by a foreigner is subject to laws regarding national security. These laws apply to all foreigners, regardless of residency, with the exception of EEC citizens, who receive the same treatment as Spanish nationals.

SPANISH INVESTMENT ABROAD

¶214 Introduction

Spanish law has been adapted to harmonise with EEC regulations regarding the free movement of capital.

Spanish investors abroad include Spanish and foreign individuals residing in Spain, Spanish companies and corporations, and offices and branches in Spain of non-resident companies and corporations. Spanish investments abroad may take the form of ordinary pesetas, foreign currency (reinvestment only), technical assistance, patents and Spanish manufacturing licences, capital goods of Spanish origin, and other types of goods and rights, including contributions of any kind chargeable against reserves and, in cases of capital increases, capitalisation of credit rights.

Fundamentally, a parallel can be drawn between Spanish investment abroad and foreign investments in Spain. The mechanism for effecting either is the same, and the principal aspects to look for are:

- who is making the investment (an individual or company);
- the form the investment is to take; and
- the applicable administrative controls.

¶215 Forms of investment

(1) Direct investments

Direct investments abroad include:

(a) the acquisition of an interest in a foreign company enabling the Spanish investor to exercise effective control. A Spanish investor is presumed to exercise effective control and influence in the company if its holdings equal or exceed 20 per cent of the share capital, or if there are other circumstances which deem the Spanish investor to have effective influence and control. This is the most common form of direct investment abroad;

(b) the establishment, enlargement, or acquisition abroad of branches, offices or businesses by Spanish companies or resident individuals;

(c) the grant of loans to foreign companies for a term of five years or more, with the intention of establishing a lasting economic relationship;

(d) the reinvestment of profits made abroad by the Spanish investor with the intention of maintaining a lasting economic relationship.

The following administrative controls for Spanish investments abroad apply:

(a) Notice *a posteriori* is required in a small number of cases, such as where profits obtained through direct investment are reinvested in the same enterprise.

(b) Prior verification by the DGTE is required for most direct investments abroad. If, within 30 days from the date of receipt of the application, the DGTE does not refuse the application or otherwise notify the applicant, the investment should be considered verified.

(c) Prior authorisation by the DGTE is needed only if changes are made to accelerate the repayment terms of loans granted to foreign corporations.

Payments and receipts relating to the above investments must be made through an authorised Spanish bank and notice given to the DGTE.

(2) Portfolio investments

The DGTE oversees portfolio investments, which include the acquisition of securities issued by non-residents, regardless of the place of issue, and of securities issued in a foreign market by a resident. This includes the acquisition by Spanish investors of shares or other securities issued in Spain by a resident, when the purchase takes place abroad and payment is made in a foreign currency.

EEC Directive 86/566 deregulates nearly all portfolio investments. Under Spanish law, all portfolio investments are completely deregulated, provided that the securities are quoted in a foreign currency exchanged in Spain and they are traded or quoted on stock exchanges or other organised markets. Similarly, securities quoted in pesetas and issued by international organisations of which Spain is a member are also deregulated. Portfolio investments which are not deregulated require prior authorisation by the DGTE.

All transactions must be effected through an authorised Spanish bank, and the securities acquired must be deposited in such a bank.

(3) Investments in real property

Such investments include the acquisition of real property abroad and the acquisition of real property rights related thereto or real property holdings. Although investments in real property have been deregulated under EEC and Spanish law, prior verification by the DGTE is always required.

(4) Other forms of investment

As a general rule, all other forms of investment need prior authorisation by the DGTE. Exceptions to this rule are the purchase or sale abroad of financial or commodity futures and the purchase or sale abroad of options for securities, futures etc., provided that such investments are made through stock exchanges or organised markets, and the acquisition of certificates representing precious metals, provided they are traded in stock exchanges or organised markets.

3 Business Organisations

¶301 Entering the Spanish market

Spanish law offers a number of choices to foreign businesses wanting to set up operations in Spain. One may start by opening a representative office and providing information services only or by establishing a more substantial presence in the form of a branch. Both representative offices and branches are directly linked to their foreign parent and have no independent liability.

Another alternative is to form a separate company under Spanish law, whether a corporation or partnership, or acquire an existing business. The decision as to how to enter the market largely depends on the type of business, the size of the business, the extent of liability to be assumed, the amount of investment to be made, and tax implications.

The various alternatives are discussed in detail in this chapter, indicating the advantages and disadvantages of each where possible. Tax considerations are dealt with in greater detail in Chapter 4 (Taxation) and foreign investment is the topic of Chapter 2 (Exchange Control and Foreign Investment).

REPRESENTATIVE OFFICES AND BRANCHES

¶302 Representative or information offices

Spanish law permits foreigners to set up representative or information offices in Spain which may not conduct business on their own behalf or on behalf of the foreign company and do not assume any independent liability. The purpose of these offices is to provide information about the business of or services offered by the foreign company and to carry out market research and gather other business information of interest to the foreign company. The general requirements for setting up a representative office are set out below. Special requirements for banks are highlighted, since representative offices are most frequently used by foreign banks and there are specific legal provisions covering them.

(1) Incorporation and registration

Setting up a representative office is deemed to be a foreign investment and as such is subject to both foreign investment and exchange control laws. Once permits and authorisations are obtained from the General Directorate of Foreign Transactions (DGTE) and the Bank of Spain (if the applicant is a foreign bank), the legal representative of the office must appear before a notary to obtain a public deed. The notary will require the following documents, duly legalised (see ¶314 regarding legalisation):

(a) Basic incorporation information required by law (*Minuta de Constitución*), including the power of attorney of the legal representative appearing, the amount of capital to be invested, and the registered address of the office.

(b) The DGTE's vertification of the proposed investment. The correct form to be presented is TE-13.

(c) The trade name certificate indicating that the name has been cleared, issued by the General Registry of Companies in Madrid run by the Ministry of Justice.

(d) Evidence, in the form of a bank certificate, of the origin of the funds used to set up the office.

(e) Form TE-1, declaring the amount of the foreign investment to be made, to be filed at the DGTE's Foreign Investment Registry.

(f) Memorandum and articles of association/certificate of incorporation and by-laws of the foreign company.

(g) Valid resolutions adopted by the board of directors and the shareholders of the foreign company authorising the opening of the representative office in Spain. Also to be submitted are the name of the office manager, the powers granted to this person, and the amount of capital to be allocated to the operations in Spain.

(h) A certificate issued by the Spanish Consul in the country where the foreign company is based, verifying that the company is duly formed and authorised under the laws of that country.

(i) If the foreign company is a bank, the Bank of Spain's authorisation for the formation of the representative office.

Once the notarised deed is obtained, the representative office must be registered, both at the Commercial (Mercantile) Registry located in the capital city of the province where the representative office has its registered address and at the Foreign Investment Registry located in Madrid, which operates under the auspices of the Ministry of Economy and Finance. If it is the representative office of a bank it must also be registered at the Bank of Spain's Registry.

(2) Costs

(a) *Start up*. The initial costs of forming a representative office are minimal. They consist of the fee for a trade name certificate (in 1989 this was 1,000 pesetas) and notary and Commercial Registry fees, which together amount to approximately 3 per cent of the initial capital investment.

(b) *Taxes*. A representative office will be liable for taxes in Spain, although if a double taxation treaty exists between Spain and the country where the foreign company is based, the representative office may be exempted, depending on the terms of the treaty. If no relevant treaty exists, tax is calculated on the basis of 35 per cent of 15 per cent of the annual cost to the parent company of running the representative office.

¶303 Branches

A foreign company may also conduct business in Spain through a branch, which is deemed to be a direct investment under Spanish foreign investment and exchange control laws and, as such, is entitled to the advantages available to any other direct investment in Spain. Direct investments are discussed more fully in Chapter 2 (Exchange Control and Foreign Investment); however, in this context, it essentially means that the foreign parent company and branch are treated as one for most purposes, although the branch is deemed to be a resident company in Spain. The parent company is wholly liable for the debts of its branch, since a branch has no independent liability.

Doing business through a branch in Spain is particularly attractive for a foreign company which does not wish to go so far as forming an independent Spanish company. The determining factors in the decision to create a branch are usually limitation of liability and taxation.

(1) Taxation

Certain provisions of corporate taxation are particularly relevant to branches. For example, if losses are anticipated initially, choosing the branch structure often proves to be advantageous due to the free flow of losses of the branch to the foreign parent company permitted under the tax laws. In addition, there is no withholding tax on the distribution of dividends or profits. The year-end statutory rate of tax on the distribution of dividends is also lower for a branch (35 per cent) than for a subsidiary (approximately 51.25 per cent). It should be noted that Spain has entered into double taxation treaties with a number of countries which specifically regulate these tax issues.

(2) Other costs

Apart from legal and notarial fees, other costs involved in forming a branch include stamp duty, amounting to 1 per cent of capital allocated by the foreign parent company to the branch as set forth in the certified resolutions, and registry and notary's fees, together amounting to approximately 3 per cent of the capital allocated by the foreign parent company to the branch. These expenses are fully deductible if they are justified by receipts and included in the branch's accounting books.

(3) Foreign investment aspects

Spanish law permits foreign companies to invest in Spain through their branches, although prior authorisation from the DGTE must be obtained in order to use foreign currency for this purpose. Acquisitions of Spanish companies through the purchase of over 50 per cent of share capital also requires the prior verification of the DGTE.

Branches in Spain of foreign companies have a duty to report to the DGTE annually in the form of an intra-company account (*cuenta de enlace*). This report is submitted by the legal representatives of the branch and allows Spanish authorities to keep a check on the branch's activities and facilitates the transfer of funds and profits of the branch to the foreign parent company. The intra-company account must contain:

(a) the total amount owed to the parent company by the branch, broken down into:
   - capital allocated to the branch,
   - assets transferred by the parent company to the branch with no obligation of repayment,
   - reserves,
   - loans from the parent company,
   - branch profits,
   - that part of the parent company's general expenses allocated to the branch, but not transferred,
   - other financial obligations owed to the parent company but not transferred; and

(b) the total amount owed to the branch by the parent company, broken down into:
   - branch losses,
   - other financial obligations owed by the parent company.

¶304 Setting up a branch

(1) Public deed

Setting up, expanding or acquiring foreign branches in Spain require prior verification by the DGTE (form TE-13-L) and registration at the Commercial Registry. The Commercial Registry must be provided with all the information which would normally be required for the incorporation of a Spanish company in the form of a public deed. The trade name to be used by the branch must be the same one used by the parent company abroad.

To obtain a public deed, the legal representatives of the foreign company must appear before a notary. The following duly authorised documents must be presented:

(a) a legalised copy of the company's articles of association/by-laws;

(b) a certificate from a Spanish Consul in the company's country of origin, indicating that the company is duly incorporated in accordance with the laws of that country;

(c) the names of the persons who are to run the operations in Spain;

(d) the authority granted to those persons;

(e) the capital allocated to the operations in Spain, stated both in the currency used in the country of origin and its equivalent in Spanish pesetas.

(2) Special regulations

Branches formed by non-private foreign companies or entities, such as foreign governments or government-owned companies, are subject to special foreign investment regulations. In addition, prior authorisation by the DGTE (form TE-1) is required for direct investments relating to gambling, television, radio, air transport, or those affecting national security. Once prior authorisation is obtained, the branch can be formed under the general rules, that is, by public deed and registration.

The parent company must apply to the DGTE for the authorisation of these kinds of branches by submitting the following:

(a) a memorandum containing the following information about the foreign company:
   - trade name,
   - registered address,
   - nationality,
   - corporate purpose,
   - share capital and reserves, and
   - members of the board of directors.

This information is normally found in the following documents regarding the foreign company, which are to be submitted as well:

- a duly legalised copy of the by-laws/articles of association;
- duly legalised copy of Memorandum of Association/Certificate of incorporation;
- a certificate from the Spanish Consul similar to that required for branches in general;

(b) a memorandum in the form of a draft of the proposed public deed, containing the following information about the proposed branch:

- trade name,
- registered address in Spain,
- capital allocated to the branch,
- names of legal representatives and managers appointed by the foreign company;

(c) a memorandum containing basic financial information about the proposed activities of the branch.

(3) Registration

The branch must be registered both at the Commercial Registry in the province where the branch has its registered address (see ¶303(2) for costs) and at the Foreign Investment Registry (located in Madrid and free of charge). Registration with the Bank of Spain is only necessary if a foreign bank is setting up a branch or if otherwise required (see Chapter 6 (Banking and Finance)).

LIMITED COMPANY/BUSINESS CORPORATION

¶305 Characteristics

The *Sociedad Anónima* (S.A.) is the most common type of company in Spain. It closely resembles the English limited company or American corporation.

An S.A. is a capital-based company with a corporate purpose, capital divided into equal shares, and shareholders (*accionistas*) who are personally liable for the obligations of the company only to the extent of their capital investment. A minimum share capital of 10 million pesetas is required by law. A limited company/corporation must indicate that it is such by having 'S.A.' or '*Sociedad Anónima*' in its name.

The internal structure of an S.A. consists of shareholders, directors and executive officers. The shareholders elect a board of directors which is responsible for the management of the business. The directors may appoint executive officers, who are responsible for the day-to-day management of the company.

The major advantage of the S.A. for a shareholder is that liability is limited to the amount of capital invested in the business. Moreover, the shares representing capital investment are, generally, freely transferable. The S.A. is a legal entity separate from its shareholders, and is capable of owning property, entering into contracts, and suing and being sued in its own name. The S.A. is also a separate entity for tax purposes and is eligible for certain tax benefits, such as deductions for expenses (see Chapter 4 (Taxation)).

Capital-based companies are strictly regulated by law and are required to make certain information, such as accounts, available to their shareholders, the public and/or the Government. In certain sectors, such as banking and finance, more than the basic annual report will be required, depending on the nature of the business and the regulatory agency.

¶306 Incorporation

(1) Deed of incorporation

The first stage in the incorporation process is to go before a notary and obtain a deed of incorporation (*escritura social*). The notary will require the '*Minuta de Constitución*', which is normally drafted and submitted by the lawyer representing the original shareholders of the company, and which contains a large part of the information to be set out in the deed of incorporation. A trade name certificate issued by the General Registry of Companies in Madrid ensures that there is no other Spanish company with the same name.

The deed of incorporation sets out the bylaws/articles of association and the following basic information:

(a) A minimum of three founders (original shareholders), although subsequently the company can function with fewer shareholders.

(b) A clear statement that the founders wish to set up the company.

(c) Details of the contribution made by each shareholder.

(d) Total cost of setting up the company, whether already incurred or estimated, e.g. notarial, registry and legal fees. This is important because these expenses can only be treated as deductions in the company's tax return if they are declared.

(e) The identity of those who will manage and represent the company initially.

(f) The terms and conditions of the agreements among the founders related to the formation of the company. Founders may agree to give themselves special remuneration or economic rights or benefits not exceeding 10 per cent of the net profits, as shown on the balance sheet, for a period of up to ten years.

(2) By-laws/articles of association

The by-laws/articles of association (*estatutos*) must be included in the deed of incorporation. They must include, at least, the corporate name, the corporate purpose, the date of commencement of operations, the registered office (which must be in Spain in the place where it is doing business or where its directors or legal representatives are located), the authorised share capital, any capital not fully paid-up, the board of directors or other managing body, and the procedure for shareholders' meetings, including when they must be called and the ways in which resolutions are to be adopted, the number of shares into which share capital is divided and the type, series, value and rights to shares. The deed of incorporation must also specify whether the shares are in the form of a certificate or book entry, the date of the close of financial year, any other contribution other than capital contributions and any special rights reserved to the founders.

(3) Registration

Once the deed of incorporation containing the by-laws/articles of association is obtained, it must be registered at the Commercial Registry. This is usually handled by the notary issuing the deed of incorporation. The deed of incorporation may only be registered once proof that all taxes relating to the incorporation of the company have been paid. Upon registration, the company acquires legal personality, which means that it can operate with all the rights and obligations allowed to corporations under Spanish law. Shares cannot be transferred until the deed has been registered.

(4) Pre-registration contracts

The validity of contracts entered into on behalf of a company before registration at the Commercial Registry is subject to its subsequent registration. Moreover, the company must ratify such contracts within three months thereafter. The organisers (*gestores*) are specifically authorised by statute to take those steps necessary to set up the company before registration and charge the company for any expenses incurred thereby. If no deed of incorporation is issued, or it is not duly registered at the Commercial Registry, the company does not acquire legal personality and is therefore not deemed to be a legal entity. It is, thus, an 'irregular' or 'de facto' company. Contracts entered into between the irregular company and third parties without notice are unenforceable against the company, and the organisers of the irregular company are held personally liable.

¶307 Share subscription

In addition to the registration requirements, at least 25 per cent of the authorised share capital must be paid-up at the time the deed of incorporation is obtained. Regulations governing banking and finance institutions may require that all capital be paid up upon incorporation. Shares may be offered simultaneously or successively. Simultaneous (private) placement occurs when the founders subscribe to all the share capital themselves. Successive (public) placement occurs when the promoters pay up at least 25 per cent of the share capital and the remaining shares are offered to the public.

(1) Simultaneous placement

A simultaneous placement requires at least three founders to execute the deed of incorporation and subscribe to all the shares of the company. The founders undertake to register the company and are jointly and severally liable to the company and third parties in respect of the payment of capital subscribed and of performance of the terms of the public deed. The founders may appoint themselves as directors of the company in the deed of incorporation. They must register the deed of incorporation at the Commercial Registry nearest to where the company has its registered office within two months of the date on which the deed of incorporation is granted. Any shareholder may request the winding-up of the company if the company has not been registered within a period of one year from that date.

(2) Successive placement

A successive placement occurs when promoters subscribe and pay up at least 25 per cent of the authorised share capital and the rest is offered to the public. Promoters are those persons who handle all the steps necessary to organise the company and issue the shares, including the following:

(a) drafting and publishing a prospectus (founding programme) giving relevant information concerning the proposed company, the by-laws/articles of association, the names and addresses of the promoters, the company purpose, the authorised share capital, and other information concerning the shares and privileges accorded to the promoters;

(b) subscription of shares and payment of at least 25 per cent of the authorised share capital;

(c) a validly held meeting of the shareholders;

(d) a deed of incorporation; and

(e) registration at the Commercial Registry.

The promoters must give notice to the National Securities Exchange

Commission (*Commisión Nacional del Mercado de Valores*) (the 'Commission') of the issue (see ¶622) and they must submit the following documents to the Commission:

(i) a complete copy of the prospectus;

(ii) a technical report on the viability of the proposed company;

(iii) documents containing information about the shares and the rights conferred on subscribers;

(iv) an informational brochure complying with the rules of the Commission.

The promoters must also file a copy of the prospectus, informational brochure and a certificate from the Commission stating that the necessary documents have been submitted to the Commercial Registry where the company is to be registered. All advertising relating to the successive placement must set forth the location where the above information is made available to subscribers.

The promoters of a successive placement do not appoint the directors. Directors are elected at the shareholders' meeting and become liable to the company and third parties for any funds received from the company, any obligations assumed by the company in respect of third parties and for the truth and validity of the prospectus.

(3) Company share subscription (treasury shares)

In general, a company may subscribe to shares of another company, but not to its own shares. There are also limitations placed on a company subsequently buying its own shares or those of its parent company. A company may acquire its own shares or parent company shares under the following circumstances:

(a) Authorisation is given in a shareholders' meeting, including the number of shares, minimum and maximum price of shares and the duration of the authorisation, which may not exceed 18 months.

(b) The total value of shares owned by the acquiring company, directly or indirectly, does not amount to more than 10 per cent of its share capital.

(c) A specific reserve is provided for on the balance sheet.

(d) The shares to be acquired are fully paid-up; if not, the transaction will be considered void.

The political or voting rights do not attach to these shares as long as they are held by the acquiring company.

(4) Loans and credits

A company is not able to advance funds or to give loans, guarantees or any other form of financial assistance in order to facilitate the acquisition by a third party of its own shares or those of its parent company. Exception is made if such facilities are to employees.

¶308 Capital contributions

The authorised share capital is a permanent entry on the books of the company, which shows the contributions made by the shareholders but does not necessarily reflect the assets actually owned by or available to the company. Capital contributions may be in the form of cash, property or rights. Non-cash contributions must be valued by one or more independent experts appointed by the Commercial Registrar. The expert's report sets forth the relevant details of the non-cash contributions and is annexed to the deed of incorporation.

(1) Form of contribution

The following basic rules apply to capital contributions:

(1) If *cash*, then payments must be made in pesetas, or if made in foreign currency, the equivalent in pesetas on the date the shares are subscribed and the deed of incorporation is issued. Documents showing proof that payments have been made must be shown to the Notary and mentioned in the deed of incorporation.

(2) If *property*, the contributor must deliver the goods with a clear title, in accordance with the provisions of the Civil Code.

(3) If *a right to receive payment*, the contributor is liable for the validity of the loan and the solvency of the debtor.

(4) If *a business, commercial or industrial establishment*, the contributor is liable for compliance with the provisions of the Civil Code regarding the transfer of businesses.

(2) 'Dividendo Pasivo'

A shareholder must fully pay up the unpaid part of the subscribed amount within the period set forth in the by-laws/articles of association or, if no provision is made, upon resolution of the Board. Once in default, the shareholder may not vote until his contribution is made nor may he receive any dividend, or exercise preemptive rights over shares or convertible bonds. If the rest of the contribution remains unpaid, the company may sue the shareholder for the amount owed, plus interest and damages, or sell the shares.

¶309 Types of shares

(1) Ordinary and preference shares

There are ordinary shares (*acciones ordinarias*) and preference shares (*acciones privilegiadas*), which give preferential rights in the distribution of profits and upon liquidation. However, a share may not bear interest of any type, nor the ratio of its nominal value to the voting or subscription rights attached thereto be altered.

(2) Form of shares

(a) Certificates (títulos)

Shares may be registered (*acciones nominativas*) or bearer shares (*acciones al portador*). Shares must be registered if the company business is specially regulated, such as banking, finance or communications. Shares must also be in registered form until the capital they represent is fully paid-up.

Registered shares show the name of their legal owner on the certificate. All share certificates are consecutively numbered and issued from a book of share certificates (*libro talonario*). These shares are also recorded in a share register. The company must be notified of all transfers of, or liens or encumbrances (*derechos reales*) on, registered shares and make the appropriate entries in the share register. Only shareholders who are registered in the share register are treated as such by the company. Transfers of bearer shares take place upon delivery.

(b) Electronic bookkeeping entries (anotaciones en cuenta)

A share may be represented in the form of a certificate or as a bookkeeping entry. A share for which a certificate is not issued cannot subsequently be represented by a certificate. An issue of shares without certificates must be made by public deed specifying the type, number and value of the shares and any other relevant information. A copy of the public deed must be given to the Commission and to the electronic bookkeeping entry centre. If the shares are quoted on the stock market, an additional copy of the public deed must be delivered to the payment securities clearing and settlement service (*Servicio de Compensación y Liquidación de Valores*). If the shares are not quoted, a copy of the public deed must be given to a securities company or agency chosen by the issuer.

The shares are represented by numbers or codes which appear in the public deed and the shares are transferred by amending the electronic bookkeeping entries.

(3) Non-voting shares

A company can issue shares without voting rights comprising up to one-half of issued and paid-up capital. The shareholders are entitled to a preferential dividend of 5 per cent of their paid-up capital contribution plus an ordinary dividend thereafter. If there is no distribution of dividends or, in any given year, the distribution of dividends to the shareholders does not reach 5 per cent of their paid-up capital contribution, the shareholders have the right to receive the amount due over the next five years and, in the meantime, recover the right to vote.

These preference shares without voting rights retain the preemptive right in respect of newly-issued shares, with or without voting rights attached, and are not affected by reductions in capital due to losses until after ordinary shares are reduced to below their nominal (par) value. Shares without votes may not be counted for the purpose of the minority's right of proportional representation on the board of directors (see ¶313).

In order to protect shareholders without voting rights, any amendment of the articles of association/by-laws which may directly or indirectly negatively affect the rights of the shares requires the consent of the majority of its shareholders holding those shares.

¶310 Rights and duties of shareholders

(1) Rights

All shares confer upon the shareholder the following minimum rights:

- the right to participate in profits and dividends,
- the right to share in the proceeds in the event of liquidation
- pre-emptive rights in the event of an increase in capital or the issue of convertible bonds,
- the right to attend and be heard at shareholders' meetings,
- the right to vote,
- the right to request any relevant information from the company.

(2) Voting

All shares bear the right to vote, except non-voting shares (see ¶309(3)). The law does not allow the issuance of shares which change the ratio of nominal (par) value and right to vote.

The articles of association/by-laws determine the maximum number of votes that any shareholder or group of companies may have. They may also require that a shareholder hold a minimum number of shares in order to attend a shareholders' meeting, provided that the required minimum does not exceed one per thousand (1°/00) of the share capital. The law permits grouping shares in order to be able to attend and/or vote at a shareholders' meeting.

(3) Who may exercise rights

There are three major variations of share ownership, which may affect who may exercise shareholder rights. They are co-ownership, usufruct, and pledges.

(a) *Co-ownership*. Shares are indivisible, and co-owners must designate one of them to exercise shareholder rights.

(b) *Usufruct*. The Roman law concept of usufruct exists in Spanish law, whereby the owner of real or personal property may transfer the rights of enjoyment of the property to another while retaining title. This concept bears some similarities to the common law life estate. In the case of shares, a shareholder may assign the profits arising from his shares to another, while retaining all other rights and benefits, such as voting rights and pre-emptive rights in respect of new share issues.

(c) *Pledge*. When shares are given as security or in guarantee of an obligation, the owner of the shares retains all shareholder rights, unless otherwise provided in the by-laws/articles of association. Although it is possible to shift voting rights to the pledgee, it is not usually done in practice. Spanish law does not allow an irrevocable proxy to be given by the titleholder of the shares to the pledgee, which would allow the pledgee to act on the pledgor's behalf and exercise his rights at the shareholders' meetings throughout the term of the pledge agreement. A proxy may only be given to a specific person for a specific meeting.

(4) Duties

The only obligation a shareholder has under the Business Corporation Act is to pay, in full, all subscribed, but not fully paid-up, shares when required by the by-laws/articles of association or, if no provision is made, by resolution of the Board (*dividendos pasivos*).

¶311 Transfer of shares

As a general rule, all shares are transferable; however, transferability may be limited either by statute, by a shareholders' agreement binding the shareholders (but not the company), or by the by-laws/articles of association. A transfer made in contravention of a shareholders' agreement may, nonetheless, be valid in the eyes of the company, leaving the contracting parties to resort to other means to enforce their contractual rights. A transfer made in contravention of the articles/by-laws would have the opposite effect and be valid as between the parties, but would not confer shareholder rights on the transferee in respect of the company.

Restrictions on the transferability of registered shares expressly set out in the by-laws/articles of association are valid as long as they do not completely prohibit transferability. Examples of typical restrictions on transfers are as follows:

(1) *Pre-emption clauses (cláusulas de adquisición preferente)*. These give a first option to purchase new stock in an amount proportionate to existing holdings to all or some of the shareholders or to the company (if permitted to purchase its own shares) before selling the shares to third parties. In practice, this is the most common clause restricting transfer of shares.

(2) *Consent clauses (cláusulas de consentimiento)*. These clauses subject the sale of any share to the authorisation or approval of the company (the directors unless the by-laws/articles of association specify otherwise) and are allowed if the by-laws set forth bases for denial.

¶312 Shareholders' meetings

The shareholders act as a body at a duly called meeting (*junta general*) held at the company's registered office, or at a meeting held by unanimous consent wherever all shareholders are physically present or represented in Spain.

(1) Ordinary and extraordinary meetings

An ordinary meeting of the shareholders must take place at least once during the first six months of each financing period in order to review the management of the company, approve the books and accounts of the preceding year, approve any distribution of dividends, and address any other matter or questions proposed by the shareholders. An extraordinary meeting is similar to an ordinary meeting, but may be called at any time.

(2) Universal meeting

A universal meeting is a convenient way of holding a meeting, particularly when there is a small number of shareholders. The only requirement is that the shareholders be present physically or by proxy and agree to hold the meeting. The advantages are numerous. There is no obligation formally to convene the meeting, thus eliminating notice requirements. The meeting may be held anywhere in Spain and is not restricted to being held at the company's registered office. As procedural requirements are minimised, there is a greatly reduced chance that shareholders' resolutions will be challenged on the basis of a procedural defect. Minutes of the meeting are usually signed by the secretary and the chairman of the meeting.

(3) Calling a meeting

Unless the meeting is universal, prior notice is a prerequisite for calling (*convocatoria*) or convening a valid shareholders' meeting. Ordinary meetings are called by the directors by means of a public announcement in the Official State Gazette (BOE) and a provincial daily newspaper published at least 15 days before the date of the meeting. The notice of the meeting must state the proposed date of the meeting and the agenda. The notice may also show the date of a second meeting in the event that a quorum is not reached at the first meeting. If a call for a second meeting is not included in the first notice, another notice must be published in the same way as the first one and with the same 15-day notice period. In order to save time, the two are usually published together, allowing for the statutory minimum period of 24 hours to separate the meeting dates. Spanish law does not provide for a waiver of notice. The notice requirements and waiting periods are therefore mandatory if all shareholders do not appear at the meeting.

Extraordinary meetings are called in same the way as ordinary meetings. They are called by the directors or upon the request of shareholders representing at least 5 per cent of paid-up capital. When the shareholders request a meeting, the chairman must call it so that it may be held within 30 days of the date of the request.

If an ordinary meeting is not called during the period required by law, or the directors fail to call an extraordinary meeting when so requested by the requisite number of shareholders, a meeting may be called by court order.

(4) Attendance and quorum

On the first call for a meeting, a quorum is reached when any number of shareholders representing 25 per cent of paid-up capital with voting rights, is present. A quorum is always reached on the second call, regardless of the number of shareholders attending the meeting. Resolutions are adopted by majority vote.

These quorum requirements are higher (50 per cent of paid-up capital with voting rights for meetings on the first call) when the resolutions include amendment of the by-laws/articles of association, increase or decrease of capital, approval of a transformation or bond issue. On the second call a quorum of 25 per cent of paid-up capital is sufficient. In any meeting in which less than 50 per cent of paid-up capital is present or represented, two-thirds of the capital present or represented must cast a favourable vote in order to adopt resolutions. The by-laws/articles may modify the requirements for convening a meeting and establishing a quorum, allowing them to be greater, but not less than these minimum requirements.

A registered shareholder may attend the meeting only if he has been registered in the books of the company or in the Commission's registry as holder of the shares at least five days before the date of the meeting. A holder of bearer shares may attend the meeting only if the shares have been deposited with the company in the manner set out in the by-laws/articles. Only shareholders or their proxies may vote, although certain other persons designated in the by-laws/articles may appear and be heard at the meeting.

The law allows a shareholder to appoint a proxy, in writing, to represent him at a specified meeting. The proxy need not be a shareholder, but the by-laws/articles may set out additional requirements if the directors or depositary or managers of the electronic bookkeeping records make a public solicitations proxy (which is assumed if one person represents more than three shareholders) the solicitation must be in the form of a public deed. The proxy deed must then take the form of a notarised power of attorney and contain such relevant information as the agenda and instructions for voting.

¶313 Board of directors

(1) Election of Directors

The law provides for one or more directors to represent and manage the affairs of the company, jointly and/or severally. Directors may be individuals or companies and are elected by the shareholders, who also determine the number of directors to be appointed within the limits set out in the by-laws/articles. The appointment takes effect once the person concerned has accepted and within ten days thereafter the resolution appointing him has been registered at the Commercial Registry.

Certain protective measures exist for minority shareholders based on the principle of proportional representation. Shareholders may aggregate their shares and elect a proportional number of directors to the Board, to the extent that the aggregate shares equal or exceed total capital divided by the number of directors. These shareholders may not participate in the election of the remaining directors.

A director need not be a shareholder, unless otherwise specified in the by-laws/articles. If the appointment is made in the deed of incorporation of the company, a director is appointed for a term of five years. Thereafter he may be re-elected for further five-year terms indefinitely. If there is a vacancy, the board may appoint an interim director until the next shareholders' meeting. Directors may receive reasonable remuneration for their services and may be removed or re-elected at any time by the shareholders.

(2) Board of directors

(a) Composition

The by-laws/articles of association may provide for a sole director (*administrador único*). However, when there are more than two directors elected by the shareholders, they constitute a board of directors. The board of directors is comprised of a chairman (*presidente*), a secretary and other voting members (*vocales*). Under certain circumstances, the law requires a legal adviser (*letrado asesor*) to attend. A quorum exists if at least a simple majority of the appointed directors is present or represented. Resolutions of the board are adopted by majority vote of those attending. These requirements may be modified in the articles/by-laws to be greater, but not less than, these legal minimums.

(b) Powers and delegation

Spanish law distinguishes between management and representational powers. Management powers (*facultades de gestión*) are established by the shareholders and are normally set out in the by-laws/articles of the company.

Powers of representation (*facultades de representación*) are inherent to directors and are provided for in the by-laws/articles. Directors may represent the company in all matters relating to the corporate purpose. In the absence of any provisions to the contrary, the board may delegate its powers to one or more managing directors (*consejeros delegados*) in a notarised power of attorney registered in the Commercial Registry, to the extent provided by law. The board may not delegate its responsibility to the shareholders to present the annual report and accounts within the legally mandated time period. Any restriction on a director's powers of representation is not enforceable against a third party, even though such restriction is registered at the Commercial Registry. The company is therefore liable in respect of third parties who dealt with directors of the company in good faith.

The directors may challenge any void or voidable Board resolution, within 30 days of the passing of the resolution. Shareholders representing at least 5 per cent of the share capital are entitled to challenge a resolution within 30 days of having notice of such resolution and not more than one year of its being passed by the Board.

(3) Directors' liability

Under commercial law, directors are liable for damage caused by them to the company or third parties. If the harm is to the company, an action may be brought either by the company itself, or by company creditors, or by the shareholders. If the harm is to third parties, an action may be brought either by the shareholders or by the aggrieved party, usually a creditor of the company.

¶314 Setting up and running the company from abroad

If a majority of the shareholders, directors or officers are not in Spain, the practical aspects of company management may pose problems.

(1) Setting up

In practice, the founders of a company need not be physically present to sign the deed of incorporation and register the company. This may all be done by duly executed and notarised powers of attorney, legalised in the form described in (5) below.

(2) Day-to-day business

The board of directors may appoint officers to represent the company and run the business. This would include a chief executive officer, called a general manager (*director general*). The general manager runs the company's operations but the directors are still obliged to supervise and manage the company, and they remain liable in respect of the shareholders. All delegated powers must be set out in a duly notarised power of attorney, filed at the Commercial Registry.

The company's business can be managed from abroad by appointing a managing director (*conserjero delegado*) from among the members of the board and giving him/her the authority to exercise all delegable powers granted to the board of directors by the shareholders and the by-laws/articles.

A company may also be organised with a sole director (*administrador único*), thus eliminating the need for meetings altogether. This may be provided for in the by-laws/articles.

(3) Board meetings and shareholders' meetings

Since there is no express prohibition in the Commercial Code, it is generally accepted that a meeting of the board of directors can be held outside Spain, although resolutions adopted at such a meeting must be registered at the Commercial Registry where the company records are kept. Meetings by telephone are not permitted, but written resolutions without a meeting are permitted, if no director opposes this procedure. Directors may appoint another director to serve as proxy.

Duly called shareholders' meetings must be held at the company's registered office or, if not, wherever all the shareholders or their proxies are physically present in Spain. As Spanish law does not recognise the concept of waiver of notice, a meeting must be duly called with a 15-day notice period or the meeting must be attended by all shareholders or their proxies. A proxy need not be a shareholder, but the appointment must be made in writing for a specific meeting.

(4) Resolutions

All resolutions must be in writing, although not all are required to be registered in the Commercial Registry. If they are required to be registered in the Commercial Registry, they are submitted in the form of a notarised certificate of the resolution signed by the secretary and the chairman of the meeting. The appointment or removal of officers or other employees authorised to represent the company, and the withdrawal of the powers granted to them, may all be accomplished by duly registered resolutions.

(5) Legalisation and the apostille

In order to set up or manage a company in Spain, certain documents originating abroad may be required to be produced in Spain. These may include powers of attorney, certified copies of documents relating to the incorporation or setting up of an office or branch, or certified resolutions passed by the board of directors executed outside Spain, but to have effect in Spain. The production of foreign documents must meet certain requirements in order to have effect in Spain. Normally the legal effect of such documents is governed by the law of the country of origination, although if a document such as a power of attorney is executed before and notarised by an authorised Spanish Consul abroad, that document is also deemed to be a Spanish document.

Otherwise, in order to take effect in Spain a document must be (a) legalised or (b) bear an apostille if the country of origin of the document is a signatory to the 1961 Hague Convention, which abolishes the requirement of legalisation for foreign public documents. In order to legalise a document it must be presented to a Spanish Consul in the country where the document originates for verification of the signatures.

The apostille is simply the stamp that must be given by the proper authority according to the domestic law of the country of origin of the document. In the United States, for example, such authority is given to the clerks and deputies of the Federal District and Appeals Courts, and to the Secretary of State of nearly every State of the Union. In the United Kingdom authority lies with Her Majesty's Principal Secretary of State for Foreign and Commonwealth Affairs at the Foreign Office.

The apostille must be in the form of a square with sides at least nine centimeters long, and appear as follows:

APOSTILLE

[(Convention de La Haye du 5 Octobre 1961)]

1. Country: ....
   This public document
2. has been signed by ....
3. acting in the capacity of ....
4. bears the seal/stamp of ....
   ....

[Certified]

5. at ....6. the ....
7. by ....
8. No ....
9. Seal/stamp: 10. Signature:

¶315 Challenging corporate resolutions

Corporate resolutions may be challenged on the grounds that they are contrary to the by-laws/articles of the company or that the interests of the company would be harmed for the benefit of one or more shareholders. This is called *impugnación de acuerdos sociales*. Agreements contrary to law are automatically void; agreements contrary to the by-laws/articles, or which are otherwise against the interest of the company, are voidable. Actions to declare a corporate resolution void or voidable are essentially the same, except that an action to set aside a voidable resolution must be made within 40 days after the resolution is adopted or one month after the resolution is registered at the Commercial Registry. An action to render a resolution void is not subject to this 40-day limitation period and may be brought in ordinary proceedings by any person connected with the company. An action to set aside a voidable resolution may be brought by shareholders who either voted against the resolution or did not attend the meeting. On the other hand, when a void resolution, the action may be brought by any shareholder and directors acting in their own names, even though they are not shareholders.

Directors of the company or shareholders representing at least 1 per cent of the share capital may require a Notary to attend a shareholders' meeting to notarise all resolutions passed at the meeting.

¶316 Amendment of the by-laws/articles of association

(1) General requirements

Any amendment to the by-laws/articles of the company must be approved by a written resolution of the shareholders in a duly called meeting. A copy of the resolution must then be registered at the Commercial Registry. The following requirements must be met:

- Reports must be filed at the Registry by the directors or shareholders explaining the reasons for the amendment itself.
- Notice of the meeting must be given describing the proposed amendments and the right of shareholders to examine the entire text of the proposed amendment and the report filed by the directors or shareholders proposing it at the company's registered office.
- Approval by the shareholder with the required quorum. A quorum is reached on the first call when shareholders representing 50 per cent of subscribed capital with voting rights attend the meeting. In the event no quorum is reached on the first call, a second meeting is called, wherein shareholders representing 25 per cent of the share capital with voting rights must be present.

The Business Corporations Act also provides some protective provisions for shareholders. For example, amendments restricting or imposing conditions on the transfer of registered shares will not apply to shareholders who did not vote in favour of those amendments throughout a period of three months. If an amendment affects the rights of one class of shares, approval by a majority of the shareholders of that class is required.

All amendments must be recorded in a notarised deed and filed at the Commercial Registry. In the case of a change of name, registered office or corporate purpose, the resolution must also be published in the daily press before being filed.

(2) Increase of capital

(a) *Cash contributions*. All issued and outstanding shares must be fully paid-up before capital may be increased.

(b) *Non-cash contributions*. A report must be submitted by the directors to shareholders explaining in detail the type of contributions, details of the contributions, the number and value of shares represented by such contributions and guarantees given in respect of the contributions.

(c) *Issue of shares to pay for debts*. Capital may be increased by converting debt into equity. At least 25 per cent of the outstanding debt is due and payable and the remaining amount becomes due within five years.

(d) *Convertible bonds into shares*. Capital may be increased by converting bonds issued by the company into shares (see ¶317(4)).

(e) *Payment out of reserves*. Shares may be issued by capitalising reserves (available reserves, surplus and legal reserves up to 10 per cent of capital as increased).

(f) *By the directors*. The directors may be authorised to increase capital by the shareholders or by the by-laws/articles of association. In such case, the authorised amount must be specified, and the increase must occur within a year.

Directors may also be authorised to increase capital one or more times. Such increases may not be greater than half of the capital of the company and the increase must be made by way of cash contributions within five years of the date the authorisation is given.

(3) Pre-emptive rights

In any increase of capital made by issuing shares, shareholders or holders of convertible bonds have the right to subscribe to shares in proportion to the nominal value of their shares or bonds. This pre-emptive right (*derecho de suscripción preferente*) is transferable in the same manner as shares.

The board of directors determines the period in which this right may be exercised, which, in any case, cannot be less than one month after the publication of the announcement of the capital increase in the Commercial Registry Gazette. In the case of registered shares, no publication is required; a notice to all shareholders in the share register is sufficient.

Under certain circumstances, pre-emptive rights can be restricted as follows:

- By shareholders in a duly called meeting. The resolution adopted must contain the restrictions on shareholders or bondholders. Additionally a Memorandum must be submitted by the Directors explaining the reasons for the restrictions.
- The Business Corporations Act prohibits the exercise of pre-emptive rights whenever an increase is due to the conversion of bonds into shares, the merger of another company ('*absorción*') or to the acquisition of a part of the corporate assets of another company.

(4) Public offerings

Shares issued due to an increase of capital may be offered to the public. This offer is subject to the provisions of the Spanish Securities Market Act (see ¶622). The formalities relating to this type of share subscription must be specified in a document called a 'Subscription Bulletin' (*Boletín de Suscripción*) containing certain relevant information, such as the name of the company, its registered office, information contained in the Commercial Registry, information about the subscriber, the number of subscribed shares and the nominal value of shares.

(5) Reduction of capital

The Business Corporations Act provides for the reduction of the capital by reducing the nominal value of shares or by redemption. Reduction of capital is usually done for the purpose of returning contributions, cancelling capital calls (*dividendos pasivos*), setting up voluntary reserves or balancing capital and assets due to company losses.

The method of reduction must be clearly set out in the shareholders' resolution and thereafter observed. Any resolution providing for a reduction of capital by returning, or disallowing, all or part of contributions made or owed by the shareholders must be published in the Commercial Registry Gazette and in two newspapers with wide circulation in the province where the company has its registered office.

Once the resolution is published in the Commercial Registry Gazette, a one-month period begins to run, during which time existing company creditors may object to the reduction of capital if the debts are not sufficiently guaranteed. This right to object must be exercised within this one-month period. The protective provisions for creditors do not apply in certain cases, such as when balancing capital and assets due to company losses, increasing the legal reserve, or in the case of a reduction due to company profits.

(6) Change of name, registered office or corporate purpose

In addition to the general requirements applicable to any amendment of the by-laws/articles, a notice must be published in two daily newspapers of the provincial capital(s) affected by the changes. The amendment must then be registered at the Commercial Registry.

¶317 Bond issues

Companies are usually financed by increases in authorised capital (discussed above) or by bond issues.

(1) Shareholder approval

Bonds are transferable debt instruments representing an equal share of the debt issue payable by the issuing company. These instruments may be payable to a named individual or to bearer. A redemption premium may be attached, as well as other express conditions and requirements. The bond issue must be approved by the shareholders in a written resolution adopted at a duly held meeting with an increased quorum (see ¶312(4)) and registered at the Commercial Registry. The board of directors may be given the power to issue bonds at its discretion, subject to any restrictions set by the shareholders. The bond issue takes the form of a contract between the company and a representative of the future holders, called the commissioner (*comisario*). The commissioner is usually the representative of the purchaser of the majority of the bond issue, which may or may not be a banking institution.

(2) Security

The amount of the issue is limited to the amount of capital of the company, unless security is provided in the form of: (a) a mortgage on real or personal property of the company; (b) a pledge of government issued bonds or debt held by the company; (c) a pledge without delivery of the pledged object (*sin desplazamiento*); or (d) a government guarantee, whether national, provincial or municipal.

(3) Formal requirements

In order to issue bonds, the law requires authorisation from the Ministry of Economy and Finance, a notarised public deed embodying the bond issue contract, registration of the notarised deed at the Commercial Registry, and publication of the issue in the Official State Gazette (BOE).

All instruments belonging to a single issue must be identical in form and content. The bond instrument must contain all of the following information:

- the precise name of the company,
- a description of the issuing company,
- the date of the deed of issue, and the name and protocol number of the Notary emitting the deed,
- the amount of the issue,
- specific terms and conditions of the bond,
- security for the bond issue, and
- the signature of one of the directors.

In the bond issue contract, the company undertakes to create and deliver the bonds under the terms and conditions set out in the notarised deed, to pay interest, and to redeem the bonds when they mature. The bond issue contract may be terminated by redemption, payment of the bonds, by any other agreement between the company and the pool of bondholders, or by conversion of the bonds into shares.

(4) Convertible bonds

Convertible bonds are becoming an attractive form of financing used by companies in Spain, and are increasingly seen in the financial markets. There appears to be substantial public receptivity to this type of relatively conservative form of investment which allows the bond purchaser an option to convert the bond into shares at some point in the future. This form of investment is of particular interest when the variable rate market is volatile, as the purchaser is assured of repayment on the terms of the bond issue contract, especially if the market is climbing and losses may result by waiting until the conversion date.

The advantages of convertible bonds are attractive to both parties, mainly due to the flexible nature of the investment. The investor is looking to acquire shares at a good price and the company has new resources available without adding new shareholders, at least until the moment of conversion.

A company may issue convertible bonds provided that shareholders' authorisation is obtained in a duly called meeting. A report by the directors explaining the terms of the conversion and an auditors' report must have been submitted to shareholders prior to the meeting. Shareholders and existing holders of convertible bonds may subscribe to the bonds pursuant to the terms of the notarised deed for the bond issue.

The company's capital may not be reduced if there are existing convertible bonds. Bonds may not be issued for less than their nominal value, and conversion of bonds is not permitted if the value of shares is less than the value of the bonds. Unless otherwise provided for in the bond issue deed, bondholders may request the conversion of their bonds at any time and the directors may issue new shares within the first month of each six-month period (usually January to June, and July to December). Thereafter a resolution of any increase of capital must be duly adopted and registered at the Commercial Registry.

A shareholders' meeting may specify the maximum period in which the conversion may take place.

¶318 Reserves

Reserves are made up of profits and surplus which are not distributed to shareholders, but are intended for future use by the company. Reserves may be either express or implicit (*tácitas*). Express reserves may be required, either by law or the by-laws/articles of association, or voluntary, by resolution of the shareholders. In any case, they must appear on the balance sheet.

A legal reserve of 20 per cent of capital must be accumulated out of 10 per cent of annual profits. This reserve may only be used to cover losses unless there are other reserves available for this purpose.

¶319 Financial structure

Because share capital is the basis of a limited company/corporation, there are particular accounting and business regulations which must be observed in order to protect that capital and secure the economic rights of the shareholders.

(1) The financial year

All accounts of the company must be closed and reviewed annually. The financial year begins on 1 January and ends on 31 December, unless otherwise specified in the by-laws/articles. There are two exceptions to this rule: the first financial year begins on the date indicated in the deed of incorporation of the company for the commencement of operations, and the final one will end on the date the company ceases operations.

(2) Accounts

The Business Corporations Act requires the production of a balance sheet, profit and loss statement, a dividend proposal and the annual report within four months of the end of the financial year.

The balance sheet is the summary of the bookkeeping entries made throughout the financial year. Its main purpose is to determine the status of company assets. The law sets out those items which must be entered as assets and liabilities.

Assets include credit extended to shareholders for shares subscribed but not paid-up and cash in hand or in a bank.

Liabilities include the capital indicated by classes of shares, legal reserves, other reserves, debts guaranteed by mortgages or pledges, other debts of the company, distinguishing those already due from those not yet due, bonds issued by the company, and the asset depreciation fund.

The annual report is prepared by the directors and explains the operations of the company and the company's progress in the last financial year.

(3) Dividends

Dividends are the distribution of profits proposed by the directors after due consideration of the balance sheet and the profit and loss statement. Under the Business Corporations Act, profit must consist of clear earnings, as dividends may be paid only out of actual profits earned (i.e. profits realised, less losses, on a cumulative basis) or unrestricted reserves, and then only if the value of the company assets is not less than capital.

Dividends are distributed to the ordinary shareholders in proportion to their paid-up capital.

(4) Auditors

The Business Corporations Act requires that the accounting books be reviewed by an independent professional auditor or auditing firm. The auditors must review the balance sheet, the profit and loss statement, the proposal for the distribution of dividends and the accuracy of the annual report (see Chapter 5 (Accounting and Auditing)). Auditors must be appointed in a duly called meeting for a term of not less than three, but not more than nine years.

Under certain circumstances a company is not required to be audited unless shareholders representing at least 5 per cent of the share capital request an audit. This happens whenever the company's total assets do not exceed 230,000,000 pesetas, turnover is less than 480,000,000 pesetas and the average number of employees does not exceed 50 during the two previous accounting periods.

CLOSE COMPANY

¶320 Characteristics

The *Sociedad Limitada* (S.L.) is a hybrid company form. The S.L. has a fixed capital, divided in equal parts which are cumulative and indivisible and represented as non-negotiable instruments which may not be called shares (hereinafter called 'holdings'). The number of members (*socios*) may not exceed 50 and their liability is limited to the extent of their contributions.

The S.L. is often associated with small or family-owned businesses. It is appropriate for entering into a joint venture with another shareholder or for introducing business to a parent company. The S.L. is characterised by its special restrictions on transferring shares to a third party, whether an individual or a company. The corporate tax advantages are similar to those for an S.A.

An S.L. must have a minimum authorised share capital of 500,000 pesetas which must be fully paid-up on incorporation. Holdings are transferable but transfers must normally be made to other members of the company and shares may not be traded on the stock market.

An S.L. must operate under a company name including the words '*Sociedad Limitada*', or '*Sociedad de Responsabilidad Limitada*' or 'S.L.'. Contributions to capital upon incorporation must be in cash or assigned a value in pesetas, or its equivalent in foreign currency expressed in pesetas. Members are liable to the company and to third parties for the delivery of the amount set out in the deed of incorporation. If the contribution is not in cash, the member must provide the warranties of title and merchantibility set out in the Civil

Code for purchase and sale agreements. If the contribution consists of credit rights, the member is liable for the validity of the credit and the solvency of the debtor. If the contribution consists of a business, then the applicable provisions of the Civil Code apply.

¶321 Incorporation

The notarised deed of incorporation must be registered in the Commercial Registry and include the name, address and nationality of each member, the company name, directors or administrators, requirements for the adoption of resolutions by the members, corporate purpose, duration, registered office, location of all branches and offices, capital and the parts into which it is divided, the contributions of each member, the form of the contribution and the value (if not in cash), and any other special terms and conditions agreed by the members.

¶322 Internal structure

(1) Management

A close corporation is run by the majority vote of the members. Usually the members appoint one or more directors or managers, who need not be members and who are restricted from directly or indirectly engaging in the same type of business as the company they are appointed to manage. A director may be removed by members holding a majority of the capital, except when an appointment is made in the deed of incorporation, in which case the resolution removing him must be adopted in a meeting with the same increased quorum as is required for amendments to the deed of incorporation, i.e. majority of shareholders representing two-thirds of capital on the first call or two-thirds of capital alone on the second call. The resolution must also be registered at the Commercial Registry.

The directors represent the company in all matters relating to the company's business and their acts are binding on the company. The extent of their authority must appear in the form of a notarised deed registered at the Commercial Registry. Any restrictions on their authority to represent the company have no effect as against third parties without notice. Powers of attorney may, however, be granted to other persons by notarised deed.

The directors are liable in the same manner as directors of limited companies/corporations.

(2) Meetings of the members

The affairs of the company are decided by a majority of the members (i.e. by resolutions adopted by members representing over 50 per cent of capital), unless otherwise provided in the deed of incorporation. A meeting is not required to adopt resolutions, unless the notarised deed so requires or the company has more than 15 members. Otherwise, members may follow any procedure which adequately demonstrates that resolutions were adopted.

Meetings may be either voluntary or mandatory. Voluntary meetings are called by the directors, in advance, in accordance with the notarised deed, giving notice of the agenda. Mandatory meetings are called by the directors at the request of the members holding at least one-quarter of the capital. A meeting may be duly convened without notice when all members are present and agree to hold a meeting.

In the absence of any provision to the contrary in the deed of incorporation, members may be represented by proxy, which may be either an individual or a company. Proxies must be in writing and specific to each meeting.

For extraordinary decisions such as increasing or reducing capital, extending the duration of the company, mergers or transformations, dissolution or any other change in the notarised deed, a majority of members representing at least two-thirds of capital must vote in favour. On a second call, members representing two-thirds of share capital will suffice.

¶323 Transfer of holdings

A member's interest in a close company is transferable, subject to the notice to the company and the procedures described below. Any condition prohibiting a transfer is void, as are transfers in contravention of the deed of incorporation or relevant law. Transfers of an interest or holdings must be made by way of a notarised deed and registered in the Commercial Registry.

A member who wants to transfer shares *inter vivos* must give written notice to the chairman of the board, or to any director, if no board exists. The chairman or director has 15 days to give notice to all other members of the intention to transfer holdings. Existing members may purchase the holdings within 30 days from the date on which notice was given. If more than one member wishes to purchase, the holdings are allocated in proportion to the holdings of each prospective purchaser. If no member is interested, the company may acquire these holdings, and if neither the members nor the company wishes to purchase the holdings, they may be sold without any further restriction.

An heir or beneficiary may accede to membership upon the death of a member, unless the deed of incorporation provides for members to acquire the holdings of the deceased member upon the terms and conditions agreed.

A registration book must be kept which records the following information:

- details of members (name, address, etc.);
- holdings of members;

- transfers of holdings.

Any member is entitled to get information from the registration book which should be kept by the directors.

¶324 Accounting and distribution of profits

Accounting rules for S.L.'s are the same as those for limited companies/corporations.

Any member has the right to examine the company's accounting books under the terms of the deed of incorporation, but in any event the company must allow the member requesting such examination a period of at least 15 days to do so.

Profits are distributed in accordance with the respective holdings held by each member and any agreement to the contrary is void. An exception to this rule is found in the so-called accessory services (*prestaciones accesorias*). The members may provide in the deed of incorporation that certain services which are rendered by some or all of them for the benefit of the company be paid out of company profits; capital may not be used for this purpose.

PARTNERSHIPS

¶325 General partnership

The Spanish general partnership (*sociedad colectiva*) is similar to the English and American general partnership. A partnership allows individuals to pool resources and to initiate and conduct their own business. Although practical for small businesses, a partnership is not usually suitable for larger operations, owing to the unlimited personal liability of each partner and to the fact that decisions are made collectively.

Partners (*socios*) have unlimited joint and several liability for partnership debts and obligations. The relationship between the partners is personal, and therefore an interest in the partnership is not transferable without the approval of all the other partners. All partners take part in management, unless any partner expressly waives this right. A partnership operates under the name of any or all of its partners, but if all the partners' names are not used, the words 'and company' (*y compañía*) must appear.

(1) Formation

Although a partnership in Spain is based on a contractual agreement between the partners, because it is deemed to be a commercial company, it must also meet certain formal requirements. Partnerships are formed by notarised deed which must be registered at the Commercial Registry. The notarised deed must contain the following information: the name and purpose of the partnership; the full name of each partner; the full names of the partners who are responsible for management; the capital contributed by each partner; the monies allocated to cover management expenses (e.g. salaries); the date of the commencement of business operations; and any other special terms and conditions agreed.

(2) Relations between partners

Partners may agree on how profits are distributed and how losses are shared. Unless agreed otherwise, distribution of profits is made in proportion to the capital contribution of each partner. Partners may not compete with the partnership directly or indirectly. Partners who contribute personal services (*socios industriales*) rather than capital may not engage in any other business activity, except by express agreement. The share of profits attributed to this type of partner may not exceed that of the partner with the smallest capital share, and he will not be liable for partnership losses unless expressly agreed otherwise.

A partnership is normally managed by all partners and all decisions are taken by unanimous consent. However, if the partnership agreement provides for the appointment of one or more managing partners, then the decisions taken by them are final, despite any objections raised by other partners. If the appointment of the managing partners was an express condition of the partnership agreement, the appointment may only be revoked by the dissolution of the partnership.

All partners have the right to examine the accounting and management books and records.

(3) Liability

A partner may demand compensation (*indemnización*) from the other partners for those expenses or damages incurred by him arising directly or indirectly from the partnership's business (e.g. a car accident occurring in company time), unless he has been negligent.

Only those partners expressly authorised to represent the partnership may assume obligations on its behalf. The partnership is not liable for obligations resulting from the acts of an unauthorised partner. However, the law distinguishes the unauthorised partner from the partner who is authorised to assume obligations on behalf of the company, but who exceeds his authority or uses it for his personal benefit. In the latter case, the partnership is bound by the acts of its appointed representative and must seek remedies in a separate action. The liability of partners is secondary to the liability of the partnership and is normally joint and several in respect of acts for which the partnership may be held liable in accordance with the above rules.

¶326 Limited partnership

The Spanish limited partnership (*sociedad en comandita*) resembles the English and American limited partnership, in that there are two kinds of partners: general partners (*socios colectivos*), who are personally liable for the debts of the partnership, and limited partners (*socios comanditarios*), whose liability is limited to the extent of their investment in the partnership. Another characteristic of a limited partnership is that the relationship between the partners is personal, and therefore an interest in the partnership is not transferable without the approval of all other partners. A major advantage of a limited partnership is that it may attract a broader range of investors, since limited partners may limit their personal liability to the amount of capital invested. The limited partnership is suitable for groups of professionals such as accountants and lawyers, who may limit their liability in respect of contractual relations with third parties but may not limit liability in respect of clients. The limited partnership is not usually suitable for larger businesses for the same reasons which apply to partnerships in general.

(1) Incorporation

The documents and procedure required are the same as for a general partnership, but the deed of incorporation must distinguish between the partners and specify the amount of the contributions of each limited partner.

(2) Relations between partners

In a limited partnership, the general partners have the same rights and obligations as they would have in a general partnership, but limited partners are subject to different rules.

Unless agreed otherwise, limited partners share in all profits in equal proportion to their capital contributions. Liability for losses is limited to the amount of their contributions. Limited partners may be given the right to inspect the books and records of the partnership in the partnership agreement, but they must at least have access to the balance sheet at the end of the year. They may not take part in the management of the partnership nor may they represent it.

Although the liability of the limited partners is limited to the amount of their contribution, if the name of a limited partner appears in the name of the partnership (*razón social*), the limited partner becomes personally liable, regardless of the amount of his contribution, as if he were a general partner with unlimited liability.

¶327 Limited partnership with shares

The *sociedad en comandita por acciones* is a special type of limited partnership in which the capital contributed by the limited partners is represented by shares (*acciones*). All requirements applicable to the limited partnerships apply, although the shares of the limited partners are governed by the general rules pertaining to shares in limited companies/corporations (S.A's).

(1) Relations between partners

All capital contributions by the limited partners are represented by shares. The limited shareholders are subject to the same provisions governing shareholders (*accionistas*) in a limited company/corporation in respect of the distribution of profits and losses. Management of the company is governed by the terms of the partnership agreement, and if none, in accordance with the provisions described above for limited partnerships.

(2) Liability

Unless agreed otherwise, the representation of the partnership is the same as for a limited partnership. General partners have unlimited liability for the obligations of the company. The liability of limited shareholders is identical to that of a shareholder to a limited company/corporation.

(3) Management

The partners must of necessity manage the partnership. Rules governing the liability, powers, rights and duties of managers are the same as those governing managers of limited companies/corporations.

The dismissal of a manager requires the amendment of the articles/by-laws by unanimous consent of all the partners. Other events requiring amendments of the articles/by-laws such as the appointments of managers, changes to the partnership purpose and duration also need the unanimous consent of all partners.

CHANGING THE ORGANISATIONAL STRUCTURE

¶328 Transformation

A commercial company is said to be transformed when the form of it is changed to another allowed under commercial law. A transformation agreement must meet certain requirements regarding the members' approval and the resolution must be put into the form of a notarised deed and registered in the Commercial Registry. In the following sections, the term 'members' is used to include shareholders and partners alike.

(1) Limited companies/corporations

(a) Transformation from a limited company or corporation into another company form

A transformation agreement must be approved by the shareholders and published three times in the Official State Gazette (BOE) and in provincial newspapers. The approved resolution must be put into a notarised deed and include all the necessary information required to transform the company. The resolution must include a balance sheet closing on the date of the resolution and a list of all shareholders having exercised their right to redeem their shares and withdraw from the company. The notarised deed must be registered at the Commercial Registry.

The law gives some protection to minority shareholders. Those who do not vote in favour of the transformation resolution have the right to withdraw from the company and redeem their shares at the price stated in the balance sheet approved in connection with the transformation. The prohibition against changes made to capital contributions is also a protective device.

If the transformation results in the acceptance of unlimited personal liability by the partners of the transformed company, as would occur in a transformation of a limited company/corporation into a general partnership, then partners assume unlimited liability for debts incurred before the transformation.

(b) Transformation from another company form into a limited company/corporation

The transformation resolution must be approved in the manner described above for each type of company and include all the information required for the formation of a limited company/corporation. The resolution must be in the form of a notarised deed and be registered at the Commercial Registry, together with a balance sheet closing on the day of the resolution.

In order to protect creditors, partners having unlimited personal liability before the date of transformation will continue to be liable for those debts, unless there is an express agreement between the creditor and the partners that the debt may be assumed by the transformed company.

(2) Close companies

Transformation of a close company requires the vote of a majority of its members representing two-thirds of the capital. If the agreement is approved in a meeting on the second call, approval will only require the approval of members holding a majority of capital.

(3) Partnerships

An agreement to transform a partnership or a limited partnership must be approved unanimously by all the partners. A limited partnership may be transformed upon the agreement of all general partners; the consent requirements for the limited partners depends on the terms of the partnership agreement. The transformation of a limited partnership with shares requires the approval of all general partners; the approval requirements of the limited partners/shareholders are the same as for shareholders of limited companies/corporations.

¶329 Mergers

Mergers (*fusiones*) are generally defined as transactions in which two or more companies agree to join their capital and their members, either by creating a completely new company and dissolving the two individual companies (*fusión*) or by one company taking over the other (*absorción*).

(1) Limited companies/corporations

The Business Corporations Act allows the merger of a limited company/corporation with another form of company as long as the new entity becomes a limited company/corporation. The merger agreement must be approved by the shareholders or members of each of the merging companies with the same requirements as set out for amending the articles/by-laws.

Before the relevant shareholders meeting takes place a report (*proyecto de fusión*) must be submitted by the directors of the merging companies containing the following information:

- Name, registered office and registration details of the merging companies.
- Details of the exchange for new shares to shareholders and any complementary cash compensation.
- Procedure for the exchange and date from which the new shares will become entitled to participate in profits.
- Date from which the operations of the companies which are to cease are to be deemed to be carried on by the company receiving capital, for accounting purposes.
- Any preferential rights or special advantages to be granted to shareholders of the new company.

Once the agenda for the shareholders' meeting is published, the following documents must be offered to shareholders, bondholders, holders of preferential rights and employees of the merging companies:

- The report (*proyecto de fusión*).
- Balance sheet, annual report and audited accounts for the three preceding financial years.
- Expert reports on, *inter alia*, the assets and liabilities of the merging companies and reasons for the merger.
- Proposed by-laws/articles of the new company or amendments to the by-laws/articles of the existing company, as appropriate.
- Existing by-laws/articles of the merging companies.
- Relevant information about the directors of the merging companies.

The formalities for the approval of a merger are as follows:

- The notice to call the shareholders' meeting and the conduct of the meeting itself must fulfil the same requirements as those specified for amendments to the by-laws/articles of association (see ¶312(4)).
- Notice of the meeting must be published at least one month before the date of the meeting.
- Once the resolution to effect the merger is adopted, it must be published three times in the Commercial Registry Gazette and in two daily newspapers in circulation in the places where the merging companies have their registered offices.

In order to protect creditors, the law provides that a merger may not occur until after one month after the date of the publication of the last merger notice. If during that period any creditor objects in writing to the merger, the merger cannot take place until the debt is satisfied; the creditor, in that case, may not object to pre-payment.

(2) Partnerships and close companies

There are no specific regulations for the merger of these types of companies. They are governed by the same rules and regulations governing their transformation. If a completely new company is created by the merger, a new entry is made in the Commercial Registry. In all other cases, a note in the margin is made in the Registry holding the records of each of the merged companies. As a merger involves a change of the legal identity of the company as a debtor in respect of creditors, the creditors' consent to the merger is necessary. Normally, notice of the merger is published in the Official State Gazette (BOE) and daily press and, unless an objection is made within the three-month notice period, consent is implied.

¶330 Split-offs or demergers

Split-off or demerger (*escisión*) is the name given to the break-up of a company achieved by dividing its operations or assets into two or more companies; it is the opposite of a merger. A split-off or demerger is usually used in order to maximise the value of company divisions or to protect certain areas of the business by separating them from areas of the business which are unprofitable or which may threaten the overall profitability of the company.

The portion which is divided off from a company must be an independent economic unit. Before any split-off can be made, the shares of the company must be fully paid-up.

A report must be submitted by the directors of the demerged company. The report must include the following information:

- the portions of assets or liabilities to be transferred,
- distribution of shares of the demerged company.

The assets to be transferred are subject to prior expert examination. The experts are appointed by Commercial Registrar where the acquiring company is registered.

¶331 Acquisitions

(1) Purchase of shares

This is the most common way of purchasing a privately held company. A share purchase means a change in capital ownership, and all assets and liabilities remain with the company.

(2) Purchase of assets

If an investor's main interest is in purchasing some or all of the assets of a company, such as buildings, machinery, industrial or intellectual property rights, it may be advantageous to purchase assets from the company and leave the liabilities of the company with the seller.

(3) Take-overs

Take-over bids or tender offers, known in Spain as OPAs (*Oferta Pública de Adquisición*), are another means of acquiring a publicly-traded company. Spain's OPAs are regulated in order to protect the interests of minority shareholders. The most relevant aspects of this type of acquisition are described here.

Securities must be admitted for quotation on the stock market, whether shares or bonds convertible into shares. The acquiring company must obtain at least 25 per cent of the target company's capital, including shares it already owns. The tender offer must be authorised by the National Stock Exchange Commission, based upon a strictly confidential notification submitted to it before the tender offer is made. The acquiring company must fix the maximum and minimum amount of securities which it intends to acquire. Once the public offer is made, shareholders of the target company may accept the offer by notifying the National Stock Exchange Commission or an authorised broker. Once the offer period is over, the National Stock Exchange Commission must confirm whether the acceptances meet the threshold requirement. If so, the acquiring company may proceed to buy the securities.

Spain's stock market is in the process of major reorganisation. The Securities Market Act of 1988 provides the basic law on the matter (see Chapter 6 (Banking and Finance)), with further changes expected.

(4) Leveraged buy-outs and management buy-outs

The Commercial Code does not specifically provide for leveraged buy-outs (LBOs) and management buy-outs (MBOs). Under the Business Corporations Act a company may not advance, lend or offer security in a transaction involving the purchase of its shares or the shares of a dominant affiliate by a third party. Nor may the transaction be secured by offering guarantees on company assets or on assets of subsidiaries of the parent company.

This provision does not eliminate the possibility of an LBO, but does require the transaction to take another form, such as having the security or guarantee come from managers, insurance companies, risk-venture capital companies, LBO companies or investments banks.

The LBO has not yet been developed in Spain's financial markets, but it may be an area that takes off rapidly in the near future. Spain has no specific regulation and offers an advantageous tax structure in comparison with other countries. Moreover, it is an area in which national banks are not active, which offers the opportunity for foreign banks to enter into the market with relatively little competition.

DISSOLUTION AND LIQUIDATION

¶332 Causes for winding up a company

A commercial company is not only a contractual arrangement between members but also a series of contractual relations with third parties. A company begins winding up when a cause for dissolution arises, which may occur upon the initiative of the members or by operation of law. Once the procedure has begun, all pending business must cease, the company must be liquidated, and all remaining capital must be distributed among the members.

A cause for dissolution is the legal or contractual basis upon which interested parties or a judge may initiate the winding-up process. Circumstances in which all types of companies may be wound up and go into liquidation include (a) when the company reaches the end of its duration under the deed of incorporation and there is no tacit agreement among the members to extend it; (b) where the company decides that it has fulfilled its company purpose; (c) where there is a complete loss of capital; and (d) where the company is declared to be insolvent/bankrupt.

(1) Partnerships

Causes for winding up general and limited partnerships include the death of a partner, when there is no express provision in the partnership agreement to continue, mental incapacity or any other disability which prevents a managing partner (*socio gestor*) from managing the business of the company, or the bankruptcy of any of the general partners.

(2) Limited company/corporations

There is a cause for winding up a company if it is a limited company/corporation or close company and there is a fixed term set out in the by-laws/articles which is not extended by resolution of the shareholders and registered at the Commercial Registry. The company may decide that it has fulfilled its corporate purpose or it is manifestly impossible to do so, or has suffered losses and thereby reduced the assets of the company to less than one-third of the share capital, or there is a merger or take-over of the company. In general, winding up may always occur upon shareholders' resolution, or for any other reason set out in the articles/by-laws. The mergers or split-off may be held as cause for winding up.

If the winding up of the corporation is discretionary, the decision to wind it up must be registered at the Commercial Registry, and be published in the Official State Gazette (BOE) and one other major newspaper with a wide circulation in the area where the company has its registered address. The Government may order the continuation of a company if it is deemed to be in the interest of the national economy or society as a whole, regardless of the reasons given for winding it up. Whenever cause to wind up a company exists, the directors must call a shareholders' meeting to adopt a resolution to wind up the company within two months of the date of the meeting. The directors are liable for the debts of the company until that time.

¶333 Partial winding up

Partial winding up occurs when one or more members leave the company which then continues to operate with those remaining.

(1) Voluntary resignation or withdrawal

A partnership may be dissolved by the resignation of one of the partners, if so provided by the partnership agreement and deed of incorporation, the only obligation being to allow the pending operations of the company to continue until concluded. However, if there is no provision made for this in the partnership agreement, the partnership continues with the remaining partners.

In the case of capital-based companies, a member may require the company to repurchase his holdings when he does not agree with the value given to his contribution, or has voted against a resolution for a merger or transformation of the company.

(2) Dismissal

(a) Partnerships

A partner may be dismissed from a general or limited partnership for using partnership capital or the partnership name for personal business, interference by a non-managing partner in the management of the business, fraud committed by a managing partner, failure to pay the stipulated contribution after a request has been made, breach of a covenant not to compete with the partnership business, where he is a working partner who absents himself and fails to return when asked, or for breach of any of the terms of the partnership agreement.

(b) Close company

A member of a close company or corporation may be dismissed for using capital or the company name for personal business, interference by a member who is not a director (*socio no administrador*) in the management of the business, breach of the terms and conditions set out in the public deed of incorporation, or for engaging in a business similar to that of the company, if a managing member.

(c) Limited company/corporation

A shareholder of a corporation/limited company may be forced to sell his holdings if he fails fully to pay up subscribed shares in accordance with the articles/by-laws or, if not specified therein, pursuant to a resolution of the shareholders. This would then take the form of a forced sale of the shares at the risk and expense of the shareholder in default.

¶334 Liquidation

(1) In general

The term 'liquidation' describes the process of determining the net worth of the company to be divided up among the members. The company continues to have legal personality and may continue to operate throughout the liquidation period, although its corporate purpose must be amended to indicate that the company is being liquidated.

(2) Liquidator

If not provided for in the deed of incorporation, a liquidator (*liquidador*) and the managers (*gestores*) and representatives of the company in liquidation are appointed by the shareholders. The sole function and powers given to the liquidator relate to winding up the company.

The liquidator prepares the inventory of assets and the balance sheet, informs the members and creditors of the state of affairs, and prepares a final balance sheet. Liquidators are liable to the members of the company for any fraud or negligence in the performance of their duties.

(3) Dividing up net assets

The last phase of the winding up is the division and distribution of the net assets in accordance with the following rules:

(a) No distribution of assets among the members may take place until all outstanding debts and liabilities of the company are satisfied.

(b) If any member disagrees with the division of net assets, he may seek remedies in court.

(c) For companies with shares, division and distribution of assets is effected in accordance with the by-laws/articles, or, if there is no such provision, in proportion to the nominal value of the shares held by each member.

The proposal for dividing up the net assets of the company must be recorded at the Commercial Registry.

4 Taxation

¶401 Outline of the tax system

As in all European countries, Spain has a very complex tax system with many different kinds of taxes, most of which are imposed by the central government. The autonomous regions (*comunidades autónomas*) and municipalities have very limited authority to tax. Most taxes are self-assessed by the taxpayer when filing the tax return. Late payments are subject to interest charges at a rate determined annually by the Ministry of Economy and Finance. Some taxes are assessed by the tax authorities on the basis of tax returns filed by the taxpayer. The filing of an appeal does not postpone the obligation to pay the tax unless an escrow or bank guarantee is provided to the tax authorities.

The most important taxes which affect foreign companies and individuals investing in Spain are as follows.

(1) Direct taxes:
  (a) on income –
    (i) individual income tax
    (ii) corporate income tax;
  (b) on capital –
    (i) net worth tax
    (ii) inheritance and gift tax.

(2) Indirect taxes:
  (a) value added tax;
  (b) transfer tax and stamp duties.

(3) Excise taxes.

(4) Import duties.

Other taxes which may affect foreign investors in Spain are as follows.

(1) *Municipal taxes.* The municipal taxes mentioned in this chapter have just been created by a new law which will enter into force on 1 January 1990, except for the business tax which will enter into force on 1 January 1991. Until then, there are a number of municipal taxes similar to the ones mentioned below. A more detailed description of such taxes is found in ¶449.

Municipal taxes can be categorised as follows:

(a) property tax on real property;
(b) business tax, for the privilege of doing business in a municipality;
(c) tax on motor vehicles;
(d) tax on the increased value of land;
(e) tax on building, construction and installation projects.

(2) *Special 'levies' (contribuciones especiales)*. These are collected in return for increases in the value of assets as a result of public works or the establishment or extension of public services.

(3) *Fees (tasas)*. These are collected in return for a public service provided by central, regional or municipal authorities.

INDIVIDUAL INCOME TAX: RESIDENTS

¶402 Scope of taxation, taxpayer and tax period

Spanish individual income tax is an annual tax on the total net income of an individual. If an individual is a member of a household, the tax is levied on the aggregate net income of all members of the household. For tax purposes, households are divided into four groups:

(1) A married couple and minor children living with their parents.

(2) In cases of annulment, divorce or legal separation, the spouse and minor children in his/her custody.

(3) Unmarried father or mother and minor children.

(4) Siblings in the care of a single guardian who live together in Spain and are not part of another household.

No person may belong to more than one household at any given time, and members of a single household are jointly subject to this tax. In March 1989, the Constitutional Court held that to require married couples to file joint returns was unconstitutional because it could result in higher tax liability than if the same individuals filed separate tax returns. In July 1989 a new law was passed by the Parliament adapting the individual income tax law to the Constitutional Court holding. The law 20/89 allows married couples to file separate returns in which each spouse will include his/her income and capital gains. The law allows married couples to elect to file joint or separate tax returns.

The tax year in Spain is the calendar year, unless any of the following events occur on a date other than 31 December, in which case the tax period ends on the date on which the events occur and a new tax period may commence to end on 31 December of the same year. The relevant events are:

(1) the death of a taxpayer filing individually;

(2) the dissolution of the household, as a consequence of the dissolution of the marriage, the death of one or both of the spouses, an unmarried parent or any of the siblings under the same guardianship;

(3) the marriage of the taxpayer.

A tax return must be filed for each tax year between 1 May and 20 June of the following year. The filing period is extended to 30 June if the taxpayer has the right to a refund. The tax return is filed at the taxpayer's local tax office or at a commercial or savings bank. Individuals or households are not required to file a tax return if gross earnings are less than 865,000 pesetas, including only salaries, pensions, investment income and capital gains, and, of that amount, no more than 206,000 pesetas are attributable to investment income and capital gains.

¶403 Residence defined

For tax purposes, a person of any nationality is considered to be a Spanish resident if he spends more than 183 days in Spain each year. Absences from Spain will not negate residency status if they are intended to last less than three years. A household is considered to be resident in Spain if either the father or the mother is a Spanish resident or, if there are no parents, all the members of the household reside in Spain. Spanish nationals residing abroad in a diplomatic or consular capacity and Spanish civil servants rendering services abroad are deemed to be resident in Spain. Foreign nationals resident in Spain under the same circumstances mentioned above will not be considered resident in Spain if the foreign country grants similar treatment to Spanish nationals.

All treaties signed by Spain provide that the criteria taken from the OECD Model Convention be applied in matters relating to dual residence status. Thus, an individual who resides both in Spain and in a treaty partner country is deemed to be resident in:

(1) the country in which he has a permanent home;

(2) if a permanent home is available in both or neither country, the country in which he has the closest personal and economic relations (centre of vital interest);

(3) if it is not possible to determine where the centre of vital interest is, the country where he has an habitual abode;

(4) if an individual has an habitual abode in both or neither country, the

country of which he is a national. If he is a national of both or neither country, the competent authorities shall determine the residence by mutual agreement.

¶404 Taxable income

Resident individuals and households are taxed on their worldwide income. The concept of income is very broad and includes any kind of revenue or capital gain. There are a few types of income which are not taxed, such as:

(1) prizes from certain recognised public or quasi-public lotteries;

(2) certain recognised literary, artistic and scientific prizes; or

(3) indemnities for losses or the deterioration of goods which are not otherwise subject to net worth tax, such as unemployment, disability or accident compensation.

Spanish taxpayers are theoretically allowed to deduct from their taxable income those expenses directly related and necessary to obtain income. Nevertheless, both the tax law and regulations have severely limited the right to deduct expenses, leaving very few deductible expenses intact.

Married couples electing to file separate tax returns should include in the return his/her income and capital gains. Income from personal services will be attributed to the individual rendering the services. Income from investment will be assigned to the owners of the assets invested. Income from commercial, agricultural, professional or artistic activities will be assigned to the person which habitually rendered such services. Deductible expenses will be attributed according to the same criteria. Capital gains and losses will be assigned to the owner of the assets. When the income or the capital gain is attributable to both members of the couple, it will be apportioned in accordance with the pro rata share each member has of the joint venture or, if unknown, by halves. If the couple is subject to community property laws, capital gains are apportioned equally between the spouses.

¶405 Net taxable income

The tax law distinguishes among the following types of income when assessing tax liability (*base imponible*).

(1) Income from dependent services or earned income

All earnings which directly or indirectly stem from employment are deemed to be dependent service income. This includes salaries, as well as:

(a) payments in kind and fringe benefits, which are included at market value except for free housing, which will not be valued at greater than

10 per cent of the taxpayer's salary. Employer contributions to private pension funds must also be included in the taxable income of the employee;

(b) pension benefits;

(c) profits distributed to a promoter or founder of a company, as allowed under Commercial Code; and

(d) compensation (*indemnizaciones*). Compensation paid to employees which exceeds limits set by current legislation. The most important one is the compensation paid as consequence of a dismissal (*despido*). Any amount paid in excess of the limit set by applicable labour law will be considered income to the employee.

From dependent service income, only the following deductions are allowed:

(a) social security payments;

(b) contributions to private pension funds up to 500,000 pesetas per family by the employer or the employee;

(c) a general allowance of 2 per cent of the gross dependent services income.

(2) Investment income

All earnings which directly or indirectly arise from capital investment, property or rights over real or personal property belonging to the taxpayer and which are not related to professional or business activities are deemed to be investment income. This category includes:

(a) income from any kind of security, loan or other form of monetary investment. The only deductible expenses from this sub-category of income are administration and custody fees and interest paid on any kind of loan taken out in order to make the investment, up to a maximum of 100,000 pesetas;

(b) income arising from the transfer of the use or the right to use any tangible or intangible property, including real estate. The law allows the taxpayer to deduct from gross income any expense required to obtain the income, including depreciation allowances;

(c) deemed income from urban property. With respect to urban property (excluding building plots) not leased to a third party, Spanish law deems 2 per cent of the value of the property (as established for the purpose of calculating net worth tax) to be income. No expenses are deductible, except for interest payable on borrowed capital used to acquire the property. The interest payable on borrowed capital used to acquire any kind of real estate is only deductible up to an overall limit of 800,000 pesetas.

(3) Earnings from commercial, agricultural, professional or artistic activities
Earnings from any kind of agricultural, livestock, forestry, fishing, industrial, commercial, service, mining, professional, artistic or business activity will be subject to income tax. Individuals engaged in these activities have to keep accounts similar to those of corporations. Net income is also determined according to rules quite similar to those applied under the Corporate Income Tax Law. From gross income, the taxpayer will be able to deduct any relevant expenses, including depreciation allowances.

Small businesses are allowed to use a simplified method of tax assessment. This method may be used by (a) professionals and artists, provided that during the previous tax year they employed no staff and the gross income did not exceed 1.5 million pesetas, and (b) businessmen or traders, provided that during the previous tax year turnover did not exceed 5 million pesetas and there were never more than two employees at any given time. Activities related to electrical power, naval construction and air transport are excluded from using this simplified method. Under this method, the taxpayer is allowed to maintain a simplified set of accounting books. Net income is determined by subtracting specific types of deductible expenses from gross receipts: (a) the cost of personnel; (b) purchases from third parties; (c) lease payments; (d) taxes other than those imposed by the central government; and (e) a general allowance for other expenses, equal to 20 per cent of gross income for manufacturing and mining activities, 10 per cent for professional and artistic activities, and 15 per cent for all the other activities.

Very small businesses are allowed to use an even more simplified assessment method. This method is available only to businessmen, and not to those involved in professional or artistic activities, provided that during the previous tax year turnover did not exceed 6,066,900 pesetas and there were never more than two employees at any given time. The net income is determined by applying certain ratios to business turnover.

Both simplified methods of tax assessment are voluntary. Notice of any change in the method used must be given to the pertinent tax office during the last month of the year prior to that in which the change is to take effect.

(4) Capital gains and losses
Capital gains or losses may arise when there is a change in the composition of the taxpayer's net worth (realisation event). There is no specific tax for capital gains, and they are treated as ordinary income.

(a) *Sale or exchange.* If the realisation event is the sale or exchange of tangible or intangible property, the amount of capital gain or loss is the difference between the acquisition cost and the selling price. The acquisition cost includes the actual purchase price (or building or manufacturing cost), together with any outlay for improvements and substantial repairs, and costs and taxes paid by the purchaser at the time of transfer, reduced by depreciation allowances. The selling price is the actual sale price, less any expenses and taxes paid by the seller at the time of the sale. In order to prevent tax evasion, the Individual Income Tax Law provides for a minimum sale price in certain types of transactions. This applies, for instance, to the sale of securities not quoted on the stock exchange.

(b) *Gift or bequest.* If the realisation event is a gift or bequest, Spanish law deems the transaction to be a capital gain in favour of the donor or deceased. The capital gain will be the difference between the acquisition cost (determined as above) and the valuation of the assets under the inheritance and gift tax provisions.

(c) *Inflation adjustment.* In order to mitigate the taxation of monetary or inflation-provoked gains on the sale of assets, Spanish law allows the taxpayer to adjust the acquisition price by applying coefficients which vary in accordance with the purchase date. For sales made in 1989, the coefficients vary from 2.333, applicable to assets acquired prior to 1 January 1979, to 1.00, applicable to assets acquired in 1988.

(d) *Deemed capital gains.* As from April 1989, in respect of transfers of properties or rights, if the sale price is lower than the assessed value of the property or right determined for transfer tax purposes, and the difference in value is larger than 2 million pesetas and 20 per cent of the sale price, the difference between the assessed value and the sale price will be considered a gift. Therefore, the seller will be taxed on the difference as a deemed capital gain arising from a gift (as in (b) above) and the buyer will be subject to the inheritance and gift tax.

(e) *Non-justified capital gains.* Any increase in the taxpayer's net worth which is not attributable to income of the period (either taxable or exempt) will be considered a non-justified capital gain and must be included in taxable income.

(f) *Loss carry forward.* Capital losses may only offset capital gains. Excess losses will not reduce ordinary income, but may be carried forward five years in order to offset future capital gains.

(5) Contributions to private pension funds

The law regulating pension funds deems any contribution to a private pension fund made by the employer to be taxable income to the employee. Nevertheless, contributions to private pension funds are deductible from a household's income up to 500,000 pesetas per household. The law 20/89 establishes that married couples will be allowed to have a deduction from income equal to 500,000 pesetas per each spouse. Contributions to certain kinds of institutions which are being phased out are treated similarly to contributions to private pension funds.

(6) Irregular income

Income or capital gains obtained over a period exceeding one year are fully taxable in the year they are realised. In order to mitigate the effect that progressive rates may have, the taxpayer may divide the net income or capital gains by the number of years it took to acquire it or them, and treat the resulting amount as ordinary income and apply the average rate of tax applied to ordinary income and capital gains to the remaining capital gains or income.

¶406 Negative taxable income carry forward

If the aggregate net taxable income (excluding capital gains) is negative, such negative amount may be offset with the positive net income of the following five years, or with capital gains of that year or of the following five years. The taxpayer may elect the form and timing in which this set-off is accomplished.

¶407 Calculation of taxable income and applicable tax rates

Net taxable income, as described in ¶405 above, is broken down into three categories to which different tax rates apply. The tax liability determined in (1) and (2) below plus net worth tax liability may not exceed 70 per cent of net income.

(1) Ordinary net taxable income

This is the aggregate of that part of net income and capital gains attributable to the tax year (including the pro rata share of irregular income and capital gains), less negative taxable income carried forward from prior years.

Ordinary net taxable income is taxed at the rates set out in Table 4.1.

(2) Irregular net income and capital gains

This is net income which is not included in ordinary net income, described in ¶405(6) above, taxed at the average rate applicable to the taxpayer. The

Table 4.1: 1989 tax rates on ordinary income

Tax brackets in pesetas	*Average rate on lower value of each bracket*	*Tax payable on lower value of each bracket*	*Marginal tax rate applicable on the remaining income*
less than 618,000	exempt	exempt	exempt
618,000 to			25.00%
1,030,000 to	10.00%	103,000	26.00%
1,545,000 to	15.33%	236,900	27.00%
2,060,000 to	18.25%	375,950	28.00%
2,575,000 to	20.20%	520,150	30.00%
3,090,000 to	21.83%	674,650	32.00%
3,605,000 to	23.39%	839,450	34.00%
4,120,000 to	24.63%	1,014,550	36.00%
4,635,000 to	25.89%	1,199,950	38.00%
5,150,000 to	27.15%	1,398,225	41.00%
5,665,000 to	28.41%	1,609,375	43.00%
6,180,000 to	29.67%	1,833,400	46.00%
6,695,000 to	30.92%	2,070,300	48.00%
7,210,000 to	32.18%	2,320,075	51.00%
7,725,000 to	33.43%	2,582,725	53.00%
8,240,000 and over	34.69%	2,858,250	56.00%

average rate is determined by dividing the tax liability on ordinary net income by taxable income.

(3) Capital gains arising from gifts and bequest

Capital gains from gifts are taxed at a fixed rate of 20 per cent. Capital gains from bequests are taxed at a fixed rate of 8 per cent.

¶408 Tax: Credits and assessment

(1) Tax credits

Spanish law provides for several types of tax credits which take into account the situation of the taxpayer or the household and how the taxpayer uses income. The main tax credits are set out below.

(a) Personal tax credits

This group includes the following tax credits:

(i) Married couples filing joint returns are entitled to a credit of 36,000 pesetas. This tax credit is not applicable when the household is entitled to the variable allowance.

(ii) Households with more than one earner of service income or of income from professional, artistic or commercial activities are entitled to a variable allowance, determined by applying a formula which takes into account the income of the different members of the household. This tax credit may not exceed 412,000 pesetas.

(iii) Each child gives rise to a tax credit of 18,100 pesetas.

(iv) Each ascendent relative living with the taxpayer gives rise to a tax credit of 13,600 pesetas.

(v) Each disabled person living with the taxpayer with income lower than 123,600 pesetas entitles the taxpayer to a tax credit of 45,300 pesetas.

(vi) The tax credit for dependent service income is 22,700 pesetas by each member of the household which receives this kind of income with a maximum of two.

(b) Medical expenses

A tax credit is allowed up to an amount equal to 15 per cent of the medical expenses paid during the year.

(c) Investment credits
Individuals who are engaged in business, agricultural, professional or artistic activities may claim the investment and employment credits granted to corporations, unless they use an objective system of tax assessment to determine taxable income.

The General Budget Law for 1989 provides several investment credits for individuals, including 15 per cent of the amount spent to acquire a permanent residence and 10 per cent of the amount invested in the acquisition of a second residence. Other investment credits relate to the acquisition of historical or cultural property, life insurance and pension funds.

(d) Gifts
Gifts or donations in favour of the State or any public institution are allowed a tax credit of between 10 per cent and 15 per cent.

(e) Dividends
Individuals receiving dividends from Spanish corporations subject to the corporate income tax may claim a tax credit of 10 per cent of the gross dividend.

(f) Foreign tax credit
See ¶410.

(g) Taxes withheld or prepaid
The taxpayer may credit against tax payable any tax prepaid or withheld (see ¶409).

(2) Tax deductions
Married taxpayers electing to file separate tax returns will not allow the 'married couple deduction' or the 'variable allowance'. The deduction for children will be assigned to the parent living with the child. If the child lives with both parents, the deduction will be apportioned by halves. The same criteria are applicable to the deduction for ascendent relatives living with the taxpayer. The remaining deductions will be applicable to the taxpayer having right to them. If both taxpayers are allowed to claim the deduction, it will be apportioned proportionally to each member of the couple. If such proportion is unknown, it will be apportioned by halves.

(3) Tax liability
Once all applicable tax credits have been deducted from the tax calculated by applying the rates to the taxable income (¶407), the resulting liability must be paid upon filing the tax return. The taxpayer may elect to pay it in two

instalments: 60 per cent of the tax liability when filing the tax return, and the remaining 40 per cent in November of the same year.

When tax liability is negative, the taxpayer has a right to a refund up to the amount of tax withheld or prepaid. The refund is made within six months after filing the tax return.

¶409 Withholding tax and prepayment

(1) Withholding tax

Income from independent services, professional or artistic activities, securities or loans is subject to a withholding tax (*retención*) if the payer is an entity resident in Spain, a permanent establishment of a foreign individual or entity, or a resident individual engaged in a business, professional or artistic activity, if the payment arises from the activity itself.

The rate of the withholding tax depends upon the type of income, as follows:

(a) *Salaries.* The withholding tax on salaries is determined in accordance with the percentages set out in Table 4.2. Special employment relationships (see Chapter 11 (Labour Law)) are subject to the same rate of withholding, with a minimum withholding of 10 per cent.

(b) *Securities or loans.* Income from securities or loans is subject to a 25 per cent rate of withholding, except for certain kinds of discount bonds which are subject to a 55 per cent withholding rate.

(c) *Professional and artistic income.* This is subject to a 10 per cent withholding rate.

(d) *Directors.* Remuneration (compensation) paid to members of the board of directors of a corporation is subject to a 25 per cent withholding rate.

(2) Prepayment of tax

Taxpayers engaged in business or commercial, agricultural, professional or artistic activities must pay 20 per cent of the difference between taxable income and deductible expenses into the Treasury on a quarterly basis. Any tax withheld during the period is credited against the tax to be prepaid. Taxpayers who determine their tax liability in accordance with the simplified methods will also be required to make tax prepayments in a lesser amount.

Table 4.2: Percentage of withholding on salaries

Annual income (pesetas)	*No children*		*Number of children*										
	Single	*Married*	1	2	3	4	5	6	7	8	9	10	11
	%		%										
Up to 840,000	–	–	–	–	–	–	–	–	–	–	–	–	–
More than 840,000	2	1	–	–	–	–	–	–	–	–	–	–	–
„ „ 900,000	5	3	2	1	–	–	–	–	–	–	–	–	–
„ „ 1,000,000	8	6	4	3	2	1	1	1	–	–	–	–	–
„ „ 1,100,000	10	8	7	5	3	3	3	2	2	1	1	–	–
„ „ 1,300,000	12	11	10	8	6	6	4	3	3	3	2	2	1
„ „ 1,500,000	14	13	11	11	9	9	7	6	5	4	3	3	2
„ „ 1,700,000	15	15	13	13	12	10	9	9	8	7	6	5	3
„ „ 2,000,000	18	17	16	15	14	13	12	11	11	10	9	7	2
„ „ 2,300,000	19	18	18	17	16	15	14	14	13	12	11	9	7
„ „ 2,600,000	20	20	19	18	17	17	16	15	14	13	12	10	9
„ „ 3,000,000	21	21	20	20	19	19	18	17	16	15	14	12	11
„ „ 3,500,000	22	22	22	22	21	21	20	19	18	17	16	15	14
„ „ 4,000,000	23	23	23	22	22	22	22	20	19	18	17	16	15
„ „ 4,500,000	25	25	25	24	24	24	23	22	21	20	18	17	16
„ „ 5,000,000	26	26	26	25	25	25	24	23	22	21	20	19	18
„ „ 5,500,000	27	27	27	27	27	26	25	24	23	22	21	20	19
„ „ 6,000,000	28	28	28	28	28	27	26	26	25	24	23	22	21
„ „ 7,000,000	31	31	31	30	30	29	28	28	27	26	25	24	23
„ „ 8,000,000	33	33	33	32	32	31	31	30	30	30	30	30	29
„ „ 9,000,000	34	34	34	34	34	33	33	33	32	31	31	31	30
„ „ 10,000,000	36	36	36	36	36	36	35	35	34	33	33	33	32

¶410 International double taxation

(1) Unilateral relief: Foreign tax credit

Spanish residents who obtain part of their income or capital gains abroad are allowed to deduct from the tax payable the lesser of the amount of tax paid abroad, either on income or capital gains, or the amount resulting from applying to all foreign income and capital gains an average rate, calculated by dividing tax liability after all tax credits (except for the withholding and prepayments of tax) by aggregate net taxable income.

(2) International tax treaties

Most international tax treaties signed by Spain grant to Spanish residents a tax credit equal to the lesser of the tax paid abroad or the tax payable in Spain on income or capital gain obtained in the treaty party country. The way in which such a tax credit is applied is the same as under Spanish law.

The treaties with Germany, Belgium, Czechoslovakia, Denmark, Finland, France, Japan, Morocco, Norway, Spain, Poland, Portugal (only with respect to permanent establishments in Portugal) and Switzerland exempt from tax in Spain income obtained by Spanish residents in the other treaty party country, except for dividends, interest and royalties, which will be taxed in Spain and for which Spanish residents are allowed an ordinary foreign tax credit.

CORPORATE INCOME TAX: RESIDENT CORPORATIONS

¶411 Overview and definitions

Corporate income tax applies to companies resident in Spain and companies not resident in Spain which have business activities there. A resident company is subject to Spanish corporate income tax on its worldwide income. A non-resident company is taxed solely on income arising out of or originating in Spain.

The concept of the company for the purpose of corporate income tax not only includes limited companies/corporations, but also partnership-like entities and any other business entities deemed to be legal persons under Spanish law. It also extends to securities investment funds (*fondos de inversión mobiliaria*), temporary associations for the management of certain kinds of funds, temporary business associations (*asociaciones y uniones temporales de empresas*), and other entities specified by statute.

A company is said to reside in Spain if the company was incorporated under the laws of Spain; or the company's business domicile (registered address) is in Spain; or the company's actual principal place of management is in Spain. Almost all tax treaties signed by Spain provide only for the 'place of management' criterion.

In addition to being subject to the corporate income tax, resident corporations must act as withholding agents with respect to both:

(1) *dividends, interest and similar payments.* All companies must withhold 25 per cent of the gross payment; and

(2) *salaries.* Employers, whether companies or individuals, must withhold a certain amount of salary which is determined by the employee's salary and number of dependents (the categories of income and rates are described in ¶409).

¶412 Basic accounting rules

(1) General

Spanish companies are required by commercial law to maintain books of accounting and to prepare regular financial statements in accordance with generally recognised accounting principles which are basically set forth in the General Accounting Rules (*Plan General de Contabilidad*). Most tax benefits and exemptions require adequate bookkeeping, and expenses must be properly entered on the books in order to be able to deduct them. Failing to maintain proper books of accounting may result in substantial tax penalties, including criminal prosecution.

(2) Tax year

The tax year is the same as the company's business year (*ejercicio social*), which may or may not be identical with the calendar year, but may never exceed 12 months.

(3) Accrual method of accounting

The company's taxable profit is determined in accordance with the accounting year, which must be identical to the tax year. Under the accrual method of accounting, all revenues and expenses will be imputed to the period in which they were earned or incurred, regardless of when they are collected or paid out. If a company seeks to apply a different accounting method, it must indicate the change and justify it on the income tax return for the first period in which the method is to be applied. It must also indicate for how long it will apply this method. A change of accounting method may not result in a failure to include any income or revenue.

(4) Valuation rules

All tangible and intangible goods will be given a value equal to their purchase price or production costs, minus depreciation allowances and plus the value of any substantial repair or improvement.

Transactions between related persons must be evaluated at market price. The arm's-length rule, requiring that the value given be equal to that which a disinterested third party would pay, will apply to transactions between a company and its shareholders, directors or persons related to them, as well as to transactions between affiliated corporations.

In order to prevent the effect of inflation, laws have been enacted to allow corporations to re-evaluate their assets without paying taxes on the revaluation, under certain conditions. There has not been a revaluation law authorised since 1983. If the revaluation occurs outside the scope of a revaluation law, on a voluntary basis, the increase in the book value of the assets will be considered a taxable capital gain.

¶413 Computation of gross income

(1) General

Any income, revenue, capital gain or increase in the book value of corporate assets is considered taxable as ordinary business income, unless the law expressly provides otherwise. Income which has been subject to withholding must be grossed up.

(2) Capital gains

A capital gain or loss may occur when there is a change in the assets of the company (realisation event). The principal realisation events are the sale or exchange of assets, the partial or total liquidation of the company, inheritance or gifts received by the company, voluntary revaluation of the assets, and destruction or loss of assets.

The capital gain or loss is determined by subtracting the net book value from the sale price or the price of the assets received in exchange, the market value of the assets in the case of liquidation, the valuation given for the purpose of calculating the inheritance and gift tax, or the accounting value given to the assets after their revaluation.

Capital gains are always taxable, except for capital gains resulting from the sale of certain tangible fixed assets, which can be rolled over tax-free if all revenues derived from the sale are reinvested in assets of a similar type in the fiscal year of the sale or within two years thereafter (it is possible to ask for an extension of up to four years). The capital gain may be recaptured and taxed if the replacement assets are sold before the expiration of their useful life.

(3) Exclusions from income
Contributions to capital made by a shareholder to a corporation, including any premium paid on the shares, are not considered taxable income of the corporation.

¶414 Allowable business expenses

A company is allowed to deduct from income any expenses required to carry on the business, provided that the expenses were produced during the tax year and were entered on the accounting books. Spanish law expressly sets out most types of business expenses, but any other kind of expenses not expressly set out by the law may be deducted if they meet the criteria of being required, accrued and entered on the books.

The most important deductible expenses may be classified as follows.

(1) Acquisition of goods and services
The costs of acquiring goods required to carry on business operations are deductible, unless such goods are on inventory at the end of the tax year. The cost of acquisition of services is also deductible. There is no limit on the deduction of interest, rental payments, insurance, etc., other than that imposed by the arm's-length rule in transactions involving related persons or related entities.

(2) Salaries and labour cost
Salaries and labour-related expenses, including social security and fringe benefits, are taxable if they are mandatory under labour law or the employment contract. Contributions to pension funds as an employee benefit are deductible by the company up to the amount of 750,000 pesetas per employee.

(3) Taxes
Taxes other than the corporate income tax are deductible, except for taxes which must be shifted to a third party by law (such as VAT and withholding taxes on dividends, interest and salaries).

(4) Bad debts
Doubtful or uncollectable accounts receivable can either be written off as soon as the inability to collect is clear (for example, bankruptcy or the outcome of litigation, or when the amount owed is not paid within six months from the expiration date) or through a reserve set up under the conditions and with a maximum annual ceiling established by law. If the receivables are subsequently collected, the revenue obtained is considered taxable income.

(5) Reserves for liabilities and for reduction of value of inventory and securities

Spanish law allows companies to create a reserve account when the company has incurred liabilities, the exact amount of which cannot be determined due to ongoing or potential litigation or assessment procedures. The amount of the reserve must be equal to the estimated value of the liability and is a deductible expense. Spanish law also allows the company to adjust the value of inventory and securities annually by creating a reserve account, which will be debited or credited, depending on the difference between the market value at the end of the tax year and the book value of the securities or inventory. Taxpayers electing to create this reserve account must then treat any loss of value as a deductible expense, and any increase in value as taxable income.

(6) Start-up and other expenses which may be capitalised

Incorporation costs and start-up expenses may be capitalised and amortised over a ten-year period (this term will probably be reduced to five years as a consequence of the application in Spain of EEC Accounting Directives). All other kinds of expenses capable of being capitalised may be depreciated over five years (for example, unsuccessful research and development expenses, or the costs of reorganising a means of production) or over the useful life of the asset or liability to which it relates (for example, the cost of issuing debentures or bonds or the expenses related to an installation project).

(7) Depreciation

Depreciation allowances for assets with a useful life of over one year are deductible from taxable income. As a general rule, assets may only be depreciated using the straight-line method. The tax authorities have issued regulations establishing the maximum and minimum depreciation rates and useful life for different types of assets and activities. The minimum depreciation allowance is mandatory. Depreciation exceeding the maximum rate allowed by the regulations is not deductible, unless the taxpayer has received express authorisation. The taxpayer may request authorisation for a specific depreciation plan with regard to assets which have a shorter useful life than the one provided by law. The taxpayer must file for the authorisation prior to using the assets involved, or within the first three months of starting to use them.

Tangible fixed property utilised in the business activity, which is acquired new and has a useful life of three or more years, may be depreciated using any of three methods: straight-line, sum of the digits, or 1.5 to 2.5 declining balance (the coefficient depends on the useful life of the asset).

Second-hand goods may be depreciated by applying either the straight-line method to the original value of the asset or by applying a coefficient which is double the regular one to the actual price paid for it.

(8) Capital losses

Capital losses are fully deductible from taxable income.

(9) Losses carry-forward

Net losses may be carried forward five years. The taxpayer may elect the amount to be offset in any given year. There is no carry-back of losses.

¶415 Alternative means of determining taxable income

If the taxpayer refuses or otherwise fails to provide the necessary accounting information to determine taxable income, either of the following methods may be applied by the tax authorities:

(1) *Fiscal equity method.* Where enough information is available, the tax authorities may simply focus on the total change on the net book value of the company (shareholders equity value) between the beginning and the end of the fiscal period.

(2) *Indirect appraisal method.* Where accounting information is not available, the authorities may rely on other evidence of income, such as average profits made by other enterprises engaged in similar operations, average income realised in previous years, profit patterns in the industry, prices and rates set by administrative authorities, value given to assets on other tax returns or in contracts, consumption of raw materials and other production input or any other method based on sound presumptions.

¶416 Tax rates

Tax liability results from application of the tax rate on taxable net income (gross income minus deductible expenses and allowances). Tax rates are revised on a regular basis by the General Budget Laws. The 1989 General Budget Law provides for a corporate tax rate of 35 per cent with certain exceptions, including, among others:

(1) insurance mutuals (*mutuas de seguros generales*) and reciprocal guarantee societies (*sociedades de garantía recíproca*) – 26 per cent;

(2) co-operatives – 20 per cent (except for credit co-operatives which are subject to special tax limitations and to a tax rate of 26 per cent);

(3) entities dedicated to public service, such as the Spanish Red Cross, religious and charitable organisations, political parties, unions, profes-

sional associations and others – exempt from corporate income tax, except for certain income subject to withholding; and

(4) collective investment entities (*instituciones de inversión colectiva*) – 13 per cent.

¶417 Tax credits and reductions of tax

Spanish law provides for a number of credits and reductions (*bonificaciones*) of tax liability, related to the kind of activity performed, the type of revenue received, or the investment made by the company. The Corporate Income Tax Law sets out the order in which the credits and reductions may be made, as some of them may take into account previous credits and reductions.

(1) Double taxation tax credit

(a) *Dividends-received tax credit.* Companies and permanent establishments of foreign companies in Spain may deduct from their tax liability 50 per cent of the proportional part of the corporate income tax relating to dividend earnings received from another Spanish company. The tax credit reaches 100 per cent when the dividends are received by a securities investment fund or company (*fondos y sociedades de inversión mobiliaria*) or by any company which owns at least 25 per cent of the stock throughout the year in which the dividends have been paid and the immediately prior year.

(b) *International double taxation tax credit.* See ¶419 below.

(2) Special tax reductions

The law provides for a number of tax reductions, depending on the type of business of the company and the source of revenue. The principal reductions are set out below:

(a) *Investment in Ceuta and Melilla.* The taxpayer company may reduce its tax liability by 50 per cent of the proportional part of the tax relating to revenues or capital gains resulting from investments made or transactions completed in Ceuta and Melilla.

(b) *Special tax reductions for industrial banks, companies for the development of enterprises, and venture capital companies.* Industrial banks and other companies having as their business purpose the promotion and development of enterprises through temporary participation in their capital may reduce their tax liability by 95 per cent in respect of that part of corporate income tax attributed to the capital gains arising from the sale of the shares, if such sale takes place within eight years of the acquisition date and the proceeds are reinvested in similar securities.

(c) *Fiscally protected co-operatives.* Tax liability may be reduced by 50 per cent.

(3) Investment tax credit

The credits listed below also permit the taxpayer to subtract a certain percentage of its investment directly from its tax liability. The total amount of all investment credits set out below may not exceed 20 per cent of tax liability once the 'double taxation tax credits' and the special tax reductions are subtracted. As an exception, tax credits allowed for investments related to the 1992 Olympics in Barcelona or to Expo 1992 in Seville, may offset tax liability up to 25 per cent. Any excess tax credit that cannot be utilised within the year may be carried forward five years.

(a) *Investment on fixed assets.* 5 per cent of investments made in fixed assets, other than land, to be used by the taxpayer for its business operations (assets to be leased to third parties are disallowed), as well as in the creation of books or films.

(b) *Export-related investment.* 5 per cent of investments made to create a foreign branch or to acquire shares or other holdings in foreign companies of which the Spanish company holds at least 25 per cent of the equity capital, when the branch or the foreign company directly promotes Spanish exports. A 5 per cent credit is also granted for certain advertising expenses incurred abroad.

(c) *Research and development.* 15 per cent of expenses for the acquisition of intangibles and 30 per cent of expenses for the acquisition of durable assets used in programmes for the development of new products or industrial processes.

(d) *Protected assets.* 10 per cent of any amount invested in the acquisition of assets which are officially listed as property of cultural or historic interest.

(e) *Olympic and international exhibition-related expenses.* 15 per cent of investments in activities related to the promotion of the Olympics or to Expo 1992 in Seville.

(4) Credit for creating jobs

Any employer is entitled to a credit of 500,000 pesetas for each new full-time job created.

¶418 Filing, prepayment and withholding

The corporate income tax return must be filed by resident corporations within 25 days of the approval of accounts by the shareholders at the annual general meeting.

Pre-payment equal to 55 per cent of the total tax paid the previous year is due as follows: on 20 July (10 per cent); on 20 October (30 per cent); and on 20 December (15 per cent). This payment subsequently is directly applied to reduce tax liability after all other credits and reductions have been applied. The payer of interest and dividends to a company must withhold 25 per cent of the amount paid on account. These amounts withheld are also directly applied to reduce tax liability after credits and reductions have been applied. If the amounts prepaid and withheld exceed corporate income tax liability, the company is entitled to apply for a refund of the excess tax paid.

¶419 Double taxation relief

(1) Unilateral relief

Spanish companies receiving income from abroad may claim a credit equal to the lesser of the amount of corporate income tax paid to the foreign government or the amount of Spanish corporate income tax payable on the foreign income. In order to quantify the foreign tax credit, income from different countries will be considered separately. Moreover, Spanish corporate income tax law provides for computation on a transaction basis. This means that if, in one country, more than one kind of transaction has taken place, the credit allowable for each transaction must be calculated separately.

Companies investing abroad through subsidiaries in the exploitation of hydrocarbons may claim an indirect tax credit for the amount of foreign corporate income tax paid by the subsidiary to its country of origin, up to the amount of Spanish taxes payable on the income of the foreign subsidiary.

(2) Tax treaties

The tax treaties signed with Austria, Czechoslovakia, Belgium, Denmark, France, Germany, Japan, Norway, the Netherlands, Poland, Portugal (for income from permanent establishments only), Morocco, Switzerland, and the United Kingdom exempt any revenue obtained and taxed in those countries from Spanish corporate income tax, except for dividends, interest and royalties. Although these types of income are subject to tax in both countries, the Spanish company may claim the regular foreign tax credit. Therefore, under the provisions of these tax treaties, profits of a permanent establishment of a Spanish company or revenues arising from real estate investments in treaty partner countries are exempt from Spanish tax.

All other treaties provide for a tax credit scheme, which allows Spanish companies to claim foreign tax credits similar to those provided by Spain unilaterally.

Some treaties also include provisions to minimise intra-company double taxation. The treaties with Belgium, Canada, Rumania, Sweden and Switzerland treat the dividends received by a Spanish company from its foreign subsidiary located in the treaty partner country as dividends from a Spanish subsidiary. Therefore, Spanish companies may claim a dividends-received tax credit similar to that applicable to intra-company distributions in Spain. Treaties with the United Kingdom and France provide for an additional scheme to minimise double taxation. The United Kingdom may refund the 'advanced corporate tax' under certain circumstances, and France may grant to Spanish shareholders of French corporations the '*avoire fiscal.*' From the point of view of Spanish tax, both amounts are deemed to be taxable income, and the Spanish companies will have the right to a full credit for the withholding tax paid in either or both countries.

Finally, Spain has granted 'tax sparing' (i.e. credit for the theoretical tax, regardless of any reduction or exemption granted by the other country) in treaties with Brazil (for interest and royalties), Finland (for dividends, interest and royalties), and Morocco and Tunisia (for certain kinds of interest payments).

¶420 Liquidation, reorganisation, mergers and split-offs

(1) Liquidations

Upon commencing liquidation procedings, the liquidating agents must first close the on-going fiscal period and prepare a balance sheet and tax return for that part of the year which has elapsed.

The liquidation proceeds received by a shareholder may constitute a capital gain to him/her if the value of the proceeds is greater than the acquisition cost of the shares. When the shareholder is a corporation, the part of the liquidation proceeds in excess of the liquidated corporation's equity is considered a dividend for the purpose of applying the dividends-received tax credit.

The shareholders are jointly and severally liable for unpaid taxes, but only up to the extent of the liquidated amount received. In addition, the liquidating agents will be liable for any negligent or wilful errors or omissions in the payment of the company's taxes.

(2) Mergers and reorganisations

The merger or reorganisation of a company may result in taxable capital gains. The assignment of assets to another company results in a taxable gain for the company assigning the assets if such assignment is made at a value greater than the net book value. The delivery of shares of a new company to the shareholders of the original company in exchange for the shares previously held by them results in a taxable capital gain equal to the difference between the stock market value, or the net book value, if not quoted, of the shares received and the acquisition price of delivered shares. Spanish Law 76/1980, dated 26 December, allows the Ministry of Economy and Finance to grant several tax advantages in connection with mergers and reorganisations which benefit the national economy.

(a) Types of reorganisations

The following types of reorganisations are eligible to apply for these benefits:

(i) the merger of two or more corporations or individual businesses into a new corporation;

(ii) the absorption of one or more companies or individual businesses by a previously existing corporation. After liquidation of the company or businesses absorbed, the shareholders receive shares in the absorbing company;

(iii) the split-off of a company's net worth into two or more parts, each allocated to another company either newly created or previously existing. The shareholders of the liquidated company receive a proportional number of shares of the company receiving the assets;

(iv) split-offs of part of the net worth of a corporation which does not go into liquidation, some or all of which is allocated to a newly created company or to a previously existing one. The shareholders of the first corporation receive shares in the companies receiving the assets.

(b) Conditions

In order to apply for the tax benefits, the following conditions must be met:

(i) Each of the companies concerned must have been operating for at least three years prior to the proposed reorganisation.

(ii) At least 50 per cent of the companies' assets, either of the previously existing companies or of the newly created ones, must be effectively connected to business activities directly related to their business purpose.

(iii) The merger or reorganisation must benefit the national economy.

(c) Maximum benefits
The Ministry of Economy and Finance must expressly approve the reorganisation, and any approval must contain the specific tax benefits to be granted. The following amounts are the maximum benefits provided by law:

(i) A 99 per cent reduction of the tax on any capital gain resulting from the reorganisation. If any of the assets revaluated during the merger or reorganisation are sold within the following three years (or five years in the case of real estate), the tax benefits may be recaptured and the capital gain calculated on the basis of the net book value prior to the reorganisation, ignoring the reappraisal made during it.

(ii) Exemption of the capital gain realised by a shareholder arising from the reorganisation from taxation.

(iii) A 99 per cent reduction of the transfer tax applicable to any transactions necessary to the reorganisation.

(iv) A 99 per cent reduction of municipal 'tax on the increased value of land'.

Any tax benefit granted to one of the previously existing companies will be passed to the new corporation or to the absorbing one if they meet all the conditions which were required of the dissolved companies to obtain the tax benefits. Any loss carry forward is not transferable.

¶421 Transparent companies, corporate groups, and other special types of tax treatment

(1) Tax transparent companies
Net income obtained by certain companies is imputed directly to shareholders without subjecting the company to corporate income tax. Tax transparent companies include:

(a) securities investment companies (*sociedades de inversión mobiliaria*), the stock of which is not quoted on the stock market; companies having more than 50 per cent of their assets invested in securities, and companies with more than 50 per cent of their assets invested in property which is not directly related to a business or professional activity, provided that more than 50 per cent of capital belongs to a family group (defined to include up to fourth degree relatives) or to no more than ten partners, all of which are private individuals or companies and not public agencies;

(b) professional corporations or companies, all the partners or shareholders of which are members of the profession.

There is no clear law regarding the taxation of non-resident shareholders of transparent companies. The tax authorities have issued two contradictory rulings; one in 1983 (with regard to a United Kingdom shareholder), in which the foreign shareholder was held to be acting in Spain through a permanent establishment, and the other in 1988 (with regard to a Luxembourg holding company), in which the imputed income was held to be 'other income' subject to a 25 per cent withholding tax in the absence of an applicable tax treaty. The treaty between Spain and Tunisia considers shareholders of transparent companies to be acting in Spain through a permanent establishment. It is highly probable that the tax authorities will try to apply such treatment in most of these cases.

(2) Corporate groups

For the purposes of filing a consolidated return, a corporate group is defined as a group of Spanish resident corporations formed by a 'dominant' corporation which controls a group of 'dependent' corporations. A 'dominant' corporation is that company which owns, directly or indirectly, 90 per cent of the equity of one or several subsidiaries and which has maintained such control during the year of the consolidated return and the two prior years. The 'dominant' corporation may not be a dependant of any other Spanish corporation, nor currently enjoy special corporate income tax treatment (for instance as an exempt company). It is required that the tax year of all companies in the group must be the same.

Generally speaking, consolidations are initiated by applications made by the 'dominant' corporation to the Ministry of Economy and Finance for authorisation to calculate the taxable base and all tax computations for the group jointly by pooling all balance sheets and profit and loss statements. On the other hand, the Ministry of Economy and Finance may require such consolidation in order to prevent tax evasion or fraud. The Ministry of Economy and Finance may also impose it on any corporate group formed by companies affiliated through direct or indirect holdings of as little as 25 per cent of corporate stock, or even less, if one or more of the companies exercises decision-making power over the others.

Tax liability is allocated among the companies of the group in proportion to the payments each company would have had to contribute if taxed separately. However, all companies in the group are jointly and severally liable for the total amount of tax liability.

(3) Other particular types of tax treatment

A number of special tax treatments exist, depending on the peculiar characteristics of the taxpayer company, the most important of which are the following:

(a) *Exempt companies.* These companies only have to pay withholding tax, because they are exempt from corporate income tax. This group includes companies with no true business purpose, for example those which are dedicated to educational, cultural or charitable activities.

(b) *Protected co-operatives.* There are some kinds of co-operative groups which receive very favourable tax treatment. Relatively recently the Government made public proposed legislation modifying the tax treatment of co-operatives.

(c) *Labour corporations.* These companies are groups of employees with a corporate structure. Such companies have some tax benefits which are regulated by a special law.

(d) *Collective investment institutions.* These are companies dedicated to the investment of funds obtained from the general public. If quoted on the stock market, they are subject to a 13 per cent tax rate and may receive a 100 per cent dividend tax credit.

(e) *Regional industrial development companies and venture capital companies.* Those are entities which are dedicated to the creation of new enterprises by participating temporarily in their equity. The law provides for some tax benefits for both dividends and capital gains arising from the sale of the investment.

TAX ON THE INCOME OF NON-RESIDENT INDIVIDUALS AND CORPORATIONS

¶422 Scope of taxation: Income and capital gains subject to tax

Non-resident individuals or companies are subject to income tax only with respect to Spanish-source income and capital gains. The definition of Spanish-source income and capital gains is not clear under Spanish law. Thc Corporatc Income Tax Law and the Individual Income Tax Regulations set out a list of items which are deemed to be Spanish-source. Nevertheless, the list can be confusing because the descriptions of Spanish-source items are vague and sometimes contradictory. The following items are those deemed to be Spanish-source.

(1) Permanent establishment income

Income resulting from a permanent establishment operating in Spain will be subject to the Spanish individual and corporate income taxes. The concept of a permanent establishment is similar to the one included in the OECD (Organisation for Economic Co-operation and Development) Draft Convention of 1977, defined as 'a fixed place of business through which the business of the enterprise is wholly or partly carried on'. It includes agriculture, forestry and cattle raising, as well as artistic and professional activities carried out in Spain. Spanish law does not exclude ancillary activities. Therefore, the maintenance of fixed places of business in Spain for any kind of activity may be deemed to constitute a permanent establishment, unless provisions of a treaty apply.

Permanent establishment income will include income resulting from the activities performed by the permanent establishment, income resulting from the lease or assignment of any asset or right effectively connected to or managed by the permanent establishment, or which is collected by the permanent establishment, and capital gains and losses resulting from the sale or exchange of assets effectively connected with the permanent establishment.

Foreign shipping and air transport companies will not be deemed to be operating in Spain through a permanent establishment if the companies' country of residence grants the same exemption to Spanish companies.

(2) Service income

Income from employment and other services rendered in Spain is deemed to be Spanish-source income.

(3) Income from capital investment

This category includes income arising from the ownership of any kind of security issued by a Spanish company, from any capital investment in a Spanish company, or from a loan to a Spanish company or to a Spanish permanent establishment of a foreign entity.

(4) Rental income

This category includes rentals from the leasing of real property located in Spain, from the assignment of rights on such real property to be exercised in Spain, and from the leasing of any kind of personal property located in Spain. It should also be noted, however, that the Individual Income Tax Regulations also include rights arising from the assignment of all types of rights created or which may be executed or performed in Spain. This category also includes royalties paid from the licensing of intangible industrial or artistic rights.

(5) Profits of foreign corporations

Income from securities issued by foreign corporations which have permanent establishments in Spain is deemed to be Spanish-source income to the extent such income is attributable to the investment in Spain. It therefore may be taxed by Spanish authorities. The wording of the law is not clear and has never been applied. A similar provision is included in the Individual Income

Tax Law, but the Individual Income Tax Regulations provide for the apportionment of profits in proportion to the net worth of the permanent establishment to the foreign company as a whole. As in the case of corporate income tax, this individual income tax provision has never been applied.

(6) Income paid by any Spanish resident

Both the Corporate and Individual Income Tax Laws deem any amount paid by a resident in Spain to a non-resident individual or corporation to be Spanish-source income. The only exclusions to this rule are payments related to the import–export trade and interest paid on non-resident bank accounts in foreign currency. From a practical point of view, this category of Spanish-source income poses very significant problems, and it is not always enforced by the tax authorities.

(7) Capital gains

Capital gains resulting from the sale or exchange of any kind of property located in Spain are considered Spanish-source. This rule is clear when applied to real and personal property because the actual location of the property governs. With regard to securities, the Individual Income Tax Regulations include capital gains resulting from the sale of any kind of security issued by a Spanish enterprise or sold in Spain. The Corporate Income Tax Law does not include a similar rule, but tax rulings issued by the Spanish tax authorities deem any security issued by a Spanish company to be located in Spain. Therefore, capital gains resulting from the sale of securities issued by a domestic corporation are deemed to be Spanish-source capital gains.

(8) Foreign source income

Article 334 of the Corporate Income Tax Regulations provides that certain kinds of income obtained in Spain will not be considered Spanish-source income for the purpose of corporate income tax. Such provisions refer to the following three kinds of income:

(a) payments made to a non-resident by a foreign permanent establishment of a Spanish resident when:

  (i) such payments are required for the business carried on by the permanent establishment of the Spanish resident abroad,

  (ii) they are made by the permanent establishment, and

  (iii) they are registered on the books of such permanent establishment;

(b) payments to a non-resident resulting from international trade transactions entered into by a Spanish resident. This category includes imports and payments related to import and export transactions; and

(c) interest paid to a non-resident on deposits and bank accounts in foreign currency or in 'convertible pesetas', unless the payment of such interest is made to a permanent establishment of the foreign resident in Spain.

The three exemptions mentioned above are included in the Corporate Income Tax Regulations. Therefore, some writers have indicated that such exemptions will not apply to foreign individuals. Nevertheless, such exemptions have been customarily applied also to individuals.

¶423 Taxing permanent establishments

(1) Permanent establishments of corporations

The Corporate Income Tax Law provides for three categories of permanent establishments for the purpose of determining taxable income.

(a) Permanent establishments with continuous business activities

This category comes within the general definition of a permanent establishment and includes all the permanent establishments that cannot be included in the other two categories. From the point of view of accounting and taxation, such establishments are deemed to be separate entities from the parent company. Taxable income is determined according to the general rules of corporate income tax. Overhead expenses are deductible from the permanent establishment's income if such expenses are allocated to the permanent establishment on a 'reasonable basis'. The Corporate Income Tax Regulations consider the following to be reasonable allocation criteria:

(i) capital used in the permanent establishment;

(ii) turnover;

(iii) overall expenses of the permanent establishment; or

(iv) investments effectively connected with the permanent establishment.

Interest payments from the permanent establishment to the parent company are not deductible.

(b) Permanent establishments with temporary activity

This category includes the following:

(i) building site or construction or installation projects with activities lasting more than 12 months;

(ii) services rendered in Spain for more than 183 days in any calendar year, unless rendered through a Spanish branch;

(iii) any kind of activity, deemed to be done through a permanent establishment, which is anticipated to last less than three years.

In the above-mentioned cases, the taxpayer may elect to be taxed as a permanent establishment with continuous activity or to be taxed as operating in Spain without having a permanent establishment (in the way described in ¶424). In the latter case, the taxpayer need not maintain the accounting records normally required of Spanish corporations.

(c) Intra-group permanent establishments

This type of permanent establishment includes any kind of office or place which renders services exclusively to the parent company and receives no income from external sources. The taxable income of this kind of permanent establishment is considered to be equal to 15 per cent of its expenses, plus any income from ancillary activities, such as investment income.

(2) Permanent establishments of foreign individuals

The permanent establishment of a foreign individual in Spain will be taxed separately from the individual's other Spanish-source income which is not directly related to the activities performed by it. Every permanent establishment of a foreign individual is taxed according to Individual Income Tax Law which does not distinguish between continuous and temporary activities.

The taxable income is determined following the separate accounting method. If the turnover of the permanent establishment is less than 15 million pesetas in any given year, and it has less than 12 employees in that year, the permanent establishment may determine its taxable income in accordance with the rules of the simplified assessment system applicable to activities performed by Spanish businessmen (see ¶405(3)).

(3) Tax year and assessment of tax

The taxable income of a permanent establishment of a corporation is computed on the basis of the parent company's fiscal year, which may or may not be the same as the calendar year, but which in any case may not exceed 12 months. The permanent establishment of a foreign individual must compute the taxable income on the basis of the calendar year. The tax rate is 35 per cent, except for permanent establishments with temporary activity which elect to be taxed on the basis of obtaining the income without permanent establishment.

¶424 Spanish-source income and capital gains obtained without permanent establishment

(1) General

As of 8 July 1989, Spanish-source income is taxed at a rate of 25 per cent of gross income, unless it can be included in one of the groups indicated in subsections (2) to (5) below, and includes dividends, interest and all capital investment income, rental income from real or personal property, and income resulting from the assignment of the right to use intangible property. Prior to that date the applicable rate was 20 per cent.

(2) Overhead and management expenses

Overhead expenses allocated to a permanent establishment by its parent company, and management fees paid by a Spanish corporation to its controlling foreign corporation, are subject to tax at the rate of 14 per cent.

(3) Types of income which are taxed on a net income basis

Income from services rendered in Spain, technical assistance, plant installations, engineering contracts, and from any kind of economic activity performed in Spain without a permanent establishment, is taxed at the rate of 25 per cent on the difference between the gross income received in Spain and salaries and social security payments payable to personnel employed in Spain and the acquisition of materials necessary to render the services.

(4) Income subject to a reduced tax rate

Income derived from leasing cinematographic films and related products, and income derived from leasing containers used in international trade, except for those used in shipping, is subject to a 10 per cent tax rate.

Non-residents receiving pensions of less than 1,500,000 pesetas per year, and non-residents who are paid employees of Spanish Embassies or Consulates abroad, are subject to an 8 per cent tax rate.

(5) Capital gains

Capital gains are determined by subtracting from the sale price the acquisition price, plus any costs of substantial repair or improvement. In order to eliminate currency gains, the Corporate Income Tax Regulations provide that the acquisition price will be determined in pesetas, using the rate of exchange applicable on the date of sale. There is no such rule with regard to individuals. On the other hand, the acquisition price will be revalued using the same coefficient table applicable to resident individuals in order to reduce the effects of inflation. Capital gains obtained either by corporations or individuals are taxed at the rate of 35 per cent.

¶425 Assessment procedures

Permanent establishments of foreign corporations or individuals must file their tax returns in the same way as resident corporations and individuals.

Non-resident corporations or individuals receiving income without a permanent establishment must file a return (Form 210) within 25 days of the date on which the income accrued or was paid. The tax on dividends and interest income can be paid quarterly under certain conditions. Presentation of Form 210 is required in order to transfer the profits of the investment abroad. The tax authorities may also make a tax audit before the profits of the investment are transferred.

Non-residents receiving income in Spain without a permanent establishment must appoint a representative in Spain to go before the tax authorities. If no one is appointed, the individual paying the income will be deemed to be the representative.

Some kinds of income, mainly interest, dividends and certain kinds of rental and service income received by non-residents, are subject to withholding or retention in Spain when the payer is not the representative of the non-resident individual or company.

¶426 Double taxation relief

Non-resident individuals or corporate taxpayers may avail themselves of the provisions of a Spanish Tax Treaty with their country of residence.

Spain has signed tax treaties with 24 countries: Austria, Belgium, Brazil, Canada, Czechoslovakia, Denmark, Finland, France, Germany, Hungary, Italy, Japan, Luxembourg, Morocco, the Netherlands, Norway, Poland, Portugal, Romania, Sweden, Switzerland, Tunisia, the UK, and the USSR. There are several treaties that are pending ratification, as, for instance, the ones with the USA, Ireland or Greece. And there are some other treaties which are in active negotiation, as, for instance, the one with China. All treaties signed by Spain follow the OECD Model Treaty. Most of them follow the 1963 Model Treaty; only the most recent ones follow the 1977 Model Treaty.

All the treaties signed by Spain exclude from Spanish tax income resulting from business or professional activities performed in Spain when such activities are not performed through a permanent establishment or a fixed base of business. Income resulting from a permanent establishment or a professional activity performed through a fixed base in Spain will be taxed in accordance with the general rules indicated above. Nevertheless, the rules regarding 'inter-group permanent establishments' are not applicable to countries which have signed a treaty with Spain, because most of such activities will be excluded from the definition of 'permanent establishment' in accordance with

Article 5, paragraph 4, of the Model Treaty. 'Permanent establishments with temporary activity' may elect to be taxed as if the income was obtained without a permanent establishment. If such election is made, Spanish-source income will be taxed following the domestic law, the Tax Treaty not being applicable to such income.

Income resulting from real estate or agricultural activities will be taxed in Spain in accordance with domestic law.

There are specific rules with regard to dependent personal services, directors of companies, artistes and athletes, pensions, government service, students, teachers and researchers, and income from shipping and air transport activities. Most treaties follow the OECD Model Treaty, but some contain certain peculiarities.

Dividends, interest and royalties can be taxed in Spain at the maximum rate indicated in Table 4.3 below.

Capital gains will not be taxed in Spain, except for the following:

(1) Capital gains resulting from the sale of real estate located in Spain. The treaties with Canada, France, Luxembourg, the Netherlands, Poland, Sweden and the USSR allow the taxation in Spain of some capital gains resulting from the sale of shares of real estate companies.

(2) Capital gains resulting from the sale of assets effectively connected to a permanent establishment in Spain.

(3) Capital gains resulting from the sale of ships or aircraft operating in international traffic, or movable property pertaining to the operation of such ships or aircraft, if the enterprise is effectively managed in Spain.

The treaty with Brazil provides that both countries will be allowed to tax capital gains which are taxable under domestic law.

Most treaties provide for the exemption method to eliminate double taxation, as, for instance, the treaties with Germany, Belgium, Czechoslovakia, Denmark, Finland, France, Hungary, Luxembourg, Morocco, Norway, the Netherlands, Poland, Portugal (with respect only to permanent establishments in Spain of a Portuguese resident), and Switzerland. In most treaties the exemption is not applicable to dividends, interest and royalties.

Most treaties provide for a 'tax sparing' credit with regard to certain kinds of interest payments which are exempt from tax or subject to a reduced rate of tax in Spain. This is the case of the treaties with Germany, Belgium, Brazil, Canada, Denmark, Finland, Japan, France, Luxembourg, Norway, the Netherlands, Sweden, Switzerland, and Tunisia.

Table 4.3 shows the maximum withholding tax provided for in the treaties signed by Spain.

Table 4.3: Tax treaties – maximum withholding taxes

	Dividends			
	General %	*Parent/Subsidiary* %	*Interests* %	*Royalties* %
Non-treaty countries	25	25	25	25
Austria	15	10	5	5
Belgium	15	15	15	5
Brazil	15	15	10/15	10/15
Canada	15	15	15	10
Czechoslovakia	15	5	0	5
Denmark	15	10	10	6
Finland	15	10	10	5
France	15	10	10	6
Germany	15	10	10	5
Hungary	15	5	0	0
Italy	15	15	12	4/8
Japan	15	10	10	10
Luxembourg	15	5	10	10
Morocco	15	10	10	5/10
Netherlands	15	10	10	6
Norway	15	10	10	5
Poland	15	5	0	10
Portugal	15	10	15	5
Romania	15	10	10	10
Sweden	15	10	10	5
Switzerland	15	10	10	5
Tunisia	15	10	5/10	10
UK	15	10	12	10
USSR	18	18	0	5

In order to benefit from the reduction of the withholding tax provided by treaty, each treaty provides for a specific procedure. Nevertheless, the Spanish tax authorities follow a homogeneous procedure. The reduced rate of tax can be applied when completing Form 210 if a certificate of residence in the treaty partner country is annexed to the form. Income subject to withholding by the payer of the income can be withheld at the reduced rate provided for in the treaty if such certificate of residence is provided to the withholding party.

NET WORTH TAX

¶427 Overview

Net worth tax is imposed on the net assets of individuals and households as of 31 December each year. Resident individuals and households are taxed on their worldwide assets, while non-residents are taxed only on assets located in Spain. The tax is applicable throughout Spain, but is administered by the regional governments, and thus some special rules may also be applied by them.

The concept of residence is the same as applied in relation to individual income tax. The concept of household is also applicable to this tax. Therefore, a resident household must add up all the assets owned by any of its members in order to assess and pay the net worth tax. The law 20/1989 establishes that married taxpayers must file separate returns. Each spouse must include his/her assets and debts. In case of co-ownership, the asset or debt will be apportioned among the taxpayers proportionally to their respective interest, if unknown it will be apportioned by halves.

¶428 Valuation of assets and debts

(1) Real property

Real property is valued in accordance with the assessed value determined for the purpose of the local property tax. Real property acquired after 1987 is valued at the acquisition price prevailing for transfer tax purposes if greater than the property tax assessment.

(2) Assets and rights relating to artistic, professional or business activities

Professional, artistic and business activities will be valued at the net book value appearing in the accounting of the activity in question.

(3) Bank accounts and deposits

These are valued by the average balance maintained during the tax year in which the tax is paid.

(4) Securities

Securities quoted on the stock exchange will be valued at the average price quoted in the last quarter of each year. Debt instruments will be valued at their nominal value. Shares of companies which are not quoted on the stock exchange are valued at their net book value.

(5) Other assets and rights

Any assets or rights not mentioned above must be included at market value. Assets or rights with an individual value lower than 250,000 pesetas do not have to be included separately.

(6) Household furnishings

Household furnishings are valued on the basis of the estimated value of all the assets owned by a household. It includes any personal property with a value lower than 250,000 pesetas. It is determined as a percentage of the value of the household assets: 3 per cent of the net worth under 20 million pesetas and 5 per cent of the excess above such amount.

(7) Debts

Debts are valued at their nominal amount on 31 December of each year.

¶429 Resident households

(1) Taxable net worth

The taxable net worth of a resident household is the difference between the value of the worldwide assets of all its members and their debts. Both assets and debts are valued in accordance with the rules described in ¶426.

(2) Personal exemptions

From net worth, the taxpayer may deduct personal exemptions as follows:

General deduction	9,000,000 pesetas
For each child less than 25 years of age living with the taxpayer	1,500,000 pesetas
For each child who is blind, crippled or physically or mentally disabled, living with the taxpayer	3,000,000 pesetas

Should the children live with both parents, each of them will be allowed to claim half of the deduction.

(3) Rates

Net worth after deducting the personal exemptions is subject to tax according to Table 4.4.

(4) Assessment of tax

The taxpayer is responsible for assessing the tax and filing the appropriate tax form, together with the income tax return.

Table 4.4: Rates of net worth tax

Taxable base (pesetas)	*Rate of tax (%)*
0 up to 25 million	0.20
More than 25 million up to 50 million	0.30
More than 50 million up to 100 million	0.45
More than 100 million up to 250 million	0.65
More than 250 million up to 500 million	0.85
More than 500 million up to 1,100 million	1.10
More than 1,000 million up to 1,500 million	1.35
More than 1,500 million up to 2,500 million	1.70
More than 2,500 million	2.00

The aggregate of the tax payable for the individual income tax and the net worth tax cannot exceed 70 per cent of the taxpayer's taxable income for the year. Any excess will reduce the net worth tax payable.

(5) Double taxation relief

If the resident household owns foreign assets or rights which are subject to a tax similar to the net worth tax in the foreign country, the taxpayer is allowed to deduct from the Spanish net worth tax payable the lesser of: (a) the foreign tax paid or (b) the result of applying the average rate of tax in Spain to the part of the taxable base taxed abroad.

The tax treatment is identical when the property is located in a treaty partner country. However, the country in which the property is located will generally exempt such property from tax, except for real property or moveable property effectively connected with a permanent establishment.

¶430 Non-resident households

(1) General

Non-resident households are subject to Spanish tax only in respect of assets located in Spain or on rights which have been created or would be exercised in Spain. Any charge or encumbrance affecting property or rights in Spain is deductible from the taxable value thereof. Non-resident households cannot claim any personal exemptions. The valuation rules, rate and methods of assessment are the same as in the case of resident households. Spanish law allows non-residents to elect to be taxed on their worldwide net worth, and such election allows the non-residents to claim personal exemptions.

(2) Tax treaties

Spain has included net worth tax in most of the tax treaties signed. Net worth tax is mentioned in the treaties entered into with Austria, Belgium, Canada, Czechoslovakia, Denmark, Finland, France, Germany, Hungary, Luxembourg, Morocco, the Netherlands, Norway, Poland, Romania, Sweden, Switzerland, Tunisia, the United Kingdom and the USSR.

Residents of these countries will only be taxed in their country of residence, except for real property located in Spain, personal property effectively connected to a Spanish permanent establishment or to a professional activity with a fixed base in Spain, vessels and aircrafts used for international transport, and any personal property effectively connected with such vehicles when the actual place of management of the business is located in Spain.

INHERITANCE AND GIFT TAX

¶431 Overview

The inheritance and gift tax covers acquisitions by reason of death, *inter vivos* gifts, and payments under a life insurance policy taken out by the deceased. The Spanish tax is not a tax on the estate, but a tax on the amount received by each individual beneficiary or donee; consequently, the law takes into account the residence and other relevant aspects of the beneficiary or donee, and the amount received by them in determining tax liability. *Inter vivos* gifts, payments under life insurance policies and transfers by reason of death basically receive the same tax treatment. Transfers to corporations are not subject to this law, as they are treated as capital gains under corporate income tax provisions.

All gifts given within a three-year period to the same donee will be considered one transaction. Gifts given within the five years immediately preceding the date of death are included in the inheritance tax return. Any taxes paid on such gifts are credited against the final inheritance or gift tax payable.

¶432 Resident beneficiaries

Each beneficiary or donee determines his/her tax liability separately. If the beneficiary or donee is a Spanish resident (applying the same definition as for individual income tax found in ¶403), all property and rights received are subject to taxation without regard to their location.

Property and rights received by the beneficiary or donee are assessed at market value. For the purposes of determining the taxable amount, the value of the property and rights received may be reduced by the debts incurred by the deceased and transferred with the gift or inheritance. In the case of transfers by reason of death, the general expenses of administering the estate and funeral or medical expenses incurred by the deceased may also be deducted. The inheritance and gift tax sets out a number of presumptions, intended to prevent any false sale of property or rights in anticipation of real gifts or inheritances.

In the case of transfers by reason of death and payments under a life insurance policy, the beneficiary is granted a personal exemption, to be deducted from the value of the property or rights received. The amount of the personal exemption depends on the degree of the relationship between the heir and the descendant. For descendants (including those by adoption), the exemption is 2 million pesetas, unless the heir is under 21 years old, in which case an additional exemption of 500,000 pesetas for each year up to the age of 21 is allowed, up to a maximum of 6 million pesetas. For spouses, ascendants and adoptive parents, the exemption is 2 million pesetas. For collaterals up to the fourth degree, and ascendants or descendants by marriage, of the spouses, the exemption is 1 million pesetas. There are no other personal exemptions allowed.

The tax rates take into account the amount received after deducting personal exemptions, the relationship between the recipient and the descendant or donor, and the net worth of the recipient prior to receiving the inheritance or gift. The rates indicated in Table 4.5 are applied to the taxable amount, the resulting tax liability is multiplied by the coefficient in Table 4.6.

If a Spanish resident receives property located, or rights to be exercised, outside of Spain, he/she will be able to deduct the lower of any similar taxes paid outside of Spain equivalent to the Spanish inheritance and gift tax, or the tax payable in Spain calculated on the basis of the average applicable tax rate on the value of the property or rights.

Spain has signed treaties with France and Sweden to prevent the double imposition of the inheritance and gift tax. Such treaties provide rules which may be difficult to apply because they are designed as an estate tax and not as an inheritance tax.

¶433 Non-resident beneficiaries

If the beneficiary or donee is not a Spanish resident, he/she will be subject to the inheritance and gift tax solely in respect of property and rights of whatever nature, located or deemed to be exercised or executed within Spain, and for amounts received as beneficiary under a life insurance policy which has been issued by a Spanish insurance company or by a foreign company issuing the policy in Spain.

The tax is assessed in the same way as for resident beneficiaries, but personal exemptions do not apply to non-residents.

Table 4.5: Rates of inheritance and gift tax

Value received (pesetas)	*Applicable rate*	*Average rate on the lower value of each bracket*
0 – 1 million	7.65	0.00
1 million– 2 million	8.50	7.65
2 million– 3 million	9.35	8.08
3 million– 4 million	10.20	8.50
4 million– 5 million	11.05	8.93
5 million– 6 million	11.90	9.35
6 million– 7 million	12.75	9.78
7 million– 8 million	13.60	10.20
8 million– 9 million	14.45	10.63
9 million– 10 million	15.30	11.05
10 million– 15 million	16.15	11.48
15 million– 20 million	18.70	13.03
20 million– 30 million	21.25	14.45
30 million– 50 million	25.50	16.72
50 million–100 million	29.75	20.23
100 million–upwards	34.00	24.99

Table 4.6: Applicable multiplier*

Pre-existing net worth (in million pesetas)	*Acquiror*		
	Groups I and II	Group III	Group IV
From 0 to 50	1.0000	1.5882	2.0000
From more than 50 to 250	1.0500	1.6676	2.1000
From more than 250 to 500	1.1000	1.7471	2.2000
From more than 500	1.2000	1.9059	2.4000

* Groups I and II include descendants, ascendants (including by adoption) and spouses. Group III includes collaterals of the second and third degree and ascendants and descendants by marriage. Group IV includes all others (persons with a remote family relationship or without any family relationship).

VALUE ADDED TAX

¶434 Overview

The value added tax (VAT) (*impuesto sobre el valor añadido*) replaced the former cascading system of general sales tax (*impuesto general sobre el tráfico de las empresas*) on 1 January 1986, as a consequence of Spain becoming a member of the EEC. The Spanish VAT Law follows closely the Sixth European Commission Directive. It is applicable in the Spanish peninsular territory and Balearic Islands. VAT does not apply to taxable transactions carried out in the Canary Islands or in Ceuta and/or Melilla.

VAT taxes the consumption in Spain of any kind of goods and services. There are two principal corollaries to this:

(1) Only consumption within Spain is taxed. Therefore, imported goods are subject to VAT, but exported goods are exempt. Regarding services, the law assumes that the consumption occurs where the service is rendered. Consequently, all services rendered in Spain are subject to Spanish VAT.

(2) Taxable transactions between merchants do not present an actual tax cost to the parties, as the seller of goods must charge the net sales price and the applicable VAT separately on the invoice. The purchaser may use the input VAT charged to him as a credit against VAT charged by him on his resale invoices, and any excess input VAT paid is refunded by the tax authorities. Thus, the tax is ultimately passed on to the final consumer.

¶435 Taxpayer

A transaction is subject to VAT when it is entered into by merchants or professionals, on a regular or occasional basis, in the course of their business or professional activity.

The taxpayer is the supplier of goods or services, when the supplier is an individual or entity resident in Spain or the Spanish permanent establishment of a foreign merchant or professional. When the service is rendered or the goods are supplied by a non-resident individual or entity and the transaction is subject to tax in Spain, the taxpayer is the Spanish resident who receives the goods or the services. This second alternative is applicable to imported goods and services rendered by non-resident individuals or entities.

Any legal entity may be a VAT taxpayer, including corporations, associations, foundations, estates, co-operatives, and any other entity or group of persons which may or may not have a separate legal identity, provided that it has capacity to enter into taxable transactions.

¶436 Taxable transactions

The following four types of transactions are subject to VAT.

(1) Supply of goods

The supply of goods or the transfer of rights over such goods, including transactions involving real property or any kind of energy (such as heating, cooling or electric power), is subject to VAT. The act of supplying is considered to take place when the authority to dispose of the goods has passed to the purchaser.

(2) Supply of services

In general terms, any taxable transaction which is not a supply of goods or importation will be considered a supply of services for VAT purposes. Any services rendered in Spain are subject to VAT. The services are deemed to be rendered at the habitual place of business of the person or entity performing the services, unless rendered by a permanent establishment maintained by the taxpayer outside the peninsular territory or the Balearic Islands. In that case, the services are deemed to be rendered outside of Spain. There are, however, a substantial number of exceptions to this general rule:

(a) Services directly related to real property are deemed rendered at the place where the real property is located.

(b) Transportation services will be deemed to be rendered in Spain only in respect of that part which actually takes place in peninsular territory or the Balearic Islands.

(c) The following types of services are deemed to be rendered in the place where they are physically performed –
   (i) services of a cultural, artistic, sporting, scientific, educational, entertainment or similar nature, including services ancillary to them;
   (ii) services rendered in connection with hotels, restaurants and camping facilities and, in general, all places where food or drinks are served on the premises;
   (iii) transportation and ancillary services, including forwarding, storage and the like;
   (iv) services performed with respect to tangible personal property, including the manufacture, alteration or repair of goods, and any kind of opinion or appraisal regarding them.

(d) Leasing transportation vehicles follows the general rules, except for two situations in which the services are deemed to be rendered in the place where the vehicles are utilised: when the place from which the vehicles are leased is located out of the EEC and the vehicles are utilised within the EEC; and when the place from which the vehicles are leased is located within the EEC and the vehicles are utilised outside of the EEC.

(e) Some services, such as the ones listed below, are deemed to be supplied in the country in which the recipient of the services maintains his business, unless the recipient does not reside within the EEC and is either not a merchant or a professional, or the services rendered are not related to his business or professional activity, in which case the general rule will apply. The following types of services are included within this 'destination' rule:

- (i) the licensing or assignment of the use or the right to use copyrights, patents, trade marks and similar intangible assets;
- (ii) advertising services;
- (iii) supplying, engineering, consulting, legal, accounting, tax and any other similar professional services, except for the ones mentioned in (c) above;
- (iv) data processing services and supply of information, including information on technical processes and know-how;
- (v) insurance and financial services;
- (vi) translation and interpreting services;
- (vii) computerised company management services;

(f) Transfer of employees (*cesión de personal*):

- (i) the leasing of personal property, except for transportation vehicles;
- (ii) preventing anyone from voluntarily or contractually engaging in any of the services mentioned above;
- (iii) agency services with respect to any of the services set out above.

(3) Importation of goods into the peninsular territory or the Balearic Islands

The importation of goods into the peninsular territory of Spain or the Balearic Islands is subject to VAT, regardless of the purpose of the importation. The importation VAT is administered by customs, and assessment and payment procedures follow customs procedures. Temporary imports are exempt from VAT to the extent that import duties are.

(4) Goods and services for the merchant's own use and transfers without consideration

Certain transactions which involve no monetary consideration are considered taxable transactions for VAT purposes. These transactions primarily take one of the following forms:

(a) the transfer of any kind of property or rights from the merchant's or professional's business activity to his/her personal assets or the personal use thereof; or

(b) any gratuitous transfer of goods or services to a third party; or

(c) the transfer of assets from one activity covered by specific VAT provisions to another activity covered by different provisions, except when the transfer of assets to this second activity allows the taxpayer a full credit for the VAT paid.

¶437 Non-taxable transactions and exemptions

Spanish law excludes certain transactions from VAT because they lack a clear business purpose or, when including them within the scope of VAT, the economy may be distorted. The two main items within this category are the transfer of all the net worth of a merchant or professional to a third party who will continue the activity, and the performance of services within a labour context.

Spanish law includes more than 40 different types of transactions which are exempt from VAT. The most notable include the exportation of goods, agency and auxiliary services in export transactions, medical, educational and cultural services, most insurance and financial services, real property transactions subject to transfer tax, and the transfer of any kind of securities.

¶438 Tax rates, credits and assessment procedures

(1) Tax rates

The regular VAT rate is 12 per cent of the value of the transaction.

There is a preferential tax rate of 6 per cent, which is applicable to some types of essential goods or services, such as basic food stuffs, books, medicine, housing, educational material, and land transportation.

There is an increased rate of 33 per cent, which is applicable to some items considered 'luxury' goods or services, a category which includes most motor vehicles, entertainments, boats and planes, jewellery and furs.

The supplier of goods or service must include VAT on the invoice, and the recipient must accept and pay the VAT charge. The invoice is required in order for the recipient to deduct the input VAT paid from the VAT owed by him.

(2) Credit of input VAT

The taxpayer may deduct from his VAT liability the creditable input VAT charged to him on his purchases of goods and services or paid by him on imports. There are some categories of input VAT which may not be used as a credit, such as:

(a) VAT charged on the acquisition of goods and services utilised in connection with exempt activities, except for the exportation of goods or transactions related to such exports;

(b) VAT charged on the acquisition, maintenance or repair of any kind of motor vehicle, plane or boat, as well as the acquisition of parts of such vehicles, except when the vehicle is going to be used for public transport services, teaching services and other very specific types of services;

(c) VAT charged on transactions which are subject to the increased tax rate;

(d) VAT charged on travel services; and

(e) VAT charged on services or goods acquired for the entertainment of clients, employees or third parties.

When a taxpayer is engaged in two or more types of activities, one or several of which do not give the taxpayer the right to credit input VAT from VAT owed, the taxpayer may apportion the input VAT among the different activities, and thus credit the *pro rata* share of input VAT against VAT owed for activities which may apply such credit.

(3) Foreign VAT taxpayers

When taxable transactions are entered into by a foreign taxpayer without a permanent establishment in Spain, Spanish law considers the taxpayer to be the Spanish resident receiving the goods or services. The foreign supplier is not required to charge VAT on the invoice or to file any tax return. The Spanish resident is required to create a document similar to the invoice, including the applicable VAT, which must be kept jointly with the original invoice. The Spanish resident then files the VAT return and pays the tax to the Spanish authorities. However, the Spanish resident is allowed to consider the tax as input VAT and, therefore, may credit the tax from the VAT payable on the next VAT return after the one in which the tax was paid on behalf of the foreign supplier.

(4) Payment of the tax

The taxpayer must file the tax return quarterly, within the first 20 days of April, July and October, and prior to 30 January. Taxpayers with an annual turnover larger than 1 billion pesetas must file within 20 days of the end of each calendar month. Taxpayers must also file an annual return, including all the transactions made during the year.

(5) Refund procedure

Taxpayers who have been charged more input VAT during the year than the VAT payable on subsequent transactions, may file for a refund of the excess VAT paid. A taxpayer who has made exports in an amount larger than 20 million pesetas during the prior calendar year, is allowed to apply for a refund when filing the quarterly or monthly VAT return. There is a special procedure with regard to goods sold to travellers.

A non-resident merchant resident in an EEC member State, or in a third country offering reciprocal treatment to Spanish merchants, is allowed to file for a refund of the VAT charged in Spain if he does not maintain a permanent establishment in Spain and does not enter into taxable transactions in Spain other than transactions in which the taxpayer would be the Spanish resident receiving the goods or services, and transportation services and services ancillary to them. The non-resident will have a right to a refund if the services or goods acquired in Spain have been used in connection with the supply of goods or services within Spain or for transportations services within Spain, or in the supply of goods and services outside Spain if such activity would have generated the right to credit VAT if it had been performed within Spain. If the taxpayer is not a resident of an EEC member State, he must appoint a representative in Spain.

¶439 Special VAT regimes

There are several special types of VAT treatment which are intended to simplify the administrative burden on small taxpayers and adjust the VAT to the specific circumstances of some special kind of services. Individual taxpayers with an annual turnover of less than 50 million pesetas may apply for simplified VAT treatment if they are engaged in some specific activities. Spanish law also provides for special treatment in connection with agricultural, livestock and fishing activities, second hand goods, art objects, antiquities and similar goods, travel agencies, and retailers.

TRANSFER TAX AND STAMP DUTIES

¶440 Overview

Under the title of 'transfer tax and stamp duty' (*impuesto sobre transmisiones patrimoniales y actos jurídicos documentados*), there are three different taxes which complement VAT and excises taxes. These are as follows:

(1) *The transfer tax.* This tax must be paid on the non-business transfers of goods or rights.

(2) *The corporate transfer tax.* This is a levy on transactions which affect the corporate structure.

(3) *Stamp duty.* This tax is applicable to certain kind of public, judicial or mercantile documents.

The State, government agencies, charitable organisations or foundations managed and represented by volunteers only, and the Red Cross, among others, are exempt from these taxes.

In addition, some transactions are not subject to or exempt from these taxes. The main ones would be the delivery of money; transfers between spouses related to community property, some corporate mergers on reorganisations, cash deposits and loans, transfers of shares, pre-emptive subscriptions rights, and bonds and analogous securities.

Input transfer taxes, as opposed to VAT, may not be credited against any other tax payable by the taxpayer.

¶441 Transfer tax

This tax applies to *inter vivos* transfers of property and on the transfer, creation or increase of any kind of right such as, for instance, real property rights (*derechos reales*), loans, guarantees, deposits, rentals, pensions and licences granted by the Government.

Only non-business transactions are subject to tax. Therefore, any transaction which is subject to VAT will be exempt from transfer tax, except for second transfers of buildings as a part of a business, which are always subject to the transfer tax.

The tax is paid by the acquiring party of the property or rights or by the beneficiary of the rights.

There are three kinds of taxable transactions.

(1) Real property transactions

The transfer of real property located in Spain, or the creation or transfer of real property rights which are created, exercisable or required to be performed in Spain, excluding mortgages and other forms of security, are taxed at the rate of 6 per cent.

The transfer of shares of a company which has more than 50 per cent of its assets devoted to real property investment is also subject to transfer tax at the rate of 6 per cent when the acquiror, as a consequence of the purchase, owns more than 50 per cent, or 100 per cent, of the company's shares. Finally, the transfer of shares received in exchange for contributions of real property to the corporation is also subject to a 6 per cent tax, unless such sale takes place more than one year after the contribution.

(2) Movable property

The transfer of movable property located in Spain, or the creation and assignment of real property rights which are created, exercisable or required to be performed in Spain, excluding mortgages and other forms of security, are taxed at the rate of 4 per cent.

(3) Rights

A rate of 1 per cent applies to the creation of a security interest in real property, such as a mortgage.

¶442 Corporate transfer tax

Contributions to the capital of any kind of corporation are subject to tax at a rate of 1 per cent on the nominal value of the shares issued, plus any premium. Capital-like contributions to other entities similar to corporations are also subject to this tax (for instance, contributions to the creation of a branch and *agrupación temporal de empresas*). The tax is also applicable to decreases of capital, liquidations and corporate reorganisations. In such cases, the rate of tax is also 1 per cent, applicable to the value of the assets received by the shareholders or partners.

There are a number of circumstances in which the Government may grant reductions of corporate transfer tax for certain kind of transactions. The most relevant are tax protected mergers and reorganisations, creation of *agrupaciones y uniones temporales de empresas*, and creation of certain entities engaged in activities which are considered beneficial to the national economy, such as co-operatives and labour corporations.

The corporate transfer tax is usually an expense which may be capitalised on the corporate income tax return. It can be depreciated over ten years at the election of the taxpayer.

¶443 Stamp duties

These constitute an indirect tax on certain types of documents which are formalised in Spain, as well as on those which, although formalised outside Spain, have legal or economic effect in Spain. The main documents which are subject to this tax are notarised documents, commercial paper (bills of exchange, drafts, warehouse bills, and other similar documents), and some public and judicial documents.

There is an additional tax on first copies of public deeds and notarial certificates related to a transaction having a quantified value and which are susceptible to registration in the Property, Commercial or Trade Mark Registries. This tax amounts to 0.5 per cent of the value of the transaction. If the transaction is subject the inheritance and gift tax, to transfer tax or to corporate transfer tax, this additional duty will not apply. Therefore, businesses should be aware of such a tax when putting transactions which are subject to VAT into the form of a public deed.

EXCISE TAXES

¶444 Overview and forecast

Excise taxes are indirect taxes levied on the consumption of alcohol and alcoholic beverages, beer, oil derivatives and tobacco. They are levied on the manufacture and importation of the goods. The taxes are paid by the manufacturers and importers, but that cost is then passed on to the buyers. The exportation of these goods is exempt from taxation if the goods are exported directly by the manufacturers; if otherwise, the exporter is reimbursed for the amount of taxes paid. These taxes are compatible with VAT.

Excise taxes apply throughout Peninsular Spain and the Balearic Islands. In the Canary Islands, the only applicable excise taxes are those levied on alcohol and alcoholic beverages, including beer, although the rates applied differ from those applied by the mainland regulations. In Ceuta and Melilla the only applicable excise tax is on tobacco.

The European Commission's Proposed Directives of 1987 are intended to harmonise all special taxes within the EEC as from 31 December 1992. The proposed Directives provide for three types of compulsory taxes: on tobacco, on alcoholic beverages, including beer and wine, and on mineral oils. Spain will therefore be obliged to impose a tax on wines on or before that date. In order to comply with its commitment to the EEC, Spain is increasing the rates of these taxes annually, but they are still generally lower than in other EEC countries.

¶445 Alcohol and alcoholic beverages

Excise taxes are levied on pure alcohol (but not on methylated spirit, since it is not for human consumption) and alcoholic products (liquors, extracts and concentrates). Wines are not presently subject to excise taxes. The rate for 1989 is 726 pesetas per litre.

¶446 Beer

For historic reasons, excise taxes on beer are different from those levied on alcohol and alcoholic beverages. The rate for 1989 ranges between 3.56 and 7.13 pesetas per litre, depending on the proportion of the dry extract of must used for its production to its weight.

¶447 Oil derivatives

Excise taxes are levied on hydrocarbons (oil derivatives), and the rate of tax varies substantially. The tax has been traditionally collected by the State Oil Monopoly, which is presently being gradually phased out, due to Spain's entry into the EEC.

¶448 Tobacco

The Spanish tax follows the patterns established in the European Commission's Directives of 19 December 1972 and 18 December 1978. Although the State tax monopoly (*monopolio fiscal sobre tabaco*) still exists, it applies only to tobacco which has not been produced within the EEC. This tax is levied on cigarettes (in 1989 two rates were applied: 150 pesetas per 1,000 cigarettes and another *ad valorem* tax at the rate of 33 per cent and 42 per cent, for black and blond cigarettes, respectively), cigars, snuff, and chewing and loose tobacco.

MUNICIPAL AND REGIONAL TAXES

¶449 Municipal taxes

As of 1 January 1990 local taxes will be classified into two groups: fees (*tasas*) and taxes (*impuestos*). There are various kinds of municipal fees, and they are usually related to the cost of certain public services or special use of public property.

The municipalities may collect the following taxes:

(1) Tax on rustic or urban real property (*contribución territorial rústica* or *contribución territorial urbana*). This is an annual tax on the ownership or beneficial use (usufruct) of real property based on an objective valuation thereof.

(2) Tax on economic activities (*licencia fiscal industrial* or *licencia fiscal de profesionales y artistas*). This is an annual tax on the mere exercise of business, professional and artistic activities, using a tariff system.

(3) Tax on the increase in value of land (*arbitrio de plusvalía*). This is charged on the difference in value between the value of developed land at the time of the acquisition of the real property (*urbana*) and its value at the time of sale. The rate of tax depends on the length of the period of time between purchase and sale, and on the amount of increase in value. The value of land is assessed by the municipality. In theory, the transferor is liable for the tax, but in practice the transferee usually pays the tax on transfers by purchase and sale (*a título oneroso*).

(4) Minor taxes. Other lesser taxes also exist, such as vehicle tax (*impuesto de circulación*) and a tax on construction works.

Valuations for the taxes in (1) and (2) above are handled by the State, although the tax rates are fixed by the municipalities.

¶450 Regional tax system

(1) In general

The Spanish State is divided into municipalities, provinces and autonomous regions which enjoy a great degree of autonomy in respect of financing. Therefore, due to the differences in the resources available to the autonomous regions, the taxes vary substantially from one to another.

Normally, of the 17 regional governments, 14 apply the same tax system. Although the autonomous regions may create new taxes, provided that they are not the same as State taxes, and place a surtax on State taxes, it is a little used prerogative in practice. The State allows the autonomous regions to handle and to collect the inheritance and gift tax, transfer tax and stamp duties, net worth tax and gambling taxes. The most important source of revenue for the autonomous regions is in fees (*tasas*). There are many such fees, and they are governed by the Organic Law of Autonomous Region Financing of 22 September 1980.

(2) Regional differences

The areas with the greatest differences in tax matters are the Basque Country, Navarra, and the Canary Islands.

(a) Basque Country

The Basque Country has a special agreement with the central government, approved by the Law of 13 May 1981. It is an autonomous region made up of three historic territories (Alava, Guipúzcoa and Vizcaya), each of which is headed by its own regional council (*diputación foral*) which handles all the State taxes (except customs and special taxes) and applies its own regulations. The most important differences from the general system are as follows:

(i) Tax liability is determined by the residence and/or domicile of the person or the location of the assets.

(ii) If business is carried on both within the territory and in the rest of Spain, corporate income tax is apportioned by a ratio based on the 'relative amount of business' (*cifra relativa de negocios*). If VAT is involved, it is applied proportionally.

(iii) Despite the fact that the regional council must adapt the regulations it passes to State norms, these local norms may offer more attractive tax incentives than those offered by the State.

(b) Navarra
Navarra's tax matters are governed by a Decree-Law of 24 July 1969. Navarra's regional council handles and collects nearly all taxes, State or otherwise, and may impose its own norms. The rules of taxation of income follow principles similar to those of the Basque Country.

(c) Canary Islands
The tax system of the Canary Islands has some important differences, since the two Canary Island provinces, Las Palmas and Santa Cruz de Tenerife, have been duty-free zones for over a century. The Canary Islands have historically had a different system from the rest of Spain and the EEC, and are not a full EEC member. With regard to customs, Spain and the Canary Islands are deemed to be different countries with special features. VAT is not levied in the Canary Islands, however; there exists a multi-phased sliding tax, the ITE, and a luxury tax and other special taxes are partially applied.

Direct taxation is the same as in the rest of Spain, with additional tax incentives to invest in the Canary Islands built in. There is also proposed legislation to create 'off-shore' centres in the Canary Islands.

(d) Ceuta and Melilla
Although they are not autonomous regions, the North African possessions of Ceuta and Melilla have a tax system similar to that of the Canary Islands, with the added advantage of a tax credit (*bonificación*) of 50 per cent for income earned in these territories.

OTHER GENERAL ASPECTS

¶451 Tax procedures and tax administration

(1) Assessment and payment
Tax assessment and payment procedures are essentially the same for all taxes.

Tax assessment commences with a tax return filed by the taxpayer, together with the payment of the amount owed as calculated by the taxpayer, except for the periodic taxes, e.g. property tax (*contribuciones territoriales*) and fiscal licences, which are within the local taxes system. The tax authorities, usually through the Auditing Bureau, checks that the tax return is correct and produces its own assessment on behalf of the Government. Normally, the tax auditors check the returns of approximately 1 per cent of the taxpayers each year.

Taxes are collected in two phases. The so-called 'voluntary period' is that in which the taxpayer should pay his taxes, within the time limits indicated for each tax. Payment should be made at the same time as the tax return is filed. If the taxpayer does not pay the amount indicated on the return, or assessed by the Administration after having checked the return, than a second, executory or compulsory period begins.

In this phase a 20 per cent default penalty and interest on late payment is charged on taxes due; in 1989 the annual interest rate was 11 per cent. The tax authorities may apply default penalties and interest directly, and do not have to go through the Justice Department. Default penalties and interest charges are completely independent and apart from any applicable sanctions.

If a taxpayer pays more tax than he owes, due, for example, to an error on the tax return or as a result of a successful appeal, the taxpayer may apply for the repayment of the excess and the tax authorities must also pay interest on late payment for delay (in 1989, the interest rate was 9 per cent).

It should be made clear that although, in general terms, the rules and regulations, such as those relating to tax audits and tax information described below, are applied by all the different tax authorities of the central government, autonomous regions and the local entities, each of these authorities generally has its own rules applicable to the taxes it assesses and collects, which nevertheless tend to follow the same general principles described above.

(2) Tax audits

The Tax Auditing Bureau checks tax returns other than those checks made by computer. Each level of the taxing authorities has its own system; therefore, there are State, regional, and local tax auditors. Although these last may have their own rules and regulations, in fact all follow the basic procedure set out in the General Regulations of the Tax Auditing Bureau, approved by Decree 939, of 25 April 1986.

The State tax authorities have several levels of auditors:

(a) the national auditors for bigger taxpayers;

(b) regional auditing units, for bigger taxpayers in each Special Tax Area (which coincide with the autonomous regions);

(c) auditing units, for taxpayers in each province;

(d) special units for international tax and tax fraud.

Auditing involves a very set procedure, in which all steps are taken in writing, ending with a written, formal report (*acta*). If the taxpayer agrees with the results arrived at by the tax auditors, the report is deemed to be approved, in which case the sanction recommended is reduced, sometimes by as much as one-half. The Auditing Bureau is endowed with a broad range of powers, and auditors are deemed to be agents of the tax authorities they represent.

(3) Tax information

The Spanish tax administration is given broad powers to obtain information, i.e. data about taxpayers, obtained through other taxpayers, professionals, public officials and public bodies. This results in a database containing millions of entries which are processed by the Central Data Bureau, and which are at the disposal of the Auditing Bureau. In this way, real property and security transactions, the amounts that companies withhold for their employees, the amount and frequency of dividends and interest paid, the numbers of all the accounts opened in the lending institutions, transactions between businesses involving over 500,000 pesetas annually, etc. are known. These investigatory powers are set out in Articles 111 and 112 of the General Tax Law and other regulations. Restrictions are few, and pertain to the protection of personal and family privacy, the duty of confidentiality of lawyers and auditors, protection of sources by journalists, and the privacy of the mail in the postal system. If the Auditing Bureau wishes to find out information about bank accounts (statements and movements), they ask the taxpayer for them; if the taxpayer refuses, special proceedings are instigated against the bank, eliminating its right to refuse to divulge information. The Auditing Bureau, however, may not examine accounts in general, but only in respect of a particular taxpayer.

The information the tax authorities have about taxpayers may be exchanged with other countries if provided for in a Double Taxation Treaty. Under Decree 1326 of 11 November 1987, certain information may be exchanged with EEC member States in order to apply income tax, net worth tax, and VAT.

If the obligation to provide information to the Government is not complied with, Articles 77 to 89 of the General Tax Law set out the applicable sanctions discussed at ¶452 below.

(4) Consultation in tax matters

Article 107 of the General Tax Law provides that taxpayers may request the tax authorities to indicate which taxes, classifications or assessments apply to them. The written reply is advisory only but, in the case of foreign capital investments, the reply is binding on the Government, which cannot later change its opinion, even if erroneous, unless the law is subsequently changed. This procedure is governed by the Decree of 23 December 1971, and it provides a guarantee for foreign investors regarding tax treatment, which is legally binding on the Government.

¶452 Penalties

If tax obligations are not met by the taxpayer, there are two mutually exclusive sanctionary measures which may be taken:

(1) administrative, whereby the Government conducts the proceedings, assesses the violation, decides the appropriate sanction and imposes it on the taxpayer; and

(2) penal, in which the criminal courts determine the offence, and impose the appropriate sanction.

(1) Administrative sanctions

These sanctions are governed by Articles 77 to 89 of the General Tax Law of 26 April 1985. Article 77.1 states that all violations are sanctionable, including those involving mere negligence or carelessness, so that all violations are subject to this objective test. However, the Constitutional Court has established that if criminal law is also applicable to administrative sanctions, the Administration must always consider the subjective element and the intent of the taxpayer. If there is no element of intent, Article 77.3 states that no violation occurs when there is a lack of capacity, e.g. minors, those who act due to *force majeur*, those who abstain or who do not attend meetings where collective decisions are made, e.g. in a company where directors are held liable, and those who pay taxes in error to the wrong tax authority, e.g. to the Basque Country or Navarra tax authorities when they should have paid them to another tax authority.

Article 77.2 states which taxpayer may be held liable and subject to these violations: taxpayers, withholding agents (*retenedores*), the parent company in the case of a group submitting a joint tax return, entities subject to flow-through taxation (*régimen de transparencia*), their members who do not fulfil their duty to provide information, and legal representatives of those who do not have capacity.

All violations are set out in the above law, but certain regulations applicable to a particular tax provide for further ones, for example VAT, special taxes, and Customs and Excise taxes.

Violations are divided into two groups, so that, applying the principle of *non bis in idem* (a person shall not be twice tried for the same crime), one act may give rise to one kind of violation but not to both at the same time.

The first group comprises minor violations (*infracciones simples*), which generally are of a residual nature in relation to serious violations (*infracciones graves*), i.e., a violation arising from the non-fulfilment of a duty or obligations in tax management, usually of a procedural nature, which does not alone constitute a serious violation.

The second group comprises serious violations, which imply a failure to pay tax liability of any kind, including such major violations as not paying all or part of taxes due within the legal time limits, or payments on account or instalments, or amounts withheld or which should have been withheld.

Article 80 sets out three kinds of sanctions:

(a) *Fines*. Minor violations are subject to a fine of a fixed amount of between 1,000 and 1,000,000 pesetas. Serious violations are subject to a fine of an amount of between 50 per cent and 300 per cent of the amount of tax which the taxpayer has failed to pay.

(b) *Auxiliary sanctions*. Such sanctions include:
   (i) the inability to receive public subsidies or loans from the State-owned banks, or to receive tax benefits for up to five years, and a prohibition on entering into contracts with the State or other public bodies for a period of five years;
   (ii) suspension from carrying on a profession, in the case of public officials such as notaries, registrars and brokers (*corredores de comercio*) who are members of a professional association, for a period of up to one year if they commit a minor violation by failing to supply tax information relating to third parties.

(c) A series of sanctions, set out in the Law of Discipline and Intervention of Lending Institutions (*Ley de Disciplina e Intervención de las Entidades de Crédito*), if a lending institution commits a minor violation by failing to supply information about its clients.

Occasionally, it is possible to request a total or partial pardon from any sanction, by applying to the administrative tax courts described at ¶453 below.

(2) Penal sanctions

Certain violations are deemed to be offences under the Penal Code, resulting in penalties of up to six years' imprisonment (*privación de libertad*) and fines of up to six times the amount of tax payable.

¶453 Assessment appeals and tax court procedures

Tax appeals (including interest for late payments and penalties) are first heard by the tax authorities themselves, and, thereafter, by courts of law.

In the case of taxes which are payable to the local fiscal authorities, the taxpayer must appeal to the same authority which decided the case, and in the case of further appeal, to the Superior Court. Decisions of the Superior Court may be appealed to the Supreme Court, if the amount is more than 500,000 pesetas.

In other cases, i.e. State taxes or taxes imposed by the regional governments (although the latter have their own peculiarities), an appeal may be brought before the authority which made the decision, or, typically, direct to one of the administrative tax courts, called the administration tax courts (*tribunales económico-administrativos*). There are 17 regional tax courts in direct relation to the 17 autonomous regions. If the decision involves an amount of less than 3,000,000 pesetas, the taxpayer may appeal to the Superior Court, from which there is no further appeal; if the matter is for an amount of 3,000,000 pesetas or more, the taxpayer may appeal to the Superior Court in Madrid. Decisions of this Court may be appealed to the National Court, and thereafter to the Supreme Court.

¶454 EEC harmonisation process and future tax reform in Spain

The following reforms are likely to take place in the future: first, an improvement of the present system and, secondly, changes as a result of EEC Directives.

Improvements of the present system are likely to consist of, at the State level, a new tax on individual net worth and changes to individual income tax (especially as regards the taxation of married couples). At the autonomous region level there will be small changes. A reduction in local taxes is envisaged.

EEC Directives, now in a preliminary stage, will mandate the harmonisation of corporation taxes and taxation of company mergers and demergers or split-offs.

It is envisaged that the harmonisation of VAT and of '*accesas*' (or Special Taxes) will take place by 31 December 1992, which will mean a significant increase in revenue from those taxes in Spain.

5 Accounting and Auditing

ACCOUNTING

¶501 Bookkeeping

Businesses are required to keep orderly accounting books which accurately reflect their business operations, including a schedule of assets and liabilities and a record of the daily operations of the company. Companies must also keep a minute book including all resolutions approved by the shareholders or by the directors and a share register. Mandatory accounting books must be audited annually, unless the company is exempt from this requirement. Books may be kept by hand or by computer and must be clear and in chronological order.

Business organisations are required to close their accounting books on a regular basis at least once every 12 months. The financial year begins on 1 January and ends on 31 December, unless otherwise stated in the by-laws/articles of association.

Tax regulations require that certain operations used to compute tax liability be reflected in the accounting books. If these bookkeeping requirements are not met, penalties may be imposed by the tax authorities, and serious breaches may lead to criminal prosecution.

¶502 Financial statements

Companies, and businesses in general, must produce annual accounts comprising a balance sheet, a profit and loss statement, and an annual report. The annual accounts must be prepared in a clear and precise manner and must faithfully reflect the position regarding the capital, financial situation and results of the company. Most Spanish companies are obliged to follow the General Accounting Plan of the Accounting Planning Institute which set out the principles and rules applicable to valuation, annual accounts and statements. The General Accounting Plan has been adapted to meet the needs of specific sectors, such as leasing, factoring and real property, and to small and medium-sized businesses.

The Commercial Code and the General Accounting Plan set out methods of valuation for tangible fixed assets and intangible assets, inventory, securities, including equity investments, commercial paper and loans and operations in foreign currency.

Annual accounts must be based on objective criteria which protect the interests of third parties. The accounting principles applied are those required for the orderly and prudent economic management of the business, such as:

(1) *acquisition price or historic cost*, as a general method of valuing fixed and current assets (except effective reduction in their value);

(2) *consistency*, so that the same method of valuation is maintained in successive fiscal years. Any change must be expressly stated in the accounts;

(3) *the accrual basis principle*, by which transactions must be allocated to the fiscal year in which they arise and not to the one in which payments are received or made;

(4) *'Going concern'*, deeming the operation of the business to be continuing;

(5) *'Prudencia valorativa'*, which prevails in the event of a conflict of principles. Only profits effectively realised are taken into account, whilst losses, actual and potential, must be mentioned in the financial statements at the time they become known. Depreciation of assets must also be taken into account whether the financial year ends in losses or profits.

The annual report as well as the management report on the progress of the business completes and amplifies the information contained in the balance sheet and the profit and loss account. The annual report of corporations/limited companies (*sociedades anónimas*) must include, *inter alia*, the valuation criteria applied to the assets and liabilities into the balance sheet, the characteristics of the different types of shares, salaries and debits of the members of the board of directors and any guarantees undertaken with third parties.

The annual accounts must be signed by the sole businessman, by the members or partners if they have unlimited liability for the debts of the company, or by the directors of corporations/limited companies (*sociedades anónimas*) or a limited liability company.

¶503 Consolidated accounts

(1) Groups affected

As from the 1991 fiscal year, Spanish company groups will be obliged to produce consolidated accounts and submit them for auditing. A company must produce consolidated accounts and an annual report if it is a shareholder of another company and any of the following circumstances apply:

(a) It has the majority of voting rights.

(b) It has the power to appoint or remove the majority of the members of the administrative body (*órgano de administración*).

(c) It has at its disposal, through agreements with other members, the majority of voting rights.

(d) Through its votes it has appointed the majority of the members of the administrative body in office at the time when the consolidated accounts are produced and during the two financial years immediately preceding that time, although if the company is associated (*vinculado*) with another in the circumstances set out in (a) or (b) above, then there is no requirement to produce consolidated accounts.

(2) Omissions

Nevertheless, consolidated accounts are not mandated for companies, unless such companies have issued securities traded on a stock market, whenever any of the following circumstances apply:

- the parent company may omit from its consolidated accounts companies belonging to the group but having no significant effect on the group accounts;
- those which present the parent company with substantial difficulties in the exercise of its rights over the capital or in the management of such companies;
- companies for which only through incurring disproportionate costs or delays can accounts be drawn up with the legal time limits;
- companies the shares of which are owned exclusively with the object of a subsequent transfer;
- companies which have such different activities that their inclusion might be contrary to the finalising of the consolidated accounts, although this does not apply simply because the companies included in the consolidation are partly industrial, partly commercial and partly service companies.

Annual consolidated accounts comprise the consolidated balance sheet, profit and loss account and an annual report. They must bear the same date as the accounts of the parent company and must be signed by the directors (*administradores*) of the parent company. The consolidated annual report must include, *inter alia*, the name and registered office of all the group companies, details of certain group debts, the average number of employees employed during the year, details of debts, guarantees and loans.

The Commercial Code and the regulations governing the preparation of accounts of groups of companies include the following definitions, consolidation methods and application guidelines:

(3) Definitions

(a) *Group*. A group is deemed to exist when one company controls one or more other companies, and all the companies are managed on a unified basis taking into account the discussion set forth hereinabove.

(b) *Association*. An assocation is deemed to exist if one company exercises significant influence over another. Such influence will be deemed to exist if one company directly or indirectly holds 20 per cent or more of the share capital of the other, or 3 per cent if the company is quoted on the Stock Exchange.

(c) *Multi-group companies*. These are defined as companies whose share capital is owned by two or more groups or the management is carried out by two or more companies belonging to the group, provided that they are managed on a combined basis. Such companies include, for example, a company whose operations are allocated in proportion to the amount of the holdings of each of the groups in its share capital.

(4) Consolidated methods and application guidelines

(a) *Global integration*. This is a method applied to groups of companies whereby the corporate assets (*patrimonio*), including all rights and obligations, of subsidiary companies are incorporated into the balance sheet of the parent company, and the income and expenditure of the subsidiary companies are incorporated into the parent company's profit and loss statement.

(b) *Equity method*. This is a method applied to associated and multi-group companies, except those which apply the proportional integration discussed at (c) below. The net value of the shareholdings in the company in which it wields significant influence is incorporated into the balance sheet of the parent company.

(c) *Proportional integration*. This is a method applied to those companies whose operations are allocated in proportion to the amount of the holdings of each of the groups owning share capital. The percentage of the share in the corporate assets of the subsidiary companies is incorporated into the balance sheet and profit and loss statement, respectively, of the dominant companies.

¶504 Legal aspects of keeping accounts

Individuals and corporations are required to keep books, correspondence, records, receipts and other supporting documents relating to the business for a period of six years from the date of the last entry. This duty continues even if the company goes out of business or into liquidation, or if a sole proprietor dies and the business passes to his successors.

The accounting books of a business are confidential and, as such, may not be used, disclosed or published without proper authority, except in the case of receivership, bankruptcy proceedings, liquidation or similar proceedings. If the company's books are found to be missing, a declaration of bankruptcy may be declared fraudulent. If business is transferred or assigned, the transferee or assignee may request a copy of the books or delivery of the original books for a limited period.

The probative value of books and other accounting documents is assessed by the courts. Books, registers and other company documents may be used in evidence against the person who made the entries or who drafted the document in respect of all clear entries. The person attempting to use any records as evidence for his own benefit must produce whole documents, including any parts which may be prejudicial. The lack of a bookkeeping entry does not prove that an event did not occur. Consistency throughout the different accounting books and records lends greater weight, and particular value is attributed to those books and records kept on a daily basis because of the short time-lapse between an event and its entry and the kinds of transactions that tend to be recorded that way.

Bookkeeping is the direct responsibility of the owners or directors of a company or persons authorised by them. In the absence of proof to the contrary, authority is presumed. Owners and directors may not delegate away this responsibility and must produce accounts within the period set out by law.

AUDITING

¶505 Scope

In 1988 a law was passed regulating the auditing of accounts, thus bringing Spanish law into line with EEC Directives. Spanish law now has minimum requirements for annual audits, regulates the auditing profession, including the creation of an Institute of Accounting and Auditing (*Instituto de Contabilidad y Auditoría de Cuentas*), and provides disciplinary measures.

An auditor's report of annual accounts must contain a statement that the accounts constitute a true representation of the net assets and financial state of the company and show the application of funds during the accounting period. The auditor's report also confirms whether the management's annual report accurately represents the accounts of the company.

Companies which are quoted on the stock exchange, make public offerings, act as financial intermediaries or participate in the insurance sector must be audited annually. The following companies are exempt from this requirement: Those to which in the last two financial years at least two of the following circumstances apply:

(1) they do not have total assets exceeding 230 million pesetas;
(2) turnover does not exceed 480 million pesetas;
(3) the average number of employees during any year does not exceed 50.

¶506 The auditor's report

The auditor's report on the annual accounts must include a brief, general description of the auditing method used, an express statement indicating that the information contained in the annual report is complete and contains sufficient information to interpret and understand the company's equity and financial position, together with any appropriate comments. The auditor must give his professional opinion as to whether the annual accounts accurately represent the company's equity and financial position and results, whether these accounts have been prepared and presented consistently and in accordance with accounting rules and principles, and whether any relevant events have occurred in the period between the close of the fiscal year and the preparation of the report. The documents examined by the auditor should be annexed to the auditor's report.

The company is required to provide all information necessary to complete the auditor's report, including those documents and accounts of other companies, if a group. The report itself should show the consolidated accounts.

Until such time as company and commercial law is fully adapted to EEC Directives, accounting rules and principles as applicable to audit reports must follow the Commercial Code, the General Accounting Plan, and accounting rules applicable to specific sectors.

¶507 Auditor's liability

An auditor's report has legal effect in respect of third parties. An auditor is personally liable for any report issued in his name and for any loss caused by his negligence. In addition to potential civil and criminal liability, an auditor may be liable under specific administrative regulations governing auditors and auditing firms. Under these regulations, negligent acts are classified as serious or minor, and sanctions are directed at the auditor's professional practice.

Auditors and auditing firms are required to put up a bond or take out insurance in proportion to the volume of business of the company being audited. They must support all their conclusions and retain all documents examined and working papers used in the preparation of the audit for at least five years. All information must be kept strictly confidential and may not be used for any other purpose.

Auditors are required to be independent during the term of their appointment, and certain activities are deemed to be incompatible with their appointment. For three years before the fiscal year audited, auditors may not perform managerial duties for or be employed by the companies they audit. They may not hold more than 0.5 per cent of the shares in the companies they audit, and in any event their shareholding may not be more than 10 per cent of their individual net worth. First and second degree relatives of the owner of a business, and of the administrators or managers, may not audit that company.

Auditors may not take up the office of administrator or manager in an audited company, nor may they be employed by such a company for three years after their appointment ceases.

Auditors may be appointed for a term of at least three years, if the company is required by law to be audited, but in any event they may not be appointed for a term of more than nine years.

6 Banking and Finance

THE SPANISH FINANCIAL SYSTEM

¶601 Regulation and deregulation trends

The Spanish financial system is undergoing significant changes, bringing to a close a long period of isolation, protectionism and state intervention in the Spanish financial markets. These changes have been brought about by a variety of factors, including the internationalisation and globalisation of financial markets, increasing innovation in the marketplace in a climate of unstable interest and exchange rates, and the fact that different types of intermediaries now have direct access to the financial markets (*desintermediación*). Securitisation is also changing the face of traditional lending transactions by utilising the stock markets. Substantial technological advances in information systems and telecommunications, and an overall policy of deregulation, are facilitating these changes and putting Spain squarely in line with European trends.

The complete harmonisation of Spanish legislation with EEC Directives has many ramifications and will further serve to open the market. Spanish lending institutions will enjoy the freedom of establishment available to all EEC lending institutions and will experience a decrease in protectionism. Intermediaries will be able to offer banking and financial services freely and handle financial investment to and from abroad. Moreover, full harmonisation with EEC Directives will mean the freedom to enter all banking and financial sectors and the disappearance of geographical barriers between member States. The development, improvement and opening up of stock markets will strengthen them by attracting more investment and resources. Together with this, a significant number of financial intermediaries will emerge. The appearance of non-banking financial intermediaries, such as insurance companies and pension funds, is already leading to the development of new products offered directly to the public.

The Government's economic policy is developing in an apparently contradictory way, by undoing the rigid controls of the past but replacing them with new ones. The purpose and effect are to replace protectionism with guarantees of solvency and stability. The deregulation process is dismantling the rigid protectionism which has characterised the Spanish financial system by imposing administrative restrictions on new competitors and on the expansion of existing ones. Past protectionism segmented the market and restricted operating capacity to certain specialised areas by imposing a series of controls, restrictions and compulsory investment requirements, and by setting maximum and minimum interest rates for financial assets and deposits. It also succeeded in isolating foreign investment through exchange controls and eliminating competition from non-banking financial intermediaries. The stock markets were closely monitored and controlled, without offering public issues at market rates or ways of freely investing in private shares.

Government regulations currently focus on reinforcing the solvency of financial intermediaries, more intensive supervision by the monetary authorities of activities in the financial markets, and the harmonisation of controls at the EEC level. The monetary authorities are imposing greater requirements regarding information to be provided to them and a greater degree of accountability on the part of financial intermediaries in respect of their customers.

¶602 Types of financial institutions

The Spanish financial system is made up of institutions offering a wide variety of financial products and services. The following serves as a description of the participants in the system. Each is described in greater detail within the context of its particular market sector.

(1) Lending institutions

Spanish lending institutions (*entidades de crédito*) comprise the following:

(a) *Banking institutions*. Included in this category are the public and commercial banks (wholesale and retail), savings banks and lending co-operatives. Unlike other lending institutions, these entities may take deposits from the public on demand and for a term of less than one year.

(b) *Specialised non-banking lending institutions*. Lending institutions specialise in particular sectors of the leading market, but may not take funds from the public for an indefinite term or for less than one year. They include mortgage companies, financial institutions specialising in instalment sales, and factoring and leasing companies.

(c) *Money market brokerage firms*. These non-banking lending institutions specialise in money markets, and in addition may receive funds from the public by way of temporary transfers of financial instruments.

(2) Institutional investors and venture capital

Financial intermediaries exist which specialise in unofficial and official securities markets and manage portfolios on the principle of spreading risk, but without controlling the companies in which they invest. They include the following:

(a) *Collective investment institutions*. The main function of collective investment institutions is to collect funds, assets or rights from the public and manage them, giving rise to a collective return on investment. They may take different forms, being either financial in nature, meaning that they invest and manage financial assets such as fixed capital and variable capital investment companies, liquid investment funds or money market investment funds; or non-financial in nature, meaning that they invest and manage real assets. Collective investment funds are managed and administered by specialised management and depositary companies of collective investment institutions.

Portfolio management companies manage portfolios, give financial advice and participate in placing public and private issues.

(b) *Pension funds*. These are private investment institutions linked to the performance and objectives of one or more pension plans. They result in payments made to participants or their beneficiaries, in the form of capital or income, upon the occurrence of certain events such as retirement, survivorship, widowhood, orphanhood or disability. They are managed and administered by specialised management companies, and controlled by committees made up of beneficiaries and participants in the plans and funds.

(c) *Venture capital companies*. The purpose of venture capital companies and funds is to foster the growth and development of non-financial privately held companies by temporarily investing in their capital. They are managed by management companies with the collaboration of depositaries.

(3) Securities companies and agencies

Specialised securities companies and agencies (*sociedades o agencias de valores*) act primarily in the commercial stock exchanges as stockbrokers. The former may act on their own account or on behalf of third parties, whilst the latter may only act on behalf of third parties.

(4) Other specialised financial intermediaries
These include companies involved in the business of insurance, reinsurance, and mutual guarantees.

(5) Regulatory bodies
The Bank of Spain is the regulatory body entrusted with overseeing the lending institutions. The National Stock Exchange Commission (*Comisión Nacional del Mercado de Valores*) oversees companies and activities related to the stock market.

THE SPANISH BANKING SYSTEM

¶603 The Bank of Spain

The Bank of Spain ('the Bank') is the country's central bank. Although the Spanish Government, through the Ministry of Economy and Finance, sets monetary and economic policy, the Bank has relative autonomy when carrying out the Government's directives. The Bank's Governor, Deputy Governor and Executive Council are appointed by the Government.

The Bank is the dominant force in the Spanish banking system. It issues bank notes and circulates legal tender. It serves as the State's free banker, performing the services of State Treasury, making interest-free advances, and providing financial and administrative services in respect of the national or public debt. In particular, it centralises the registered debt and supervises the market by means of the electronic bookkeeping entry system centre for public debt (*Central de Anotaciones en Cuenta de Deuda del Estado y del Tesoro*).

The Bank serves as the bank for banks and other lending institutions within the system, and is the ultimate lender in the banking system. It manages the Money Market Telephonic Service and bank clearing houses. The Bank implements the Government's internal and foreign monetary policy, administers Spain's foreign currency reserves, and oversees payments from abroad and all foreign financing involving residents. Most of these last functions are delegated to the lending institutions themselves and to other financial intermediaries, which are permitted to maintain stop and forward positions in the foreign currency market within certain limits, and enter into other transactions involving foreign currency.

The Bank has the power to oversee and discipline lending institutions. Lending institutions submit periodic reports to the Bank of Spain and are subject to internal inspections by it. The Bank plays a major role if a lending institution goes into a financial crisis, and administers the deposit insurance fund. It runs the Central Office of Risk Information for the use of participating lending institutions and maintains a central data base containing the financial statements of non-financial businesses. Finally, the Bank provides consumers with a complaints service where they can air their grievances concerning treatment by or transactions related to lending institutions.

¶604 State-owned banking institutions

As in the rest of the EEC, and notwithstanding the constitutional commitment to a free-trade economy, the State has direct involvement in the Spanish banking system through the lending institutions it owns or controls (*la Banca Publica*). In this way the State is able to correct imbalances in the domestic markets, provide financing on favourable terms to strategic sectors or sectors undergoing rationalisation, and finance long-term or job-creating projects.

The public banking sector is being reorganised and rationalised. It has felt the effects of deregulation and increased competition in the Spanish financial system, and is reacting by offering more competitive services.

The following institutions are owned partially or entirely by the State.

(1) The Official Credit Institute

The Official Credit Institute (*Instituto de Crédito Oficial* or ICO) supervises and co-ordinates the public lending sector. It is comprised of the Mortgage Bank of Spain (*Banco Hipotecario de España*), the Local Lending Bank (*Banco de Crédito Local*), the Rural Lending Bank (*Banco de Crédito Agrícola*), and the Industrial Lending Bank (*Banco de Crédito Industrial*). It also administers Development Aid Funds.

(2) The Exterior Bank of Spain

The Exterior Bank of Spain (*Banco Exterior de España*) is technically a private bank in which, by law, the Spanish State must hold a majority interest in the share capital in order for it to administer public funds in the area of exports. The remaining stock is owned by private shareholders. In all other respects, it operates under the same rules and regulations as other banking institutions.

(3) The Post Office Savings Bank

The Post Office Savings Bank (*Caja Postal de Ahorros*) is a savings bank linked to the state postal and telecommunications system. All transactions are guaranteed by the State.

¶605 Opening a new lending institution

The rules and regulations governing the creation of new banks and the establishment of foreign lending institutions in Spain have been adapted to

EEC Directive 77/780 and have two objectives: to reinforce the solvency of new banks, and to assure their viability and stability. Notable among these regulations is the discretionary power reserved to State authorities to act in response to the needs of the market. This power may be exercised in connection with any proposal for the creation of a new bank or other lending institution in Spain, applications regarding the establishment of subsidiaries or branches of foreign banks or other lending institutions (savings banks, leasing companies, finance or mortgage companies, or lending co-operatives), regardless of the nationality of the applicant, until 31 December 1992. New projects may be refused if they offer insufficient guarantees, would not add to the productivity or competitiveness of the system, or do not widen the range of services offered.

However, after 31 December 1992 this discretion may no longer be exercised in respect of applications made by applicants from EEC member States, whilst the principle of reciprocity will apply to those from outside the EEC.

(1) New commercial banks

New commercial banks require a favourable report from the Bank of Spain and prior authorisation from the Ministry of Economy and Finance. An application may only be refused for legitimate reasons. Once incorporated and registered at the Commercial Registry, the new bank must also be registered at the Bank of Spain's Special Registry.

Any new bank must take the form of a corporation/limited company, be formed in a 'simultaneous' incorporation procedure (see ¶307(1)), and have a minimum share capital of 1.5 billion pesetas, paid-up, in cash, and represented by registered shares. By law, its corporate purpose must be limited to that of a lending institution, and there must be at least five persons on the board of directors. Certain restrictions are also imposed on operations during the first few years of existence. During the first three years no dividends may be distributed and all profits must be allocated to reserves. There may only be up to three offices, including the head office, unless the express authority of the Bank is given. During the first five years, in addition to continuous supervision by the Bank of Spain, the new bank may not authorise loans to its partners, directors or chief executives. Any one company or non-financial group may hold no more than 20 per cent of its share capital, and *inter vivos* transfers or charging assets require the prior authority of the Bank. Moreover, during this period the new bank is prohibited from acting solely in the stock market.

(2) The establishment in Spain of foreign lending institutions

Chapter 3 (Business Organisations) describes in detail the requirements for setting up representative and branch offices in Spain under the Commercial Code. Foreign lending institutions and banks are subject to the following additional requirements:

(a) *Representative offices*. These offices may not receive or make investments or offer financial or banking services; they may only act as information offices. They must be authorised by the Ministry of Economy and Finance, and notice must be given to the Bank.

(b) *Branch offices*. The requirements for setting up a foreign branch office are the same as for Spanish commercial banks, with the following differences: a foreign branch must have permanent, unrestricted capital reserves equal to 1.5 billion pesetas available to secure any losses of the branch, and appoint at least two people directly responsible for its management. As stated in ¶304, the documentation accompanying the application for the creation of a foreign branch must contain information regarding the legal and financial basis of the foreign bank filing the application and adequate proof that it is authorised to open a branch in Spain.

The entry of Spain into the EEC and the gradual harmonisation of Spanish law with EEC regulations have broken down the geographical and trade barriers which used to affect the subsidiaries and branches of banks and lending institutions in Spain. On 31 December 1992, the general restriction on expansion will be eliminated in respect of EEC member States. Originally limited to three offices, four will be allowed by 1990, and two more will be allowed in 1991 and in 1992. By 1993 expansion will be unrestricted.

Although branch offices have been prevented from receiving direct deposits from the public in excess of 40 per cent of lending assets and securities plus those assets covering the cash ratio or required cash reserve (*coeficiente de caja*), this percentage has been increasing by 10 per cent annually since 1988 and will continue to do so until it reaches 100 per cent.

(c) *Subsidiary banks or lending institutions*. These are Spanish commercial banks or other lending institutions in which a foreign lending institution, its holding companies or foreign subsidiaries hold a majority share interest. For member States, the same requirements applicable to Spanish commercial banks and other lending institutions apply to the creation of these foreign-held subsidiaries. However, if the entity incorporating the subsidiary has its registered office in a country outside the EEC, reciprocity will apply, and a guarantee may be required in respect of all activities in Spain.

(3) Acquiring capital of existing banking institutions
Spanish banking regulations provide for tight supervision of shareholdings in banking institutions. Apart from the general requirement that capital must be represented by registered shares, the Bank requires a periodic declaration of shareholdings greater than 0.25 per cent of capital and a declaration of any changes in such shareholdings.

Any direct or indirect acquisition of an interest equal to or greater than 5 per cent of capital, must be reported to the target institution and to the Bank within ten days of the effective acquisition. Authorisation must be obtained from the Bank if the shares acquired give the purchaser control of 15 per cent or more of the share capital of the Spanish bank. Any exercise of voting rights remains subject to this notification or authorisation, as applicable. Any resolution adopted in the meantime may be challenged on these grounds.

BANKING SECTORS

¶606 Overview

The trend towards specialisation by all banking and other lending institutions began as a result of the acute banking crisis which Spain suffered in the 1980s. This crisis was largely due to excessive concentration in industrial assets, the value of which suffered a severe decline at that time, and put into question the legal separation of commercial and industrial banks.

The law only permits banks to take deposits on demand and for a term of less than one year. They may offer any other kinds of financial services and engage in all kinds of lending operations, including leasing as from 1990. Banks may freely specialise to meet the needs of the market and increase competition, but this process of specialisation has been slowed due to a number of factors. Among these can be cited the relatively low level of competition among the banking institutions, the effects of the national deficit and the direct activity of the Government in the market in order to finance it, thereby taking business away from the banks, and the many changes in banking regulations and tax implications.

The banking sector can be divided roughly into the wholesale sector (corporate, investment or merchant banking) and the retail sector. Many institutions, both in Spain and in EEC member States, carry on both types of business.

¶607 Wholesale banking

(1) Overview

The wholesale banking sector (*banca al por mayor*) is made up of:

(a) the big national banks, either directly or through specialised subsidiaries. They are still the traditional bankers of larger Spanish companies, in which they often exercise a certain degree of control as shareholders;

(b) branches of foreign banks, whose penetration in the market has been through multi-nationals. They also provide financing to businesses not linked to the banking sector and act as second or third bankers to the large Spanish companies;

(c) some smaller commercial banks orientated towards wholesale banking;

(d) some of the larger savings banks (*cajas de ahorro*).

This is the most competitive and innovative sector of banking in Spain today. There are virtually no entry barriers, since a wide network of branch offices is not necessary to compete, and there are fewer fixed costs. There will be even more competition in this sector in the future because of competition from EEC member States and increased interest on the part of resident companies or groups in specialising in wholesale banking.

Multi-nationals, their subsidiaries in Spain and big Spanish companies, which are the main customers in the wholesale banking sector, will also be the main beneficiaries of the increase in financial services being offered by non-residents, and of the increase in the international movements of capital. At the same time, securitisation and the appearance of specialist securities brokers will facilitate cash management and portfolio investments of these companies and erode the use of traditional bank financial instruments.

The Spanish wholesale banking sector, pressured by the need for results, will have to consider the financial market as a whole and expand operations both nationally and internationally. It will have to maintain a very active and innovative presence in the stock markets and increase the quality of the services offered to the large companies. A major limiting factor to competition in this sector continues to be found in the traditional strong links between the banks and the large national companies. However, progress has been rapid since 1978, when foreign banks were first authorised to set up business in Spain. The national market has assimilated international expertise to launch new financial products.

(2) Financial products

Innovation has been the main cause of increased international activity and of the change in traditional services and products. This process has been brought about by the increased application of interest rates which are variable or indexed to loans or deposits, the channelling of traditional loan operations through organised markets in the form of negotiable instruments, and the standardising of off balance sheet operations to cover interest and exchange rate risks.

Other financial products which have been developed in wholesale banking, some of which are also found in other parts of the banking sector, include:

(a) securities and bond issues at variable interest rates and with zero-coupons, without periodic interest payments;

(b) money market accounts with earnings pegged to inter-bank interest rates;

(c) loans with interest pegged to profits of non-financial companies;

(d) subordinated bonds, which are deemed to be resources and appear on the creditors' list after ordinary creditors in case of insolvency;

(e) sale of shares in a loan in which the lending bank keeps all credit risks;

(f) 'Off balance sheet' transactions, such as interest rate 'swaps' in which the interest payments on transactions in different markets are interchanged; foreign currency 'swaps'; futures and options on foreign currency to cover foreign currency risks or speculation; transfers of loans with all credit risks; and stand-by credits; forward rate agreements and futures to cover interest risks.

Other services offered by the banks in the wholesale sector include advising businesses when they go public, insuring share issues, bonds and company promissory notes, and taking part in company acquisitions and mergers, all with increasing impact on the profit and loss statement.

¶608 Retail banking

(1) Competition

The relatively low level of competition in the retail banking sector exists largely because of the need to have a network of branch offices. Convenience and personal service are still important to Spanish customers. The traditional habits of Spanish customers and the low quality of service offered by the Spanish banks are the main reasons why retail banking in Spain is not as advanced as in other countries.

The competition for small and medium-sized businesses and private customers is mainly among:

(a) the big banks, which already have extensive branch networks in place. The banks in this sector also overlap with their own subsidiary banks which tend to be concentrated in particular geographical areas;
(b) medium and small-sized commercial banks, which cover a smaller geographical area and tend to specialise in certain services;
(c) subsidiaries of foreign banks which are expanding their presence in the sector;
(d) savings banks and lending co-operatives, which are concentrated in particular provinces or areas of Spain.

In addition, the Government and large companies are a source of growing competition, trying to attract small and medium-sized investors in the primary market. The larger department stores and distribution companies are also starting to compete in the field by offering credit directly to the public.

The need for geographical coverage and the lack of specialised intermediaries are the principle reasons that the placement of public debt and certain private securities has continued to be channelled through the existing bank networks. Because of the relatively limited distribution of credit cards and the ties the large companies have maintained with the banks, the banks predominate in attracting funds.

The obstacles to entering the retail market today can only be overcome by acquiring or taking control of a bank or other financial intermediary, such as an insurance company with a branch office network, or by a collaboration scheme giving access to a distribution network.

Future competitors in retail banking will still have to count heavily on entry barriers. However, the freedom of banks to expand outside their traditional geographical areas, and the entry of foreign banks in the market, either by directly forming their own branch network or by acquiring Spanish banks, points to a rapid increase in competition. There will also be more competition as financial services become available to a wider segment of the public, who, in turn, will be better informed and more price-conscious when choosing among the types of financial products available. In the meantime, the retail banking sector must rationalise its branch network and retrain its staff to increase cost-effectiveness and efficiency.

(2) Attracting funds

Financial innovation began in 1987 with the total deregulation of interest rates on deposits. Subsequent changes in tax treatment have also influenced the creation of new financial products.

Traditional current (checking) accounts and money market accounts with a higher return and on which cheques may be drawn are both available, although bank cheques are not widely used in Spain as a means of payment. Alongside the traditional time deposits, it is increasingly common to see accounts with staggered interest, monthly and fortnightly deposits, and 'sweep' accounts with overnight investment of available amounts. There is also a noticeable increase in investments in fixed and variable interest investment funds and various combined insurance and pension plans.

(3) Credit

Consumer credit is experiencing rapid growth in Spain. Credit with fixed or variable interest rates is offered at the point of sale or by finance companies. Applications are commonly evaluated on the basis of a point system or 'scoring'.

It is now a speedier process to obtain a mortgage for the purchase of a home. Normally the interest rate is variable and relative to the prime rate. The tendency in the market has been to increase the amount capable of being financed and the length of the term, which now averages between ten and 20 years. Sccond mortgages are also becoming available. Banks offer assistance and advice as to the different kinds of loans available, including those which protect the purchaser from unexpected increases in interest rates by establishing maximum limits and fixed payment terms, and variable interest loans convertible into fixed interest loans.

(4) Payment

Direct salary deposits and direct payment of bills by the bank out of the client's account (*domiciliación*) are widely used services. A relatively large number of people take care of household accounts in this way, as do small and medium-sized companies.

Credit cards are not widely available and are used mainly to obtain money from automatic banking machines and as a way of payment, rather than as a means of obtaining credit.

¶609 Savings banks and lending co-operatives

Savings banks (*cajas de ahorro*) and lending co-operatives directly compete with banks in the retail banking sector. The capital base of savings banks and lending co-operatives is fundamentally different from that of the commercial or public banks. The savings banks are founded with base funds (*fondos fundacionales*) and the lending co-operatives have contributions (*aportaciones*) incorporated into their capital. Both include, as capital resources, non-liquid quasi-charitable or civic (*benéfico social*) funds. Savings banks may increase their resources by issuing a participative interest (*cuota participativa*). This type of holding must be in registered form and may not confer voting rights. Earnings thereon may only be paid out of available surplus, and may be used to compensate losses in the same proportion as other reserves and base funds.

(1) Savings banks

Savings banks began as non-profitmaking institutions in the nineteenth century to protect against usury. From these beginnings they have developed into powerful institutions, their customers mainly drawn from family savers and small and medium-sized businesses. Depending on their origins, they may be publicly or privately held, and they attract just less than half the resources of the banking system. Of the ten largest Spanish banks, two are savings banks. One of the main differences between savings banks and commercial banks is that once reserve requirements are met they are required to invest part of their profits in such areas as health, research, teaching, and cultural and social services.

The Ministry of Economy and Finance and the regional governments authorise the creation of new savings banks, which must have minimum capital of between 150 and 750 million pesetas, depending on the number of inhabitants in the municipality where the savings bank is located. Since 1988 they are authorised to open offices anywhere in Spain. Foreign savings banks opening subsidiaries, offices or branches in Spain are also subject to the restrictions discussed in ¶605(2) above.

The Spanish Confederation of Savings Banks (*Confederación Española de Cajas de Ahorros* or CECA) exists to represent savings banks and provide them with certain administrative and financial services.

Spanish savings banks may carry on the same operations as other banking institutions and must comply with the same requirements relating to resources, liquidity and risk limits.

The savings banks were affected to a much lesser degree by the economic crisis of the 1980s because of their natural diversification and their traditional strong presence in the mortgage market. They are preparing for the EEC single market to come into effect in 1992 by concentrating on a regional level and improving the quality of services.

(2) Lending co-operatives and rural banks

Lending co-operatives and rural banks (*cooperativas de crédito* and *cajas rurales*) play a lesser role in the Spanish banking system. Their presence is primarily found in the agricultural sector and the professions, since the professional associations often have their own lending co-operatives.

The Ministry of Economy and Finance, the Ministry of Labour and the regional governments supervise the creation of these entities. Base capital contributions from members of these co-operatives varies between 50 and 300 million pesetas, depending on the geographical area in which they operate.

Lending co-operatives are subject to the same regulations and controls as banks. They are, however, required to give priority to their members, and only up to 50 per cent of their resources may be lent to non-members. In the case of rural banks, there are certain requirements for lending peculiar to the rural environment in which they operate.

The rural banks also suffered a crisis in the 1980s, owing to weak management and the general economic climate. They are now undergoing a process of takeovers, mergers, reorganisations and associations, both on the inter-provincial and international level, bringing them up to modern banking standards.

BANKING REGULATIONS

Banking regulations focus primarily on solvency. Banking institutions are required to make certain investments in accordance with the Government's economic and monetary policy, and provide greater access to information by customers. Discipline and enforcement are also emphasised.

¶610 Solvency requirements

This body of regulations is characterised both by the type of preventative measures to be taken by all banking institutions and by the specific regulations to be applied in the face of an impending bank crisis.

(1) Risk-base capital

Banking institutions, depending on their risk assets and off balance sheet liabilities, must maintain minimum base capital, calculated on a twice-yearly consolidated basis and accounted for separately. Failure to comply with this requirement may restrict the annual distribution of dividends and the opening of any new offices without prior authorisation.

(2) Coverage of bank assets and risk reserves

The accounting rules applicable to lending institutions require that there be a sufficient level of reserves allocated to specific risks such as bad debts, country risks, and present and future pension obligations in respect of bank personnel. General coverage of all credit risks and transfers is also required.

(3) Limits on assumed risks

These are limits placed on the concentration levels of credit risks and on exposure to exchange risks. Banks may not maintain risks of over 40 per cent of the consolidated base capital with any one individual or company or group of companies. The minimum level of base capital required to be maintained is increased if the credit risks maintained with a given person or group exceed 15 per cent or more of consolidated base capital, or if there are credit risks maintained with non-consolidatable affiliated companies, or with the directors or managers of the consolidated banking group or with companies controlled by them.

This charge on bank base capital excludes public debt issued by the State, the autonomous regions, public bodies or State-run businesses, and money market assets for terms of less than three months. Branches of foreign banks are not subject to these requirements regarding concentration of credit risks in respect of their own resources.

The restrictions on exchange risks vary according to the individual base capital of each bank, which affects the exposure of each currency and the sum of short or long exposures of different currencies.

(4) Good banking practices

Certain operations are considered to be contrary to good banking practices and are prohibited. Such prohibitions include banking institutions participating in a transfer of assets at nominal value or at other than market value. Earnings from the sale of assets to a company or persons connected with the banking institution may not be included on the profit and loss statement if the price is paid directly or indirectly with the bank's own funds; nor may an increase in value be entered on the books based on a reappraisal made for a sale and later repurchase of the assets. In the case of lease-backs where the asset leased is still being used, the excess over the accounting value is credited to the profit and loss statement periodically, together with the depreciation and the residual value of the leased asset. Losses may appear on the profit and loss statement on the date of the lease-back contract. Circular lending between institutions is prohibited, i.e. those operations in which a banking institution offers loans to businesses connected to another banking institution so that the latter, in turn, finances the related businesses of the former.

(5) Crisis intervention and deposit insurance

If a lending institution finds itself in a state of financial crisis or its solvency or stability is threatened, the Bank may appoint receivers to take part in its management or replace the entire board of directors.

Commercial banks, savings banks and lending co-operatives all have deposit guarantee funds which insure deposits up to 1.5 million pesetas per depositor. These funds are financed by their contributions, which are matched by the Bank. The Bank may also deem it necessary to increase the fund up to a legal maximum.

The deposit guarantee funds are managed and administered by the Bank through a managing committee made up of an equal number of members from banking institutions and the Bank. The governor of the Bank acts as chairman of the Commission and has the casting (tie-breaking) vote. In order to stave off a crisis, the committee may buy unsubscribed shares at an agreed amount so that the value can be adjusted to its real value and later resold. Other measures include the assumption of losses, the purchase of assets, and offering guarantees.

¶611 Compulsory investments

Currently, a bank must maintain with the Bank of Spain a maximum reserve of 20 per cent of all its deposits received from the public. The level varies according to the monetary policy of the Government, but, in any event, only part of the reserve with the Bank accrues interest. Additionally, the investment ratio obliges banking institutions to make certain compulsory investments in public funds – State and Treasury bonds – at a percentage equal to 11 per cent of resources. In order to harmonise with EEC treatment of lending institutions, banking authorities have agreed to reduce the cash ratio to around 5 per cent, and are gradually reducing the investment ratio through quarterly reductions so that by the end of 1992 it will be abolished.

¶612 Informed customers

This is a relatively new concept in the Spanish financial system, which offers a degree of protection to bank customers in their banking transactions. Notwithstanding the freedom to contract that governs private commercial transactions, certain banking practices are being standardised for the sake of a greater clarity and uniformity in bank-customer relations. Banks must express the effective yield of deposit or credit and lending operations which they advertise and actually apply in a standardised way, by stating it in terms of a transaction with interest payable annually. They must publish their prime rate (defined as that rate applicable to private clients with good credit standing in short-term credit transactions involving significant amounts of money), the rates of interest applicable to overdrafts in current/checking accounts or credit accounts, the rules of valuation used to calculate interest, and all the applicable commissions on lending or borrowing transactions and services.

Banks must also give their customers copies of all contractual documents in transactions involving less than 10 million pesetas and in all lending, credit or deposit transactions. Banks may not index transactions to a variable rate of interest calculated on its own prime rate, and may not increase fees on less than two months' notice.

The Credit Customers Complaint Service is a part of the legal department of the Bank and receives and handles complaints from banking customers concerning bank services. If the parties do not resolve the problem themselves, a report is written up which may be used in legal proceedings. It is also sent to the inspection department of the Bank if a breach of regulations is alleged.

¶613 Disciplinary framework

Law 26/1988 sets out banking violations in great detail and classifies them as very serious (*muy grave*), serious (*grave*) and minor (*leve*). Sanctions applicable to banks can go as far as revoking their banking licence (authorisation). Individuals in administrative or managerial positions may be held personally liable for violations.

The Bank handles those cases involving minor or serious violations. The Ministry of Economy and Finance deals with very serious violations, and the Council of Ministers considers the revocation of the authorisation to carry out banking operations.

SPECIALISED NON-BANKING LENDING INSTITUTIONS

¶614 Applicable regulations

Non-banking lending institutions may not take deposits from the public for terms of less than one year. They specialise in specific sectors of the lending market and must comply with the following fundamental regulations, also applicable to banking institutions:

(1) These lending institutions must obtain the prior authorisation of the Ministry of Economy and Finance, file a report with the Bank and be registered at the special registries before commencing business. They must take the form of a corporation/limited company (*sociedad anónima*) with a minimum share capital represented by registered shares. Minimum share capital for finance companies is 300 million pesetas, for mortgage and leasing companies, 500 million pesetas, and for money market brokerage firms, 750 million pesetas.

(2) In order to establish a subsidiary, branch or representative office of a foreign lending institution of this type in Spain, banking regulations apply, along with the share capital requirements described immediately above.

(3) Notification and publication of shareholdings is required. All holdings which directly or indirectly give title and control of 5 per cent or more must be notified to the institution itself and to the Bank.

(4) The compulsory cash ratio must be maintained.

(5) The capital requirement, calculated according to weighted risk assets,

is applicable. Calculation methods, however, differ from one institution to the next, depending on their particular activity.

(6) The discipline, supervision and control by the Bank, including the measures for intervention and substitution of administrators in exceptionally serious cases where the resources, stability, liquidity or solvency of the institutions is threatened, are the same as for banking institutions.

(7) Customer relations are provided for by law, although adjusted to the specific activities carried on by the specialised lending institutions.

(8) These non-banking lending institutions are allowed general participation in the financial system and may hold accounts in the Electronic Bookkeeping Entry System for Public Debt, have access to the interbank market, act as authorised banks (*entidades delegadas*) in exchange control transactions, to the extent permitted by their operations, and have access to the Bank's Central Risk Information Office.

¶615 Finance companies

These are specialised companies which provide financing for developers, construction companies, manufacturers, distributors, and consumers. They are active in many sectors, although in terms of volume, the housing and car industries stand out.

In 1988, finance companies were brought into the framework of lending institutions. This rationalised and standardised their legal status and laid down the legal parameters of the business. The most distinctive features of finance companies may be briefly described as follows:

(1) Finance companies may not own each other's shares without express authorisation.

(2) Insolvency funds of not less than 1.5 per cent of total lending investments and company risks (*riesgos de firma*) not guaranteed by public entities or secured by mortgage are required.

(3) The solvency ratio must be calculated according to the finance company's risks, less amortisations and specific reserves, with risks ranked according to type. In any event, the ratio of risk–base capital may not be less than 4 per cent of total risks.

(4) The maximum risk limit in respect of one person or group of companies may not exceed 5 per cent of own resources.

¶616 Leasing companies

Spanish law applies the term '*arrendamiento financiero*' to the concept of leasing. It describes the contractual relationship whereby goods or property are purchased by one party in order to lease them to another party (lessee) for a set period of time, at the end of which the lessee has the option to purchase all or part of the goods or property at a pre-determined price. Leasing agreements may cover tangible goods (e.g. plant and equipment) or intangibles (e.g. software, trade mark or patent rights). Leasing agreements may be either real or personal, depending on the type of property. The leased assets may only be exploited by the lessee.

Spanish law provides for three general types of leasing agreements: the standard contract (*alquiler*); the operating contract (*leasing operativo*); and the hire purchase (installment sale) agreement (*leasing financiero*). Unlike the standard lease, the operating lease also includes a package of maintenance, upkeep and repair services, such as those commonly provided in car rental agreements. The hire purchase agreement includes an option to purchase the leased goods at the end of the lease period, the sales price having been paid, wholly or in part, through the lease payments. The contract is irrevocable throughout the lease period, and all risks are assumed by the lessee.

Other types of leasing are classified by the type of goods. Equipment financing in Spain generates the greatest volume of business. Other major areas include vehicle and car sales and data processing.

The term 'lease-back' is used to describe the purchase of property by a lessor, which is immediately leased back to the seller for his continued use. The term 'cross-border leasing' includes all international leasing operations.

Leasing contracts must have a minimum term of two years if the subject of the lease is personal property, and ten years if real or industrial property is involved. The annual amount of that part of the leasing payments allocated to the recuperation of costs is required to remain the same or increase during the contract term.

As from 1 January 1990 banking institutions may carry on the business of leasing or hire purchase.

There has been a spectacular increase in the number of leasing companies and the volume of business in Spain since 1984, during which time private investment began to recover from a long slump. This expansion is largely attributable to the fact that there have been essentially no legal limits placed on the operations of these companies, and the customers have enjoyed favourable tax treatment. The customer (lessee) is allowed to accelerate depreciation on goods purchased through leasing and the costs are totally deductible from income tax. However, this rate of growth may change in light of future competition from banking institutions and the treatment of leasing companies as specialised lending institutions subject to banking regulations (e.g., resource requirements, supervision by the Bank of Spain, control of shareholdings, foreign investment regulations, and customer relations regulations). These changes, along with the change in the preferential tax treatment of these types of investments in 1988, have opened the doors for realignment in this sector.

¶617 Mortgage companies

The Spanish mortgage market has traditionally been dominated by the Mortgage Bank of Spain (*Banco Hipotecario de España*) and the savings banks. The economic crisis in the 1980s and the subsequent recession in the construction industry provided the impetus for the changes experienced in the market. One of these changes was the creation of specialised lending institutions called mortgage companies (*sociedades de crédito hipotecario*). The sole corporate purpose of these companies is to participate in the mortgage market. They must comply with a resource ratio requirement of 8 per cent and a cash ratio. The maximum risk limit with one person or group of companies is 2.5 per cent of total resources, and they must set aside 10 per cent of liquid surplus in a special reserve each fiscal year until the reserve amount equals share capital.

(1) Securitisation

Allowing the securitisation (*titularización*) of mortgage loans through such vehicles as mortgage bonds, mortgage obligations and participation mortgages has increased and facilitated liquidity in the secondary market. These instruments can be described as follows:

(a) *Mortgage bonds*. These securities are secured by all those mortgages held by the lender which are not covered by other obligations.

(b) *Tied mortgage bonds (bonos hipotecarios)*. These bonds are directly tied to specific mortgages in the issuer's portfolio.

(c) *Mortgage securities (obligaciones hipotecarias)*. These securities are globally guaranteed by a mortgage on property.

(d) *Mortgages participations (participaciones hipotecarias)*. The security lies in the part of a mortgage loan allocated to the participant. The loan itself is on the balance sheet of the issuing institution.

In general, it is not permissible to negotiate more than 90 per cent of the mortgage loan portfolio. The transfer of these securities does not require the intervention of a public intermediary (*fedatario*), as long as the parties are authorised to operate in the mortgage market.

(2) Secondary markets

The most important secondary markets for mortgage securities are:

(a) the official secondary stock market, where qualifying securities may be traded;

(b) the market created by issuing institutions which repurchase the securities they issue, up to a maximum limit of 5 per cent of its issued securities;

(c) the market created by lending institutions participating in 'mortgage market liquidity funds' (*fondos de regulación del mercado hipotecario*) which were created to lend liquidity to the market by facilitating the sale and purchase of mortgage securities. These funds must have assets of at least 100 million pesetas and be managed by specialised management companies, in which at least ten issuing companies participate.

¶618 Money market brokerage firms

The sole corporate purpose of the money market brokerage firms is to act as money brokers in the money market. They deal in liquid assets, give depth and liquidity to the money markets, and provide a second line of liquidity to lending institutions. They are the only non-banking lending institutions which may take deposits from the public through the sale of financial assets with an obligation to repurchase (*repos*).

Money market brokerage firms must comply with a set of regulations peculiar to the business, such as notifying the Bank in advance of any change in ownership of shares. They are also subject to the direct supervision of the Bank, which may inspect their activities as often as deemed necessary. In order to supply these companies with cash, the Bank may repurchase assets from their portfolios, within given limits. Changing conditions in the money markets constantly alter the governing regulations and controls, which basically relate to the:

(1) *solvency ratio*. The investments of these companies are treated in accordance with the respective maturity dates of the assets, excluding arbitrage transactions with Treasury assets. They may not exceed 450 times net worth (*neto patrimonial*) less real assets, net depreciation (*inmovilizaciones materiales netas*), and foreign investments;

(2) *investment ratio*. Investments in Treasury bonds must make up at least 20 per cent of total assets;

(3) *risk limits*. Commercial promissory notes and bills of exchange bought on the stock exchange may not exceed 10 per cent of all investments.

Money market brokers may not invest more than 10 per cent of that amount in certificates of deposit and promissory notes issued by any banking group participating in the capital of the brokerage firm.

These companies have access to the Telephonic Inter-bank Market Service and may act as dealers and 'market makers', placing public debt with other financial intermediaries and the public in general by means of the electronic bookkeeping entry system.

SECURITIES MARKETS

¶619 Regulatory and market trends

There is an indistinct line between the capital market, in which brokers trade financial assets with a maturity of over one year, and the money market, in which short-term or liquid assets are traded. In the securities markets fundamentally long-term assets are traded, but transactions and assets characteristic of the money markets are also found. The securities markets in Spain, by legal definition, include any securities issued, traded and marketed in Spain.

After a decade of lethargy, the Spanish securities markets, both primary and secondary, are undergoing a period of rapid growth. This is attributed to many factors, such as Spain's economic recovery, heavy foreign investment (due in part to favourable interest rates on the peseta), corporate reorganisations, the growing need for financing in the public sector, and the increasing sophistication of both institutional and private investors. This rapid growth is seen in the new financial products offered by banks, and is accentuated by the increase in non-banking financial intermediaries. Modernisation can be seen in such things as securitisation (*titularización*) and '*desmaterialización*', which dispenses with the necessity of physical embodiment of securities.

These changes are being brought about by the growing tendency to save and to access the stock market through institutional investors, i.e. through investment funds, pension funds and insurance companies, rather than keeping money in bank deposits. Corporate investors are seeking cost reductions by taking advantage of the growing circumvention of the bank and directly accessing the market. The markets are opening up due to greater diversification in the type of securities offered, by companies and by the State (public debt), and by the growing opportunity for foreign investment in and outside the national markets, especially at the EEC level.

There is a trend towards deregulating the movement of capital and the securities market. On the other hand, the trend is towards regulation of intermediaries specialising in these markets, the assumption of risks off the balance sheet, the use of privileged information, and an increase in the type and quantity of information to be submitted to financial and tax authorities.

The regulations governing the securities markets are designed to maximise competition and meet the needs and reflect the changes in the market by:

(1) shaping and developing a specific market for debt issued by the State and Treasury to meet the ever growing need to attract investment, largely due to the deficit;

(2) implementing legislative changes in the Spanish stock markets, which affect the primary (issuing) markets and the secondary (trading) markets;

(3) fostering the emergence of a new type of securities brokers in the form of companies to replace the individual broker system; and

(4) enforcing a code of conduct based on EEC recommendations which are mandatory for all those taking part in the market.

¶620 The National Securities Exchange Commission

The National Securities Exchange Commission (*Comisión Nacional del Mercado de Valores*) ('the Commission') supervises the securities markets. It is governed by a board appointed by the Government, the members of which are not professionally connected with the markets.

The Commission's main functions are to ensure the accessibility and accountability of the different markets, to correct pricing within the markets, and to protect investors. It also oversees the development of the primary and secondary markets. The Commission ensures compliance with codes of conduct, advises the Government, and exercises the disciplinary and sanctionary powers granted to it; it notifies the Ministry of Economy and Finance of the creation of new stock market companies and agencies and collective investment institutions.

The Commission is endowed with broad supervisory powers which reach not only the governing and compensatory bodies of the secondary market, securities companies and agencies, collective investment institutions and security investment companies and funds, but also individuals, companies and financial intermediaries, to the extent of their activity in the market.

The Commission exercises its functions over the securities markets, except in respect of public debt traded by electronic bookkeeping entries under the supervision of the Bank.

¶621 Code of conduct

Rules of conduct within the securities markets apply to all participants in order to ensure honesty and fair dealing in the marketplace. The law deals with insider trading and requires immediate publication of all matters and decisions which could influence the market price of a company's securities. Specifically, advisers and dealers must give absolute priority to the interests of their clients. They may not create artifical price movements for their own or others' benefit, unnecessarily duplicate transactions, allocate securities to themselves on preferential terms or give priority to the sale of their own securities over the sale of their clients' securities. Those who have access to privileged information may not engage in any direct or indirect dealing in the market on the basis of that information. Privileged information is that which is not available to the general public and which, if it were made public, would have a significant effect on trading. Issuers of securities must inform the public at the earliest possible moment of any act or decision which may substantially affect prices quoted. This is a requirement which may be waived by the Commission.

In accordance with a proposed EEC Directive, securities transactions are not subject to Value Added Tax (VAT) nor to transfer tax. In 1992 commissions are to be deregulated.

¶622 The primary market

Issuing securities in the primary market is not, in principle, subject to prior administrative authorisation. Nevertheless, the Ministry of Economy and Finance may prohibit an issue or require administrative authorisation for it under certain conditions, such as:

(1) if the principal or interest thereon depends on a price index, or if earnings thereon are partly or totally payable, according to its terms, in a period of over one year; or

(2) if the transaction is carried out in Spain and involves foreign currency or non-residents; or

(3) if the transaction gives rise to a tax benefit or any other advantage provided by law, unless the benefit is one offered by an autonomous region, in which case the autonomous region is the competent authority.

In order to issue securities in the primary market, the issuer must notify the Commission in the form required for subsequent publication by them, and file the issue agreement, a description of the securities to be issued, the rights and obligations of holders and the procedure to be followed. In addition, the Commission will require to see the auditor's report of the issuer, and the issuer must file a prospectus in the form dictated by law, giving all the information necessary for investors to evaluate the proposed investment. The law also spells out minimum waiting periods which must be observed between mandatory filings, notices, and the actual issue.

Securities issued by the State and autonomous regions are not subject to the above requirements. The auditing requirement does not apply to public entities exempted by the Government, nor to international organisations to which Spain belongs. The Government may waive all or part of the above requirements for certain types of issues, depending on the issuer, the size of the issue, the restricted number or type of investors, or other circumstances which might warrant it.

¶623 The secondary market

There are two official secondary markets for securities. One consists of the stock exchanges and the other is the public debt market. The public debt market is described further at ¶626 to ¶628 and consists of the Government bond market electronic bookkeeping entry system and any other securities market electronic bookkeeping entry system which may be created in the future by the Government.

¶624 Stock exchanges

A stock or securities exchange may be created by the Government or by the autonomous regions with the consent of the Government. Spanish stock exchanges are expected to grow in keeping with demand and the range of securities available. Although these markets are experiencing increased activity by Spanish and foreign non-banking financial intermediaries, it cannot be over-emphasised that the Spanish banking system still receives the biggest share of the increased demand, because most orders to sell and buy securities are handled through the bank branch network. The banks also tend to be major shareholders in the brokerage firms.

There are four stock exchanges in Spain; the largest is in Madrid and the others are located in Barcelona, Valencia and Bilbao. Spanish stock exchanges are characterised by continuous strong growth in share prices, broken only by the crash of October 1987, which has substantially raised capitalisation to levels comparable to those of other EEC countries, in respect of gross domestic product. The breadth of securities offered is narrow and sharply inclined towards the financial sector. No foreign company is quoted in Spain. Despite this, more non-financial companies are quoted on the stock exchange than in Germany or France. This narrowness can be explained by the role of the banks in the economy (*bancarización*) as the main vehicles of financial activity, the lack of specialised intermediaries which would widen the scope of and lend liquidity to the market, and the prevalent ownership structure of Spanish companies, consisting of either family-run businesses or businesses having a large amount of foreign capital.

The future strength of the stock markets, apart from the constant increase of foreign investors who tend to make highly speculative investments, will be found in the increase of institutional investors such as investment funds, insurance companies and pension funds. Due to their importance, these entities are treated in a separate section (see ¶629 to ¶632).

In order to cope with the challenges of the future, the Spanish stock markets have been reorganised to meet EEC standards. As a result, companies have been created to manage and supervise the exchanges in Madrid, Barcelona, Valencia and Bilbao. An inter-exchange company has been created to join up the information systems of the stock exchanges. Another new entity which has appeared is a securities clearing and settlement company (*sociedad de compensación y liquidación bursátil*), the capital of which is formed by financial companies directly related to the securities' clearing and settlement process. Non-resident institutions with analogous functions abroad may hold an interest in the capital of the Spanish financial companies, which, in turn, capitalise this clearing and settlement company.

The Commission may, on its own initiative, or as requested by the issuer or by the governing body of a securities exchange market, withdraw securities from all official secondary markets if it finds that special circumstances exist which distort normal trading of the securities or it is necessary to protect investors. The Commission may also exclude securities from trading which do not meet the legal requirements relating to concentration, frequency and volume of trading. If exclusion from trading is considered detrimental to the interests of shareholders, it may deny such a request or make it conditional upon the issuer making a public offer.

The issuers of securities admitted to trade must be audited annually and must publish a provisional balance sheet and profit and loss statement on a quarterly basis, containing essentially the same information as required for the annual report.

Trading on the official secondary market, in the exchanges, is defined as the purchase and sale of securities admitted to trade in that market. All transactions must include the participation of at least one member of the market, otherwise they are null and void. Therefore, on the official secondary market, purchases are made either between members of the market, between members of the market and non-members, between non-members with a member acting as broker, or between non-members who have agreed to the terms of the transaction with the consent of one of the members.

¶625 Securities companies and agencies

Securities companies and agencies (*sociedades y agencias de valores*) are the only brokers allowed to trade securities on the stock exchange, provided that they are members of it. They specialise in trading all securities which may be quoted there and have replaced the '*Agentes de Cambio y Bolsa*' who previously had acted as licensed individual stockbrokers. The main difference between a securities company and a securities agency is that the former may trade on its own account and that of third parties, whereas the latter may only act on behalf of third parties.

Securities companies and agencies are authorised by the Ministry of Economy and Finance upon the recommendation of the Commission, and they take the form of corporations/limited companies with an initial authorised share capital of 750 million pesetas for securities companies or 150 million pesetas for agencies. Capital must be fully paid-up upon incorporation. The chief executive officers, managing director or general manager, and the members of the board of directors, which must be at least five for companies and at least three for agencies, must be well-respected in their business or profession and have previous experience in the stock markets.

There are also strict rules governing capital participation, supervision and advertising. Other securities companies and agencies, investment and pension fund management companies and portfolio management companies may not hold shares. Other individuals or companies holding shares in other securities companies or agencies at the same time may not hold shares, unless the scope of their activity is mutually exclusive. The shareholdings of the board of directors and those who are on the payroll of other securities companies and agencies, portfolio management companies and investment and pension funds, are limited to 10 per cent. The Commission must be notified of all acquisitions of 5 per cent of the share capital and successive multiples of 5 per cent. Until 1 January 1992, non-EEC residents may not hold shares in companies and agencies which are members of the stock exchange.

The financing methods available to these companies and agencies only allow them to obtain financing from other financial intermediaries, and directly from the market through shares issues, subordinated loans, fixed-income securities which have a term of no less than one year and may be traded on the stock market, and funds acquired temporarily from the public to carry out their own share trading.

Securities companies and agencies must maintain a liquidity ratio (i.e. the relation between liquid assets in respect of total assets) of between 5 per cent and 10 per cent, and a solvency ratio. This means that the company or agency must maintain a level of resources weighted by different risk assets which may not be below 5 per cent of total assets.

The concentration of risks in any one individual or company or group of companies may never exceed 40 per cent of own resources.

Securities companies and agencies may act as authorised entities (*entidades delegadas*) in connection with foreign currency operations, and may act as management companies for public debt.

THE PUBLIC DEBT MARKET

¶626 Overview

The sole purpose of the Government Bond Market Electronic Registry is to trade in public debt and securities issued by public institutions.

The economic policy implemented by the fiscal and monetary authorities in Spain is designed to finance the substantial and budget deficit of the public sector by applying orthodox methods, yet avoiding undesired macro-economic effects. The Government has also pursued a policy of openness and accountability to the public (*transparencia*) in respect of the management and costs of the public debt.

The Government's policy has been to issue short-, medium- and long-term public debt, based on competitive bidding. It has set in motion an electronic bookkeeping entry system to facilitate the negotiation and transfer of assets issued by the Treasury. This, along with the development and specialisation of financial intermediaries active in the field, has ensured the liquidity of the market and an efficient method of pricing; these have been the co-ordinates around which the public debt market has revolved since 1987.

This policy has had its effects on the market. The channelling of these assets has given quantity and depth to it. Public debt instruments, although receiving a certain amount of fiscal protection, have taken advantage of the banks' distribution network and are more competitive in the market. New mechanisms and innovative financial practices have been introduced into the system – *inter alia*, the electronic bookkeeping entry system, obviating the need for documentation, the generalised use of '*repos*' or purchases with an undertaking to sell on, futures and the development of an options market for public debt.

The appearance and strengthening of the secondary market have accelerated the process of direct market access (*desintermediación*), in spite of the fact that small savers still use the banks' branch network for distribution and access to the market. The banking system itself shows interest in the public debt market by making investments beyond obligatory requirements. The secondary public debt market has allowed more flexibility and speedier implementation of monetary policy by the Bank, whose operations in the open market are beginning to include assets issued by the Treasury and the State. This has given a second line of liquidity to lending institutions and other intermediaries, which in turn has lead to a widening of the inter-bank market and the creation of a wholesale public debt market. The practice and methods of portfolio management on the part of those in the market has improved, adding sophisticated methods of controlling price risks.

¶627 Treasury and State assets

Securities issued by the Spanish Treasury are mainly channelled through the electronic bookkeeping entry system, since there is no need for certificates. They take the form of treasury notes (*pagarés del tesoro*), issued at a discount with a nominal unit value of 500,000 pesetas for a term of 18 months, which, since 1987, have been issued at a fixed price. Treasury bills (*letras del tesoro*) are another form of public debt, issued at a discount with a unit value of 1 million pesetas, for a term of a year, and awarded in competitive bidding. Bonds and Treasury Bonds (*bonos y obligaciones del Estado*), with interest dividends each half-year, with a nominal unit value of 10,000 pesetas, and falling due after three or more years, are also awarded in competitive bidding. They may still be found in certificate form, although the electronic bookkeeping entry system is clearly the more widely used method of distribution.

¶628 Organisation of the market

(1) Decentralisation

The registered public debt market in Spain is decentralised, and business is done over the telephone. It works through a central electronic bookkeeping office which is a public service supervised by the Bank on behalf of the Treasury. The Bank also supervises the general functioning of the system by overseeing the accountability (*transparencia*) built into the regulatory system. The Bank has the authority to allow the participation of financial intermediaries in the public debt market, and defines and regulates the procedures for trading, quotation, clearing and settlement.

(2) Financial intermediaries

There are specialised financial intermediaries who are involved in the public debt market:

(a) *Account holders (titulares de cuenta)*. These are lending institutions and other financial intermediaries which may maintain an account in the electronic bookkeeping entry centre for their investments in Treasury and State assets. They must have own resources of at least 200 million pesetas and comply with the rules and regulations of the electronic bookkeeping entry system.

(b) *Management companies (sociedades gestoras)*. These are account holders which may maintain an account for investments made on behalf of third parties in the electronic bookkeeping entry centre, as well as their own account. They must have at least 1 billion pesetas in own resources and maintain a balance of at least 7 billion pesetas in favour of third parties who are not account holders.

(c) *Securities dealers (negociantes de deuda)*. These are managing companies which are authorised to enter into 'blind' (*ciega*) public debt transactions. They must quote at least six issues of public bonds, and must deal in more than 0.75 per cent of spot transactions in the public debt market.

(d) *Market makers (creadores de mercado)*. These are managing companies which quote at least 60 per cent of registered public debt issues and maintain very broad portfolios. They must regularly attend the debt auctions, have access to sufficient material and professional resources, practice adequate methods of risk control and have a substantial presence in the market. These entities must deal in more than 1.75 per cent of spot transactions in the public debt market.

(e) *Brokers for securities dealers (mediadores entre negociantes de deuda)*. These brokers facilitate the information going from the network of dealers to the market makers, close transactions between them and assure anonymity between the parties (blind transactions). They must have a minimum liquid capital of 300 million pesetas, adequate staff and resources, act under a code of conduct which guarantees anonymity and optimum pricing, and demonstrate that their services are required by securities dealers, who together represent at least 50 per cent of third party accounts in the electronic bookkeeping entry centre.

(f) *Private individuals* are third parties in the electronic bookkeeping entry system, and have access to securities offered by the State and Treasury only through the management companies.

(3) Functioning of the market

The secondary public debt market is composed of a wholesale market, in which account holders, management companies, debt dealers and market makers participate, with or without brokers, and a retail market in which management companies operate on behalf of their individual clients.

The wholesale market is the arena for three kinds of transactions:

(a) The traditional buying and selling of Treasury and State securities on account, with or without an undertaking to repurchase, done over the telephone in the inter-bank market.

(b) The 'blind' transaction through the brokers for the securities dealers, based on the anonymity of the parties and using screens where the prices are shown. Buying and selling public debt, with or without the undertaking to repurchase, and term transactions are also done over the telephone.

(c) Futures and options will be transacted through a centralised market being created, where transactions will be carried out over the telephone through a clearing house, and the earnings settled daily. Futures operations will be traded at a fixed price, a price based on an average price of a given group of securities (*cesta de valores*), or a notional price. Options with a fixed value or stock futures, which will be able to be executed at any moment during the option period or upon maturity, will also be traded.

Table 6.1: Distribution of the market*

			Trader brokers (5)	
Accounting system	Account holders (250)	Managing companies (84)	Securities dealers (28)	Market makers (11)
(SACDE)				Other dealers
			Other managing companies	
		Other holders		
	Third parties (through the securities dealers)			

* Information available as of May 1988.

(d) The market makers channel the Bank of Spain's participation in the money market in order to inject liquidity into the system, through options contracts of the issuing bank in the electronic bookkeeping entry portfolio belonging to the marketmakers.

(e) The retail market is composed of the management companies and their clients and is decentralised. Transactions may be made for cash, with or without the obligation to repurchase, on demand or for a fixed term, or term transactions involving not less than 100 million pesetas, in which it is possible to agree to settle accounts on any date within the term or upon maturity. The numbers in parentheses show the number of lending institutions and financial intermediaries.

INSTITUTIONAL INVESTORS AND VENTURE CAPITAL

¶629 The role of the non-banking institutions

Non-banking institutions are playing an increasingly larger role in stock market trading and public debt. These are institutional investors which, although varied in form and subject to specific rules and regulations, have some characteristics in common.

These specialised institutions attract funds from a number of investors and channel them into financial assets traded mainly on the stock markets. This type of investment company attempts to produce high earnings with low risks through a balanced portfolio. The purpose is not to gain control of the business. Earnings are allocated to individual investors in accordance with the collective yield of the funds invested or set aside for the purpose of ensuring future payments, e.g. pensions.

Pension funds are regulated through their capital funds, made up of moneys derived from one or more pension plans. The difference between pension funds and other so-called investment funds is the control the participants may exercise in the management of funds through committees (*comisiones*) set up for that purpose.

Venture capital companies and funds limit their capital investment activities to companies not quoted on the stock market.

¶630 Collective investment institutions

(1) Definitions

Collective investment institutions (*instituciones de inversión colectiva*) are financial intermediaries which receive funds from the public to turn them into financial or real assets. The purpose is to produce a collective income by spreading risks, with no attempt to take control of the businesses in which they invest. They operate both as limited companies and as capital funds.

Collective investment institutions include stock investment companies, stock investment funds, money market investment funds, and any other institutions which receive funds or assets from the general public and manage or invest them and the earnings thereon.

Collective investment institutions may be classified as financial or non-financial. The financial companies specialise in the investment or management of financial assets, such as money, bonds and securities, promissory notes, bills of exchange, and certificates of deposit. At present there are no regulated non-financial funds.

Collective investment institutions and their management and depositaries must be located in Spain. Express regulations cover transactions involving managers and directors, transactions to be made in open and organised markets, and the registration, authorisation, information and naming of such institutions. General regulations applicable to stock investment companies, investment funds and money market investment funds require that the share capital of such companies be represented by registered shares of equal value with equal rights. The equity of investment funds is divided into 'participations' which confer upon each holder proprietary rights in the funds. These participations are registered and negotiable. Minimum starting capital required is presently 200 million pesetas for investment companies, 500 million pesetas for investment funds and 1.5 billion pesetas for money market investment funds. All capital contributions must be in the form of cash, securities quoted on the stock exchange, or other financial assets permitted to cover investment and liquidity ratios. The number of shareholders of these collective investment institutions and the number of participants in the funds may not fall below the required number for companies quoted on the stock exchange (currently 100).

(2) Restrictions and ratios

Existing legislation dictates the proportion and type of assets which may be held by the companies and funds by imposing certain investment ratios, shown in Table 6.2.

At least 90 per cent of the assets of a collective investment institution must be invested in real assets with fixed or variable rates quoted in the stock market, and in other financial assets traded in organised and officially recognised markets.

Liabilities to third parties may not exceed 20 per cent of assets, or 10 per cent if they are capital funds or companies with variable capital. They may not receive loans or deposits from the public, unless they are fixed capital investment funds (*sociedades de inversión inmobiliaria de capital fijo*), which may take funds direct from the public, but not for an indefinite period or for a period of less than one year.

Liquidity ratios applicable to variable capital companies and investment funds are presently set at 5 per cent and 3 per cent respectively, subject to review by the Ministry of Economy and Finance. These percentages may be raised up to 10 per cent, depending on the market for shares of the variable capital companies or level of investment in the fund. All securities and assets shall be held in the custody of an authorised depositary.

Table 6.2: Maximum investment limits of collective investment institutions

Investment made by	In securities issued or guaranteed by	Not to exceed a maximum of	Of	Calculated over	Observations
An IICO	another IICO	5%	total assets IICO	Effect valuation of assets and security in question	An IICO is prohibited from participating in issued securities guaranteed by investment company of the same group, or funds managed by companies of the same group.
	1 single entity	5%			The limit is extended to 10%, provided that the investments exceeding 5% of the assets of the IICO do not together exceed 40% of the assets.
	state/CCAA/OOII	35%			IICOS are authorised to invest up to 100% in these securities if the investment is diversified at least in six different issues and the securities of each issue do not exceed 30% of the IICO's assets.
	entities from the same group	15%			
	1 single entity	5%	total securities in circulation of one and the same company		
An IICO belonging to the same group or managed by companies of the same group		15%			

IICO – Collective Investment Institutions
CCAA – Autonomous Regions
OOII – International Organisations

(3) Types of collective investment institutions

(a) Investment companies

The sole corporate purpose of investment companies (*sociedades de inversión mobilaria*) is to acquire, hold, manage and transfer securities and other financial assets of sufficient diversity to maintain a portfolio with a proper balance between risk and return, without having a controlling interest in other companies in either an economic or political sense. They may have fixed or variable capital. Investment companies with fixed capital have the following characteristics: The management of an investment company may be entrusted to a third party from outside the company and registered as a management company (*sociedad gestora*), and shareholders, who are not members of the board of directors, may form a supervisory committee, overseeing management and the appointment of auditors.

Variable capital investment companies (*sociedades de inversión mobiliaria de capital variable*) are companies in which the share capital may be increased or decreased within the legal limits, although it may not be increased by more than ten times the initial share capital. The company may purchase its own shares and keep them in its portfolio without shareholders' approval.

Investment company shares must be traded on the stock exchange. Furthermore, when the market value deviates from the book value by more than 5 per cent, the company must sell or purchase stock to equalize the difference.

(b) Investment funds

Investment funds (*fondos de inversión mobiliaria*) have the same purpose as investment companies, but consist of equity capital owned by a number of participants and administered by a professional management company, which has possession of the fund and may exercise administrative powers over it. The exclusive object of the funds is to purchase, hold and transfer assets traded on organised markets. If they specialise in money market assets they are called money market investment funds (*fondos de inversión en activos del mercado monetario*).

The law regulates the investment of the fund's equity, its administration by a management company, the commissions to be received by the management company, the issue and repurchase of participations, valuation of the assets, distribution of profits, and the dissolution and liquidation of the fund itself.

(c) Investment fund management companies

Money market investment funds are managed by professional management companies (*las sociedades gestoras de los fondos de inversión*). They must have resources of at least 100 million pesetas at any given time, increasing by

0.5 per cent, of the real value of the managed assets up to 10 billion pesetas and 0.3 per cent, of the excess above that amount. Share capital must be represented by registered shares. They must be registered at a special registry kept by the National Stock Market Commission.

The depositary institutions are lending institutions or securities companies or agencies which carry out the instructions of the management companies and oversee them. Each investment fund may only have one depositary, and no one entity may be both manager and depositary.

(d) Portfolio management companies

Companies which have as their corporate purpose or normal business the management and administration of stock portfolios and other financial assets (*sociedad gestora de cartera*) must be registered in the Registry of Portfolio Management Companies. The shareholders of the company must be made public, and the company's managers or representatives may not engage in similar activities to those of companies whose shares form part of the portfolio or assets being managed by the management company, unless the registered owners of the securities and assets being managed have been duly notified. Management companies are required to publish an annual report containing specific information, and their accounting books are subject to mandatory audits. Currently, the level of resources may not fall below 0.5 per cent of the total value of the managed assets, up to 10 billion pesetas, and 0.3 per cent of assets exceeding that amount.

¶631 Pension plans and funds

Regulations covering pension funds are governed by a complex set of administrative provisions.

(1) Pension plans

The pension plan determines the rights of participants to receive payments, pensions or annuities based on retirement, survivorship, widowhood, disability or being orphaned, the obligation to contribute to the plan, and the regulations governing the application of the assets in order to meet obligations arising from the exercise of the rights of the participants of the plan.

Pension plans involve two parties – sponsors or promoters, which set up or develop the pension plan, and participants, who are the contributors and beneficiaries.

Pension plans are classified according to the nature of the relationship between the sponsor and the participants: Employer-employee, where the participants are employees of the sponsor; association-member, where the sponsor is an association, union or collective group and the participants are their associates or members; or financial institutions-individuals, where the sponsor is a financial institution and the participants are any individuals, except employees of the financial institution and their relatives to the third degree.

Pension plans may take the form of 'fixed-benefit payment plans', 'fixed contribution plans', in which both the sponsor's and the participant's contributions are fixed, and 'mixed plans', which specify the amount of payments and contributions. Employer-employee and association-member plans may take any of the forms described above, but institution-individual plans may only take the form of a fixed contribution plan.

Every pension plan must have a pension fund. An individual's maximum annual contribution may never exceed 750,000 pesetas. Depending on the pension plan, the benefits may be paid upon retirement, early retirement, disability or death, with capital, term or life annuities or capital earnings.

Pension plans are supervised by a committee of representatives of the sponsor(s) and the participants (including beneficiaries), with participants having an absolute majority. The functions of the supervisory committee and the specifications of the pension plans are tightly regulated.

(2) Pension funds

Pension funds must receive prior authorisation from the Ministry of Economy and Finance, be recorded in a notarised deed executed by the sponsor, and be registered in the Special Administrative Registry and the Commercial Registry. They are not a separate legal entity and must be managed by a professional management company, together with a depositary, under the supervision of a supervisory committee. Should a fund serve several pension plans, representatives of each individual plan must sit on the committee.

(a) Regulations

Pension funds are subject to the following financial regulations:

(i) Restrictions on the concentration of risk (maximum investment of 5 per cent of securities issued by a company). If a number of pension funds are managed by companies belonging to the same group, then the maximum investment of all those funds may not exceed that limit.

(ii) At least 90 per cent of funds invested must be invested on stock markets, in bank deposits (maximum 15 per cent), mortgage loans (*préstamos hipotecarios*) and real assets.

(iii) At least 1 per cent of their assets must be liquid.

(iv) Liabilities to third parties may not exceed 5 per cent of the assets of the fund.

(b) Management companies
The Ministry of Economy and Finance supervises and inspects management companies and pension funds. Management companies are corporations which must receive prior administrative authorisation before starting up business. They have a paid-up share capital of 100 million pesetas, represented by registered shares plus 1 per cent of assets of the fund over 1 billion pesetas.

Management of pension funds is the only permissible corporate purpose. Their registered offices must be in Spain, and they must be registered in the Special Administrative Registry. Management companies may not issue debentures or apply for loans, and their capital must be invested in specified assets laid down by regulation. Life insurance companies authorised to operate in Spain may act as pension fund management companies, if they meet certain requirements.

(c) Depositaries
The custodian and depositary of the assets of a pension fund must be a banking institution domiciled in Spain. Each pension fund may have only one depositary and no one entity may be both manager and depositary.

¶632 Venture capital companies and funds

Venture capital companies and funds are financial intermediaries whose sole object is to foster and develop the growth of non-financial companies by temporarily investing in their capital. In this way they channel market resources towards business growth and also serve as holding companies. They are legally prohibited from investing in companies quoted on the stock exchange, which limits their operations to a nucleus of small and medium-sized businesses or those which voluntarily are not quoted.

Venture capital funds are made up of assets administered by a management company under the supervision of a depositary, and have the same exclusive corporate purpose as venture capital companies but not the same company form. The minimum capital of a venture capital company is 200 million pesetas. The initial assets of venture capital funds must be at least 275 million pesetas. Both funds and companies must be authorised by the Ministry of Economy and Finance, and must be registered at a special registry before starting up operations.

Venture capital companies or funds may not have a majority interest, whether direct, indirect or interposed, in the companies in which they invest. Fifty per cent of the venture capital assets must be invested in shares or other holdings not quoted on the stock exchange, but no single investment may reach more than 45 per cent of the paid-up capital of the issuing company. Additionally, up to 75 per cent of the assets of the venture capital company, including the 50 per cent of assets invested in shares or other holdings not quoted on the stock exchange, must be made with investments having a maturity date of over three years.

The law regulating these companies and funds takes into account the temporary character of this type of shareholding. This temporary investment gives the companies invested in the time to prepare to go public, and thus facilitates the eventual divestment of the shares. There are important tax advantages applicable to the capital gains derived from the divestment which allow for a variable percentage rate to apply, depending on the number of years for which the shares were held.

The law regulates the investment of the assets of venture capital companies and funds, their registration in the Special Registry of the General Directorate of Treasury and Financial Policy, incorporation requirements, authorisation by the Ministry of Economy and Finance, preferential tax treatment, and quotation in the stock exchange.

Management and depositary companies of venture capital funds must meet the requirements applicable to collective investment institutions.

OTHER FINANCIAL INTERMEDIARIES

¶633 Private insurance

The 1984 Private Insurance Law ('the 1984 Law') focuses on the insurance market, the supervision of insurance companies, and providing insurance to the public. It governs all private insurance transactions which take place in Spain. Compulsory social security contributions and coverage are not considered to be private insurance. Within the scope of the law are found insurance, capitalisation, preliminary or complementary activities related to insurance or capitalisation, the management of group retirement, disability, widows' and orphans' funds, insurance guarantees in respect of preservation of capital or minimum interest, agents and brokers, and insurance surveyors and adjusters.

Insurance companies may manage group retirement funds and the reserves for death, survivorship or disability benefits, pursuant to the law governing pension funds. Without special authorisation, they are prohibited from entering into transactions which are not based on actuarial principles, involve equity account contracts or which are outside the insurance field. They may not accept liabilities or issue guarantees unrelated to insurance, or act as agent or broker between insureds and other insurance companies, unless as a lead co-insurer.

Insurance may only be offered in the private sector by corporations/limited companies, mutuals with a fixed or variable rate of return, pension funds, social security mutuals and co-operatives. The public sector may be active in the insurance field through companies incorporated in any of the above forms, with a direct or indirect majority interest held by the central government, its agencies or the autonomous regions.

The Ministry of Economy and Finance may authorise foreign insurance entities to establish subsidiaries in Spain. Insurance companies must have their registered offices in Spain and must maintain their capital or mutual funds above the legal minimum, depending on the types of insurance provided (e.g. life, liability, accident, sickness, travel, property, or reinsurance).

Insurance companies must issue registered shares in exchange for cash or non-cash contributions. In the latter case, the Ministry of Economy and Finance may value the assets and, if they are found to be insufficient, may require the company to reduce its capital or make up the difference. Life insurance companies may not engage in any unrelated activity. Insurance companies must keep their own accounts and make available any necessary documents and information. The Government, through the Ministry of Economy and Finance, oversees the operations, disclosures and financial state of insurance companies.

(1) Reserves

Insurance companies are required to maintain the following reserves: actuarial; current risks; accident; expired capital; unclaimed income or benefits; settlements or payment; a marginal fund for accidents; and a reserve for unpaid premiums. In each fiscal year the insurance company must provide for a solvency margin, consisting of its own non-committed assets after deducting the value of office equipment and other tangibles, as permitted by law. The minimum solvency margin depends on the type of insurance contracted. One-third of the margin will constitute a guarantee fund, which is also subject to a legal minimum. Insurance companies not complying fully with the reserve provisions, or failing to maintain the minimum solvency margin, are not allowed to expand their business to other locations or sectors, open new branches, or provide other forms of insurance.

(2) Restrictions

The law imposes certain restrictions on insurance companies during the first three fiscal years of their existence. It also regulates portfolio management, mergers, changes in the corporate entity, revocations, dissolutions and liquidations, reinsurance, protection of the insured (loan preferential rights and settlement commissions), administrative supervision, and sets out breaches and sanctions. Insurance law closely follows the disciplinary system provided for lending institutions. In addition, the Insurance Companies'

Settlement Commission (*Comisión Liquidadora de Entidades Aseguradoras*) has been operating since 1984 in order to provide greater stability in the insurance sector.

¶634 Providing private insurance

Providing private insurance is a service reserved exclusively to professional agents and brokers, which may be either individuals or companies. It includes those who are involved in marketing, advising or acting as an agent or broker in respect of private insurance and reinsurance contracts entered into between individuals or companies on one side, and legally authorised insurance companies on the other, or between insurance companies themselves. It also includes advising policy holders, insureds or beneficiaries.

Agents and brokers may be classified as follows:

(1) *Representatives*. Those persons contracted by an insurance company with no authority to bind it (*agentes afectos no representantes*).

(2) *Agents*. Those contracted by an insurance company with authority to act on its behalf (*agentes afectos representantes*). Agents may not act simultaneously in insurance and reinsurance.

(3) *Insurance brokers*. Agents or brokers who do not act as representatives or agents of any one insurance company (*corredores de seguros*). Their business involves finding adequate insurance products to meet the needs of potential insureds.

(4) *Reinsurance brokers*. Companies may be formed for the sole purpose of offering services as an insurance agent, insurance broker or reinsurance broker (*corredores de reaseguros*). Directors or managers of these companies must be licensed agents or brokers, and associates must also be agents or brokers for either insurance or reinsurance, as the case may be.

Private insurance agents and brokers must be licensed by the Ministry of Economy and Finance and belong to the appropriate professional association. Foreign individuals or companies may engage in this activity in Spain on an equal basis. Those not from an EEC member State are subject to reciprocity.

The law governs many aspects of the insurance industry in detail, including conflicts of interest, obligations of agents and brokers and insurance companies, agency agreements, commissions, professional organisations and associations, and violations and sanctions. It very clearly states that the legal relationship between private insurance agents and brokers and insurance or reinsurance companies is purely commercial, as opposed to being an employment relationship, or one governed by Civil Code provisions.

¶635 Mutual and joint guarantee companies

(1) Mutual guarantee companies

Mutual guarantee companies (*śociedades de garantía reciproca y sociedades de reafianzamiento*) are variable capital companies with the exclusive corporate purpose of providing accommodation or performance guarantees, or any other type of guarantee permitted by law, for the benefit of its members in connection with the normal business activities of those individuals or businesses.

The variable nature of the capital of these companies distinguishes them from the typical corporation/limited company. Their capital may range from the minimum set out in the articles of association/by-laws (in any case no less than 50 million pesetas) to three times that amount. The variation in capital within these limits may be made by resolution of the board of directors without the necessity of shareholder approval. Capital is divided into parts of equal nominal value, cumulative and indivisible, which are non-negotiable and may not be called shares.

(a) Guarantee fund

The law requires that all mutual guarantee companies maintain a guarantee fund to secure the guarantees granted to their members in the event of non-payment of the underlying debt. The guarantee fund is composed of the contributions made by those members having guaranteed debts, as well as all earnings thereon. The articles of association/by-laws may allow the company to require a supplementary contribution from members if the guarantee fund is inadequate to cover defaults. The law regulates investments of the guarantee fund and sets a maximum limit for guaranteed debts at 25 times total capital plus asset reserves.

When a debt which has been guaranteed by the guarantee fund is satisfied, the contributing member has the right to reimbursement of the contribution made to the guarantee fund to secure that debt, as well as any interest thereon. In the event that a member defaults on a debt guarantee, the outstanding amount is paid out of the guarantee fund. The guarantee company must first apply the contribution of the defaulting member and then turn to the amounts paid by the remaining members of the guarantee fund in proportion to their contributions. The company then has the right to claim from the defaulting member the total amount of the debt. All proceeds obtained from the defaulting member must be used to reimburse the guarantee fund.

(b) Mixed companies for secondary guarantees

As additional support, there exist mixed companies for secondary guarantees, which consist of corporations capitalised mainly with public funds which back up the guarantee given by the mutual guarantee insurance company. The law closely regulates the capital investments and reserves of these companies. This second guarantee is ancillary, and only comes into effect to cover a debt which the mutual guarantee company fails to pay due to lack of available assets (except for the minimum capital and the legal reserve). A mixed company guarantee covers 75 per cent of the guarantee granted by the mutual insurance company and may only cover the debt principal, excluding expenses, interest and damages. A debt paid by a mixed company gives rise to the right to reimbursement and preceeds the mutual guarantee company in order of preference.

(2) Joint guarantee companies

Joint guarantee companies (*sociedades de reafianzamiento*) provide bonds, accommodations or any other form of guarantee permitted by law to mutual guarantee companies to secure a part of the risks undertaken by those companies.

The capital of these companies must be greater than 500 million pesetas, with at least 25 per cent fully paid-up. The majority of capital must be held by mutual guarantee companies, although no individual one may hold more than 10 per cent of the total capital held by all the mutual guarantee companies collectively. Public companies and agencies of the autonomous regions may not hold more than 25 per cent of capital. The law closely regulates capital investment and the reserves of these companies.

7 Real Property

¶701 In general

This chapter attempts to provide the reader with an introduction to the law relating to real property in Spain, by covering the main areas of concern to a foreigner wishing to purchase real property there. The chapter deals with the acquisition of real property from three main angles: (a) from the point of view of foreign investment and exchange control; (b) zoning and planning; (c) legal requirements. The Spanish conveyancing system is different from the English and American systems, and although the Spanish system does give protection to those who understand its principles, it can provide pitfalls for those who do not take as much care with real property transactions in Spain as they would do in their home country.

Unless otherwise stated, it is assumed throughout the chapter that a purchaser is not a Spanish resident, and that the term 'real property' includes real property both for personal and for commercial use, since there is little or no difference in the procedural and legal aspects involved in the sale and purchase of the two types of property.

FOREIGN INVESTMENT REGULATIONS

¶702 Foreign investment and exchange control

Spanish exchange control and foreign investment regulations are set out in Chapter 2 (Exchange Control and Foreign Investment), where the relevant terms used in this chapter are defined and procedures are explained. These regulations are of specific interest in respect of the acquisition and use of real property in Spain.

Certain administrative controls still exist in Spain in respect of real property purchases by foreigners, depending on where the property is located, the status of the purchaser and the property in question. Purchases of real property by foreigners are divided into three categories:

(1) *Deregulated purchases.* These do not require prior verification or authorisation and may be effected freely. Purchases of real property

made by individuals and purchases which do not require prior verification or authorisation are all deregulated.

(2) *Prior verification.* Certain real property purchases require prior verification by the Spanish authorities. This is a procedure whereby the authorities check that all legal requirements have been met and verify the investment by stamping the application and returning it to the purchaser. Purchases requiring prior verification must not be made before obtaining positive verification.

The following transactions require prior verification:

(a) purchases made by foreign companies or corporations;
(b) purchases of rural land or land which may not be developed;
(c) purchases of more than three dwellings in one building;
(d) purchases of urban plots (*solares*); and
(e) purchases of business premises.

(3) *Prior authorisation.* This is a procedure whereby the Spanish authorities not only check that all legal requirements have been met, but also use their discretion as to whether or not they authorise the transaction. Purchases requiring prior authorisation must not be made before authorisation is given. Examples of transactions requiring prior authorisation are:

(a) where the purchaser is a foreign government or a state-owned foreign company or corporation;
(b) where the property is located in a strategic area affected by national security regulations, although this example applies only to non-EEC nationals whether resident or not in Spain.

The areas named as being of restricted access to foreigners include Cartagena, the Straits of Gibraltar, the Bay of Cadiz, the Portuguese border area, Galicia, and the French border area. In principle, the total amount of real property owned by non-EEC foreign investors in these areas may not exceed 15 per cent.

¶703 Repatriation of funds

Certain requirements must be met when real property is purchased and sold in order for a foreign purchaser to have the right to repatriate funds after sale, whether the sale takes place in Spain or abroad.

(1) Purchase requirements

The purchase requirements are as follows:

(a) The purchase price must be paid wholly with funds from abroad through a Spanish bank account, either in foreign currency or in convertible pesetas. If the purchaser becomes a Spanish resident at the same time as purchasing the property, he must use a Spanish bank account in ordinary pesetas. In this latter event a permit from the General Directorate of Foreign Transactions (DGTE) must be obtained to pay with ordinary pesetas, so that the investment is deemed to be free and transferable to any person and to any country.

(b) A certificate from an authorised Spanish bank must be obtained, stating that payment is made with funds from abroad. The certificate will be required by the notary when the deed of transfer is notarised.

(c) The purchase must be made by way of notarised public deed and be registered both at the Land Registry and at the Foreign Investments Registry which is kept by the DGTE in Madrid.

(2) Sale requirements

The requirements to be fulfilled on the sale of property are as follows:

(a) The proceeds of sale or rental income cannot be repatriated until the vendor has paid all taxes due as a resident or as a non-resident.

(b) It is advisable to apply for a written permit from the DGTE before selling property and before transferring rental income abroad. Any problems which may arise in respect of the repatriation of funds are thereby identified in advance.

URBAN PLANNING

¶704 Zoning and planning law

The use of land in Spain is governed by the 1976 Land and Urban Planning Law (*Ley del Suelo y Ordenación Urbana*) ('the 1976 Land Law'), regional and provincial regulations, and municipal planning provisions.

(1) Types of plans

The 1976 Land Law provides for land planning to be carried out at a variety of levels, the most important being the following:

(a) *National Plan (Plan Nacional de Ordenación)*. There is one national plan which applies to the whole of Spanish territory. The national plan provides the main directives for organising not only general land planning but also economic and social planning, e.g. population, industrial areas, natural reserves, and medium- and long-term schemes.

(b) *Territorial Plans (Planes Directores Territoriales de Coordinación).* These plans co-ordinate in greater detail the specific requirements of the national plan. They develop the urban policy of the autonomous regions.

(c) *Municipal Plans.* These plans are the most important in respect of development because their content is directly applicable to particular projects. These are various types of municipal plans –

  (i) *General Municipal Plans (Planes Generales Municipales de Ordenación).* The provisions of the General Municipal Plans (GMPs) vary, depending on the category of the land, i.e. whether it may be developed or is deemed to be urban land (see (2)(a) below).

  (ii) *Partial Plans (Planes Parciales).* Partial Plans (PPs) are intended to develop in detail land categorised as that which may be developed in the GMP.

Other regulations and plans exist to complete the GMP. There are also detailed studies which exist to provide for complex technical problems, special plans for artistic buildings, protected areas, rural land, etc., and urban action programmes where GMPs do not exist.

GMPs and PPs are of the greatest interest to a potential purchaser of land in Spain. GMPs are approved by each municipality and they define land use within each municipality. PPs relate solely to land which may be developed (*suelo urbanizable*) and go into greater detail in the regulation of a particular part of the municipal territory covered by the GMP. These plans can be inspected in the local Town Hall (*Ayuntamiento*).

(2) Classification of land under a GMP

The GMP classifies the land it applies to as follows:

(a) *Urban land (suelo urbano).* Urban land has access for vehicles, water and electricity supply, sewage, and at least two-thirds of the land is built up. Further building is allowed in urban land if it is designated a 'plot' (*solar*), provided that it is developed in accordance with the GMP.

(b) *Land which may be developed (suelo urbanizable).* This is land which is destined to be developed, and is either scheduled (*programado*) or non-scheduled (*no programado*). If it is scheduled, then improvements may be made to the land in accordance with a PP. If it is not scheduled, then improvements may only be made if an urban action programme (*programa de actuación urbanística*) is specifically approved.

(c) *Land which may not be developed (suelo no urbanizable).* Land which may not be developed comprises areas which are not included in the above categories, or land singled out for special protection because of its value in terms of agriculture, forestry or ranching, because of its natural resources, landscape, history or culture, or for the protection of the environment.

(3) Classification of land without a GMP

In the event that there is no GMP, then land is divided into:

(a) urban land, i.e. where there is access for vehicles, water and electricity supply, sewage, and least one half of the land is built up.
(b) land which may not be developed, which is all land which does not come under the above description of urban land.

¶705 Coastline

The Spanish Coastline Law of 1988 (*Ley de Costas*) is intended to protect public property on the Spanish coast and is based on EEC recommendations on coastal protection. It defines the following areas as coastline public property: sea and saltwater rivers up to high tide line, saltwater lakes and saltwater marshes; cliffs, beaches and sand dunes; and areas created by artificial landfill of the sea. Such land may not be transferred, thus assuring public use and rights of way. Any special use of such land requires a licence.

Coastline public property is either in a protected zone or in a zone of influence. If it is a protected zone, then a coastal strip of 100 metres width is protected. This means that certain activities and constructions which block the view of or access to the coast may not take place, unless a concession was granted before the 1988 Coastline Law came into force. If land is in a zone of influence, then a minimum of 500 metres is protected. These protected zones are broken down in further detail, according to whether the land is classified as urban land or land which may or may not be developed.

Other uses of public coastal property are subject to specific concessions awarded by the Spanish government, and are usually subject to competitive bidding.

ACQUISITION BY PURCHASE AND BY INHERITANCE

¶706 Pre-contractual considerations

(1) Land registries

The Spanish property system is based on a registry system. All real property must be duly registered at the Land Registry. District registries are located in town or cities and are maintained by the Ministry of Justice. The Land Registry is a public registry, and any person may obtain information from its records and books in two ways:

(a) by doing a personal search at the Land Registry, taking a passport or equivalent personal identification document. This search facility is free of charge and can be made during normal working hours;

(b) requesting an official search, which means that any information requested is obtained in writing. The Registry can be requested to provide two kinds of search –
  (i) simple note (*nota simple*), which is merely a legalised photocopy of the Registry records. Its contents are not guaranteed, but it is cheap and quick to obtain, and
  (ii) certificate (*certificado*). This is issued by the Registrar who guarantees its contents about the registered owner, measurements, mortgages or encumbrances, etc. It usually takes about three to four weeks to obtain this certificate.

Property details which are registered include measurements in square metres, the location and a description of the property, the names and title of ownership of the different owners since the property was first registered, and any other encumbrances or rights over the property, such as mortgages, building restrictions and rights of way.

The registered owner is the only person who is able to sell a property, although the owner may grant a power of attorney to a third person to conduct negotiations and sign the contract on his behalf. The power of attorney must be executed before a notary.

(2) Searches

Before entering into a contract to purchase a property in Spain it is advisable to make the following pre-contract searches:

(a) a search at the local Land Registry to check that the property is registered in the vendor's name and that the property is free from encumbrances; and

(b) a search at the local Town Hall, to check that there are no outstanding local taxes or fees in relation to the property and, if relevant, that all planning consents and building licences have been duly granted in relation to the property.

Many purchasers, especially those who do not live in the area where they are buying property, use a local '*gestor*' who specialises in a variety of administrative matters, including real property matters, and who can obtain the certificate from the Land Registry and approach the Town Hall. If the purchaser uses a lawyer (*abogado*) for his purchase, then the lawyer can do this.

¶707 The contract

The contract (*contrato de compra-venta*) must include:

(1) a description of the parties;

(2) a description of the property in the same terms as it is described in the Land Registry;

(3) the purchase price and the date on which the balance is to be paid;

(4) a statement as to which party is to pay fees, taxes and other costs. The purchaser normally pays capital transfer tax, Land Registry fees and the costs of the first copy of the deed of transfer; the vendor normally pays the tax payable on the increased value of land, known as *Plusvalía* tax, and the costs of obtaining the original deed of transfer;

(5) a statement that all taxes and bills relating to the property have been paid;

(6) a statement as to whether or not the property is sold subject to any mortgages or other encumbrances; and

(7) any other special conditions or warranties, for example a warranty by the vendor as to hidden or latent defects.

Once signed by the parties, the contract at this stage is merely a private contract. As such it does not transfer the legal right of ownership to the purchaser, nor does it have any effect on the rights of third parties, and it may not be registered at the Land Registry. For all this to occur the parties (or their legally appointed representatives) must appear before a notary, who prepares the deed of transfer (*escritura*). Once the parties have signed the deed of transfer, the purchaser should request a copy (*copia simple*) from the notary so that the purchaser can be registered at the Land Registry as the new registered owner without delay. The notary's fee and Land Registry fees are each 1–2 per cent of the purchase price. The vendor usually pays the notary's fee, and Land Registry fees are usually paid by the purchaser.

¶708 Registration

The importance of registering the notarised deed of transfer immediately cannot be stressed enough. Mere possession of the deed is not sufficient. To illustrate the point, if the registered owner of a property sells to A on Monday and then fraudulently sells it to B on Tuesday, the first of the two buyers to register his purchase will be the new registered owner. A would, however, have a criminal claim against the vendor. Similarly, a purchaser who acquires a property free from encumbrances would have to accept any mortgage that was registered on the property before he registers the purchase.

¶709 Checklist

In summary, whenever purchasing real property in Spain, attention should be paid to the following matters:

- Ensure that the purchase does not require prior verification or authorisation. If it does, the appropriate consent must be obtained.
- Check current exchange control and currency regulations and that appropriate bank accounts are opened, so that money may be repatriated without problems when the property is eventually sold.
- Enquire at the local Town Hall to ascertain that all planning matters and building licences are in order, and that all local taxes and rates in connection with the property have been paid.
- Make a search at the Land Registry to check the official existence of the property and to ascertain the identity of the registered owner. A further search should be made immediately before the deed of transfer is notarised to ensure that no mortgages or other encumbrances have been charged to the property.
- Check that all electricity, gas and other bills relating to the property have been paid up to date.
- It is not advisable to purchase property under a private contract, i.e. one which is not notarised and therefore not registrable at the Land Registry.
- Documents should not be signed without fully understanding the contents and full implications of the documents.
- Local professional legal advice should be sought, in the same way that one would in all likelihood do when purchasing property in one's home country.
- The notarised deed of transfer should state the full price paid for the property.
- Ensure that the notarised deed of transfer is registered at the Land Registry without delay, and that any mortgages or other encumbrances are also registered.

¶710 Purchase price and deposits

(1) Reasonable price

In any purchase of property the purchase price must be reasonable. For transactions which require administrative authorisation, it is a determining factor in the authorisation process that the price is reasonable and relates to the objective value of the property. In many cases, the Ministry of Economy and Finance asks for an expert valuation of the property.

Until recently it was quite normal in Spain for a purchase price much less than the price actually paid to appear in the notarised deed of transfer. The full purchase price must now be declared in that deed. By declaring the full price in the notarised deed of transfer, a foreign purchaser ensures that the transaction is valid and secures his rights to repatriate his full investment on sale. Also, if the price in the notarised deed of transfer is less than the value assessed by the Ministry of Economy and Finance, and the difference is over 2 million pesetas or 20 per cent of the purchase price, whichever is the greater, then the difference is deemed to be a gift for tax purposes. The vendor is taxed on the difference as a deemed capital gain arising from a gift, and the purchaser is subject to the inheritance and gift tax. A further point to be made is that if the next purchaser declares the full price, then the vendor who did not declare the full price on purchase will appear to have made a larger capital gain than he has actually made and will be liable to pay tax on that amount.

(2) Pre-construction deposits

Deposits made by purchasers to promoters or construction companies before construction is completed are regulated by law. If deposits are taken before or during construction, the promotors must guarantee the repayment of the moneys paid plus 6 per cent interest per annum, by means of an insurance policy issued by an insurance company or by a joint guarantee from a commercial bank or savings bank, and place purchasers' deposits in a specially designated account.

Contracts of sale requiring a pre-construction deposit must expressly state the amount payable, the terms of the guarantee or insurance policy, the name of the bank, and the account through which the purchaser is to make payments. Once the time limit for the commencement of construction or for the completion of construction has expired, and neither event has taken place, the purchaser may either rescind the contract and demand the return of his money, together with interest at an annual rate of 6 per cent, or grant an extension of time, which is noted in the contract, specifying the length of the extension period and the proposed date of completion and sale.

¶711 Financing

(1) Instalment terms

Payment for the purchase of property by non-residents may be made in instalments without prior authorisation, provided that the instalments are paid on the due date and with foreign capital. The purchaser must obtain a certificate from an authorised Spanish bank which confirms the transfer of foreign funds, how they are to be applied, and the amount of the payments actually made.

If the property purchased is not a deregulated investment and requires prior authorisation, the fact that the payment is made in instalments is stated in the application for authorisation, and this is a determining factor in the authorisation process.

(2) Spanish mortgages

Non-resident Spanish or foreign individuals may obtain a loan secured by a mortgage in pesetas from Spanish banks, lending institutions, savings banks or mortgage companies for the acquisition of property, provided that the following conditions are fulfilled:

(a) The money is used for the acquisition of newly constructed property or property which is being transferred for the first time to a Spanish national residing in Spain.

(b) The loan is not made on more favourable terms than those generally given to residents.

(c) Repayment is made in the equivalent in pesetas of foreign currency exchanged at the Spanish rate of exchange, or pesetas coming from foreigners' accounts in convertible pesetas, or according to regulations in force at the time.

(d) The loan is used to pay for the property which is to be mortgaged.

Mortgages are usually granted for a term of ten years, and the trend is for longer-term mortgages to be granted.

¶712 Tax

A detailed discussion of Spanish taxes applicable to real property transactions can be found in Chapter 4 (Taxation), but, briefly, foreign owners of real property in Spain are liable for the following taxes:

(1) Taxes payable on purchase

(a) *Value added tax (IVA).* This tax is payable on brand new properties, and different rates apply depending on what kind of property is purchased, and from whom it is purchased. Examples are the purchase of commercial premises from a promoter (12 per cent of the purchase price); the purchase of an apartment or a building plot from a promoter (6 per cent).

(b) *Transfer tax (Impuesto de Transmisiones Patrimoniales or ITP).* This tax is payable on purchases of second-hand property. Transactions are normally taxed at a rate of 6 per cent.

(2) Taxes payable on sale

(a) *Tax on the increase in value of land (Arbitrio de Plusvalía).* This is a municipal tax on the increase in value between the value of urban land at the time of acquisition of the real property and its value at time of sale. The rate of tax depends on the length of the period of time between purchase and sale. The maximum rate is 40 per cent of the official increase in the value of land, which is assessed by the municipality. This tax is in theory paid by the vendor, but the purchaser usually pays the tax on transfers by purchase and sale.

(b) *Capital gains.* If the vendor is a Spanish resident, any capital gain on sale is deemed to be income and charged to income tax. If the vendor is a non-resident, then any capital gain is subject to withholding tax at a rate of 35 per cent.

(3) Taxes payable as a result of ownership of property

(a) *Net worth tax (Impuesto sobre Patrimonio).* This is an annual tax on the owner's net assets, including real property. The tax is payable by all non-resident foreigners on their assets located in Spain.

(b) *Property tax (Contribución Territorial).* This tax is levied annually by the Town Hall and is payable by all property owners in Spain.

¶713 Acquiring property by inheritance

Acquisitions by foreigners by inheritance do not require authorisation for the purpose of exchange control or foreign investment law. If, however, the inherited property is situated in a strategic zone, the foreign beneficiary must either apply for military authorisation within three months of the date on which the beneficiary legally assumes title, or transfer the property within one year of that date or, if authorisation is refused, of the date of refusal. Otherwise the Ministry of Defence may expropriate the property.

Although no authorisation is needed, foreigners who inherit property in Spain must still declare the acquisition on form TE-7. If the property was not originally made with foreign capital or with ordinary pesetas, the value in pesetas will not be recorded on form TE-7, only the fact that the transfer was made.

If the deceased met all the requirements under the Foreign Investments Law when the purchase was made, and the investment was made with foreign capital or with convertible pesetas, a simple change of title takes place and the new owner must notify the DGTE in writing.

TYPES OF OWNERSHIP

¶714 Leases

There are few differences in the procedural or legal aspects involved in leasing real property for residential or commercial use in Spain.

Until 1985, lessees of residential property had an automatic right to renew their lease with or without the lessor's consent, Since then, residential leases have not been subject to such compulsory extensions, and the terms of both residential and business leases may be freely agreed by the parties. All leases must be in writing.

Initially, the lessor will usually require a deposit of one month's rent for an unfurnished apartment. The deposit for a furnished apartment or business premises is normally two months' rent, but in practice this can be negotiated.

The terms of the lease may provide for an annual rent review according to the Spanish Consumer Price Index or some other formula agreed by the parties. If the apartment is furnished, the rent for the apartment itself is treated separately from the rent for the furniture. During the term of the lease, the lessee must pay rent to the lessor, and, in order to vacate the premises before the end of the lease, the lessee must give the lessor 30 days' notice and indemnify him for the amount of rent remaining on the lease, unless a right of termination is included.

The repair and maintenance of the premises is the responsibility of the lessor, unless the damage is due to the lessee's negligence. The lessee, however, may make urgent or necessary repairs in order to avoid serious problems or damage and charge it to the lessor. Premises may be sub-let by the lessee only with the express written consent of the lessor.

Leases of business premises do, however, have different regulations in respect of use and change of use. No change of use is permitted unless the lessor is given notice of change and he has given his consent for the change of use. It is advisable to obtain this consent in writing. Taxes, repairs, internal decoration and insurance are usually the responsibility of the lessor, and superficial internal alterations are paid by the lessee. The parties, however, are free to agree otherwise.

Business premises may be assigned by the lessee to a third party without the need to obtain the consent of the lessor. The third party will be subrogated to the lessee's rights and obligations in respect of the lease. If the lessee is a company which is transformed or which merges with another, or which demerges, an assignment will not be deemed to have taken place, but the lessor has the right to review the rent as if an assignment has taken place. Business premises may also be sub-let under the same conditions as residential property, i.e. with the written consent of the lessor.

A lease expires at the end of its term, unless it is renewed or terminated by either party if the other is in breach.

¶715 Horizontal ownership

(1) General characteristics

Horizontal ownership usually comes about when an owner of a building divides it up into separate units for use as flats or offices, when co-owners partition a building, or when joint owners develop a property which is subsequently divided up between them. Condominiums are governed by the 1960 Law of Horizontal Ownership, the Law of Mortgages, the by-laws of the building or complex, conditions in the sales contracts, or the rules of internal management laid down by the owners' association and the Civil Code.

Title is given to each unit-owner on the basis of ownership of a unit, and title to the units must contain a description of the entire building, the services installed and the proportion each unit bears to the whole in terms of surface area expressed in square metres.

The individual units must be capable of independent use and have their own entrance. Title may also include a garage space, attic or basement. The ownership of a unit includes a right of co-ownership in the public areas of the building necessary to its proper use and enjoyment, such as the land, airspace, foundations, hallways, walls, pipes, drains, and rights of way.

Each unit must pay an annual fee, calculated as a percentage of the total value of the building. This percentage is used to determine the share of charges and benefits to be allocated to each unit. Improvements to or the deterioration of any unit will not alter the percentage, which is calculated on the basis of the relation of useful floor surface of each unit to that of the whole building, its position within the building, and the estimated use of the public areas and communal services. The percentages are fixed by the owner of the building when the units are sold off and may only be changed thereafter by unanimous agreement of all the individual owners of the units.

(2) Rights and duties of the owners

(a) *Private areas.* Each owner must keep the unit in good repair. He may modify architectural features, fixtures or utilities, if in so doing the safety of the building, its general structure, its exterior and the rights of other owners are not affected. Notice of such modifications must be given to the chairman of the owners' association. Additionally, an owner or occupant of a unit must observe the by-laws of the owners' association and not carry on any immoral, dangerous or unhealthy activities, or do anything which might damage the building.

(b) *Public areas.* In addition to the rights of use and enjoyment over the public areas of the building, co-ownership rights impose the following specific obligations:

(i) To consent to repair works to common services within the owner's unit.

(ii) To respect the building's fixtures or fittings, including those within the unit which are enjoyed in common with the other owners in the building.

(iii) To take due care of the building, being liable for any damage done to the building by any occupant of the unit, without prejudice to any action which may be taken against the occupant directly.

(iv) Not to make alterations to the building, and to notify the building manager of the need for any urgent repairs.

¶716 Timeshares

The timeshare market is an important and growing market in Spain. The idea of timesharing has largely been imported from abroad, and many existing schemes follow one of the systems used in EEC member States and Scandinavian countries.

As yet there are no specific Spanish regulations governing timeshares, which means legal uncertainty for both developers and purchasers. Various systems have, however, been used in Spain with varying degrees of success, and legislation providing a clear framework for timeshares is envisaged in the near future.

Many timeshare schemes in Spain are based on the English model, whereby a club is formed and a trust is set up outside Spain, each timeshare owner becoming a member of the club. Each unit (i.e. apartment or house) is owned by a company, the shares of which are held by a trustee for the benefit of the members of the club. The club constitution shows details of the units which are part of the scheme, and provides for the setting up of off shore companies, each owning a unit. Each club member undertakes to comply with the club by-laws.

Other schemes may be run on a condominium basis, whereby the timeshare system is fitted into the Spanish law of co-ownership, or condominium system. The deed of co-ownership contains the rules and regulations or by-laws which govern the community. As each period of ownership relating to each unit is sold, a notarised deed is created which includes a clause declaring that the purchaser accepts the conditions of the community by-laws.

In conclusion, as no specific regulations exist in Spain, developers and purchasers should take Spanish professional advice, to ensure that any proposed scheme is properly registrable and complies with Spanish law.

MISCELLANEOUS

¶717 Improvements and alterations

(1) Foreign investment aspects

Additions and improvements made to property by non-residents with foreign capital are deemed to be foreign investments if the following conditions are met:

(a) For newly constructed buildings or improvements to a building all rights and modifications or encumbrances must be set out in a notarised deed and be registered at the Land Registry.

(b) Justification (e.g. receipts) for the need for or application of funds from abroad must be given.

(c) Prior verification must be obtained from the DGTE if the new construction is for business or commercial use.

(d) Notice must be given to the Foreign Investment Registry.

It is important to bear in mind that no improvement or expense on a property will be recognised by the tax authorities if receipts are not issued with VAT included.

(2) Building licences

In order to carry out almost any construction works an appropriate licence from the Town Hall (*Ayuntamiento*) is necessary. Works requiring a licence include:

- construction of new buildings,
- additions to existing buildings,
- modifications or improvements which affect the structure of existing buildings,
- modifications to the exterior or interior lay-out of buildings,
- projects of a temporary nature,
- installation of public services,
- development of an individual building plot,
- sub-divisions,
- moving earth, unless this forms part of a previously approved plan to urbanise or build on the land,
- the first use or occupation of buildings in general,
- temporary uses,
- use of property above existing buildings and installations,
- change of use of a building, in general,
- demolition of buildings (unless they have been declared uninhabitable or illegal),
- underground car-parks or any other underground premises used for industrial, commercial, professional or public purposes,
- cutting down clusters of trees in areas for which there exists an approved plan,
- any other acts specified in the plans, regulations and by-laws of the Town Hall.

¶718 Options

Options held by a non-resident to purchase property, the purchase of which does not require prior authorisation, will require prior verification and notice given to the Foreign Investments Registry. If the option to buy is not exercised, the holder has the right to transfer a sum of money equal to the amount paid originally in foreign currency. In order to be considered a foreign investment, the option contract must take the form of a notarised deed. In order for the notarised deed to be registered at the Land Registry, it must include an express agreement between the parties to register it, the stipulated purchase price of the property and the period of time given in which to exercise the option, which may not exceed four years.

Although as a general rule leases do not require prior verification or authorisation, a lease with an option to buy requires prior verification, and an application for verification must be made before the option is exercised.

The period of time in which the option may be exercised expires at the end of the original lease term, even if the lease is extended.

8 Investment Incentives

¶801 In general

Investment incentives in Spain are intended to encourage investment and promote certain types of investments in specific economic sectors and geographical areas which are either depressed or which offer prime development opportunities. Spain classifies regions into four zones of economic development (*zonas de promoción económica*), according to per capita income and the level of unemployment. Regions with severe industrial problems are classified as zones of industrial decline (*zonas industriales en declive*). Incentives take the form of cash subsidies, subsidised interest rates on bank loans and subsidies for redeeming bank loans. An employer can obtain a reduction of up to 50 per cent of employer social security contributions for up to two years for creating new jobs. Incentives are available to both Spanish and foreign companies.

Investment incentives in Spain may be offered by central government, the autonomous regions, or the EEC. The incentives may take different forms, depending on their purpose. The kind of assistance given by the EEC is more likely to be a loan on favourable terms. Spanish incentive programmes have been harmonised with those of the EEC.

¶802 Application

Spanish and foreign companies and individuals can qualify for incentives if they offer investment in fixed assets or provide new jobs, technological development or growth in a particular activity, sector or geographical area. The investor must be able to provide at least 33 per cent of the cost of fixed assets.

Application procedures for investment incentive programmes depend on whether funds are provided by the central government, which are administered by a department of a Ministry, or by the autonomous regions. In most cases, the initial enquiry as to the availability of incentives is made at the local or regional level where the investment is contemplated. There one can find out what programmes are available and which government agency administers them. Although the application procedure can vary, the following information, as a minimum, will be required:

(1) if the applicant is a company, its latest annual report;
(2) a report on the activities or projects for which a subsidy is sought;
(3) the specific investments planned, including the amount needed for each stage of the project, together with an overall summary;
(4) the amount of capital to be invested and if such capital is to be invested in a company, specifying whether the investor is a company, an individual, or a third party;
(5) details of the investments, scheduled on a monthly or yearly basis, financing conditions and repayment terms of any loan; and
(6) the expected results.

Once the application is received, the viability of the project and its financing are reviewed. The ultimate decision is given by way of a ministerial order or a resolution which is published in the Official State Gazette (BOE) or in the equivalent regional publication.

¶803 Transfer of benefits

As many foreign investments involve a foreign investor setting up a Spanish company, the law allows benefits or incentives obtained by a foreign company to be transferred to its Spanish subsidiary or branch. These rights and benefits may be transferred whenever any of the following events occurs:

(1) transfer of ownership, which may involve a change of the company name or a change of corporate legal status;
(2) change of registered office to an address in the same area or to an address in a different area also qualifying for subsidies;
(3) transfer of rights, which involves a corporate acquisition of all or part of another company receiving subsidies;
(4) corporate merger or acquisition involving a business which trades in a subsidised sector.

¶804 EEC incentives

The European Community offers aid in Spain through the following entities:

(1) The European Investment Bank

The European Investment Bank (EIB) grants a variety of loans for projects involving regional economic development, areas of community interest, and the modernisation and restructuring of companies. The amount of the loan may never be higher than 50 per cent of the share capital of the applicant company.

(a) *Individual loans*. Loans are granted for terms of between seven and 20 years, with interest rates at international market levels. The EEC grants several kinds of loans, all of which have a minimum sum of 2 million ECUs.

(b) *Global loans*. Global loans are granted to financial institutions, which in turn distribute the loans between different projects. This kind of loan is intended for small and medium-sized projects. The amounts of the loans fluctuate between a minimum of 20,000 ECUs and a maximum of 7.5 million ECUs.

(2) The New Community Instrument

This is a source of funds which can be called upon in cases which do not come within the EIB's scope. The New Community Instrument was created by the EEC Council and Commission, and its main purpose is to grant loans to companies or organisations investing in projects promoting technological innovation, job creation, energy-saving and improvements in regional infrastructures, as well as other projects of benefit to the Community.

(3) The European Fund of Regional Development

This fund is essentially aimed at correcting regional imbalances within the EEC, and projects may qualify for subsidies of up to 55 per cent of their cost. Investments in the industrial, handicraft and service sectors may qualify for subsidies of up to 50 per cent of the costs of a project, plus a percentage of infrastructure costs.

(4) Other EEC incentives

(a) *Agriculture*. The EEC promotes and subsidises the processing and marketing of agricultural and fishing products. The following products receive subsidies from the EEC: fruits, vegetables, tubers, cereals, dried fruits, flowers, plants, seeds, nursery plants, wines, oilseed, animal feed, beet molasses feed, eggs, tobacco, olive oil, milk, meat, fish, cotton, sugar, and rice. Subsidies may amount to up to 30 per cent of the investment.

(b) *Energy*. The European Coal and Steel Community grants benefits for the mining of coal, iron and steel, technical and economic research directed at improving efficiency and the quality of iron and steel products, which may include forming companies producing and marketing coke coal. Investment incentives usually take the form of long-term, low-interest loans.

(c) *Technology*. Other sectors which receive subsidies include biotechnology, advanced telecommunication technology, non-nuclear energy, research regarding applied methodology and reference materials, basic technological research and new technology, information technology, technology of the future, and environmental research. The EEC also offers subsidies to encourage co-operation between universities and institutions for the teaching of technology, innovation in technology, and programmes allowing access to advanced telecommunication services.

¶805 Incentives at the national level

Incentives vary according to the industry affected. Tax benefits are the most common form of incentive, although subsidies and loans are also available.

(1) Tax benefits

Tax benefits are offered to companies or individuals, and a number of different types are available, including the following:

(a) *Industrial licences.* An industrial licence must be obtained when a new company is incorporated. Up to 95 per cent of the industrial licence fee may be waived during the period in which the company is being set up or plant and machinery installed.

(b) *Taxes on the transfer of assets.* Depending on the sector, this tax benefit is granted in connection with corporate transactions, domestic or foreign loans, and mergers and acquisitions. The amount of benefit depends on the transaction involved.

(c) *Customs duties.* Certain imports qualify for a reduction in customs duties. The beneficiary must submit the ministerial order granting the benefits to the customs authorities. The amount of such benefits depends on the product and may vary from time to time. The customs authorities deduct the amount of the benefits directly from the amount owed at customs.

(d) *Corporate taxes.* Benefits include, *inter alia*:
   - (i) a 99 per cent reduction in the tax payable by companies owning shares in foreign companies;
   - (ii) a 99 per cent reduction in the tax payable by companies in the publishing business;
   - (iii) a 99 per cent reduction in the tax payable on loans and credit facilities to be used for so-called 'real' investments, that is those which involve the actual management or running operations of a business;

(iv) a 50 per cent reduction in the tax payable by companies doing business in Ceuta or Melilla.

(e) *Real property taxes.* Tax benefits are granted in the municipality in which the property in question is situated.

(f) *Repayment plans.* These types of benefits consist of special repayment plans for companies which invest in fixed assets. They are granted by the Ministry of Economy and Finance in the province where the company's registered office is situated.

(2) Subsidies and loans

Subsidies are normally granted and funded by the department of the Ministry of Economy and Finance which handles the economic sector or geographical area concerned. Loans granted on advantageous terms may be available from public lending institutions in quantities and on such terms as provided by law.

(3) Sectors affected

The sectors affected by national incentives are as follows:

(a) *Tourism.* Certain areas with special features may be designated as 'Areas of National Tourist Interest' and may qualify for certain benefits, which usually take the form of tax relief, subsidies and long-term, low-interest loans.

(b) *Industry.* In the industrial regions of Cantabria, Asturias, Murcia, Castilla–La Mancha and Aragon, subsidies are given in the sectors of mining, iron and steel, high technology, energy and energy-saving, tourism, agriculture, as well as job-creating industries investing in newly incorporated companies (minimum investment 15 million pesetas), development (same minimum investment) and modernisation of industry (minimum investment 45 million pesetas). Subsidies vary between 30 per cent and 50 per cent of the cost of the investment project.

(c) *Agriculture.* Investment incentives are granted –

(i) to small and medium-sized agricultural and food-producing companies with a capital of 200 million pesetas or less, or having less than a 20 per cent interest in a company with a capital of more than 200 million pesetas;

(ii) for assistance in planning technical and managerial support for food-producing associations, public companies, unions, and other similar organisations;

(iii) to the agricultural and food industry, whether individuals or companies. The subsidies granted consist of low-interest loans amounting to 70 per cent of the investment or 25 per cent of the total capital required. Other subsidies are granted for slaughterhouses, dairies, and bottling plants for perishable goods.

(d) *Energy*. Benefits are granted:

(i) to promote hydro-electric production in small power stations with a production capacity of less than 5,000 Kw, for which benefits may consist of subsidies up to 30 per cent of expenses of research, tax reliefs, and government loans;

(ii) for investments aimed at energy conservation or the creation of alternative energy sources, for which benefits may consist of subsidies up to 40 per cent of the investment; and

(iii) for investments in solar energy by companies who have installed domestically-produced panels.

(e) *Electronics, computer science and innovation.* Incentives are granted:

(i) for projects of technological development and innovation and industrial design;

(ii) for technical and financial consultancy in electronics;

(iii) for research and development in micro-electronics;

(iv) for research projects;

(v) for technological modernisation of small and medium-sized companies;

(vi) for research organisations; and

(vii) for industrial diagnostic services.

(f) *Mining*. There are a variety of projects which are financed by the General Directorate of Mining under the auspices of the Ministry of Industry, such as:

(i) research, development and testing projects by companies with experience in the mining sector. The amount of the subsidy depends on the merits of each individual case;

(ii) improvement of the mining environment and the recovery of minerals and residues. Again, the amount of the subsidy depends on the merits of each individual case;

(iii) non-energy producing raw materials. Subsidies are given of up to 20 per cent of the investment;

(iv) coal-producing companies. Benefits will consist of subsidies of up to 20 per cent of the investment, a reimbursement of 35 per cent of the fixed investment, and a subsidy of 6 per cent of the rate of interest.

(v) the mining of non-energy-producing materials. Benefits

consist of long-term, low-interest loans for up to 70 per cent of the investment.

(vi) mining safety. Benefits consist of long-term, low-interest loans of up to 70 per cent of the investment.

(g) *Handicrafts and art.* The Spanish government gives assistance to this sector by designating certain regions as eligible to receive aid. The provinces of Salamanca, Pontevedra and La Coruña currently qualify for the protection of this sector. Benefits consist of subsidies of up to 40 per cent of the value of the investment and preferential government loans.

(h) *Shipping.* Subsidies are granted for ship-building, major repairs to vessels, conversion of vessels, acquisition of ship-fittings, conversion of fishing boats, purchase of equipment for fishing boats, export of ships converted in Spain, and improvements to technology.

¶806 Incentives offered by the autonomous regions

The 17 autonomous regional governments have independent incentive programmes, which are co-ordinated by the General Directorate of Regional Economic Incentives. Tourism is an important sector in Spain, and the autonomous regions may declare a specific area to be especially appropriate for tourism and offer the following benefits: preferential loans for construction in and development of the area and for financing working capital and investments, financial assistance (which can be given by both the national and regional governments), and technical and other kinds of assistance.

Table 8.1 indicates which of the autonomous regions offer incentives in a variety of industrial sectors:

Table 8.1: Incentives offered by the autonomous regions

Region	*Shipping*	*Industry*	*Agri-culture*	*Energy*	*Elec-tronics*	*Mining*	*Handicrafts & art*
Madrid					x		
Andalucia	x	x	x	x			x
Aragon		x			x		x
Asturias		x	x				
Canary Islands	x	x		x			
Cantabria		x	x	x	x		
Extremadura		x	x	x			x
Galicia		x	x			x	
Murcia		x		x	x		
Navarra		x	x	x	x		
Basque Country		x		x		x	
La Rioja		x		x			x
Valencia	x	x	x		x		
Castilla-Leon			x				x
Catalonia			x	x	x		

9 Importing

¶901 Introduction

Imports into Spain are governed by a variety of regulations, imposed by Spanish law, EEC law and international treaties. The mechanics of importing goods into Spain are complex, and the basic framework of import regulations is set out in broad terms.

Spanish customs regulations are governed by the Order of 21 February 1986 ('the 1986 Law'), which was passed in order to harmonise Spanish regulations with EEC legislation to the extent required by the 1986 Accession Treaty whereby Spain became a member State of the EEC. The ultimate objectives of the EEC regulations are to allow the circulation of goods within the EEC and eliminate artificial trade barriers between the member States. As a part of the Accession Treaty, Spain has been allowed a transition period with special privileges. The 1986 Law also seeks to harmonise Spanish regulations with the objectives of the General Agreement on Tariffs and Trade (GATT) to which Spain is a party. Of the various agreements and protocols which comprise the GATT, the most important commitment is the limitation of tariffs, whereby GATT countries agree to charge a tariff which will not exceed an amount specified in their respective tariff schedules. The remaining GATT obligations pursue the objective of eliminating non-tariff barriers to trade.

SPANISH IMPORT REGULATIONS

¶902 Import zones

(1) Zones

There are three types of procedure applied to imports into Spain, depending on whether the imports are deregulated, controlled, or require administrative authorisation. The procedure applied to imported goods depends both on the type of goods being imported and on the country of origin of the goods. The four main geographical zones are as follows:

- Zone A, which includes EEC member States.
- Zone B, which includes countries within the European Free Trade Association (EFTA), Mediterranean, African, and Pacific countries not included in Zones A, C, and D, and overseas territories of the Netherlands, France, Great Britain, and Denmark.
- Zone C, which includes the GATT countries, and all other countries or regions not included in Zones A, B, and D.
- Zone D, which includes non-free market economies or state trading countries, such as East Germany, Russia, Poland, China, Hungary, and Romania.

(2) Special treatment

Imports into Ceuta, Melilla and the Canary Islands, and imports of certain goods into Spain, receive different treatment, which in most cases is more restrictive.

(a) *Ceuta, Melilla and the Canary Islands.* Imports from these territories into mainland Spain are deemed to have their origin in Zone C. Imports into these territories are generally subject to much fewer import restrictions.

(b) *Textile products.* Over 100 textile products from countries including Argentina, Brazil, Uruguay, China, India, Thailand and Taiwan are afforded different treatment and are subject to quota restrictions. Textile products not included in this special category are governed by the general provisions of the 1986 Law.

(c) *Iron and steel products.* Imports into Spain of some iron and steel products are governed by the rules of the European Coal and Steel Community (ECSC).

(d) *Agricultural and fishing products.* Imports into Spain of some agricultural and fishing products are governed by the EEC Common Agricultural Policy (CAP).

¶903 Deregulation

Deregulated imports may be brought into Spain on a free trade basis (*régimen de libertad comercial*) and are subject only to minimum controls for statistical purposes, unless specific restrictions are imposed. No import permit documentation is required, except for a Statistic Import Payments Declaration form (DEPI), which is a payment form that has to be submitted to the office of the Secretary of State and Trade (*Secretaría de Estado y Comercio*) or to any of the territorial or provincial Directorates of Economy and Trade (*Direcciones provinciales o territoriales de Economía y Comercio*). The DEPI form is not required if the import transaction involves less than 500,000 pesetas and the financing terms are of less than one year, in which case the sales contract will be enough for Customs clearance. An invoice or other documentation which implies a contract between the foreign seller and the buyer may be sufficient for these purposes.

¶904 Trade controls

Statistical verification is required for the purposes of controlling certain products imported into Spain, such as goods of Zone D origin. The import documentation required by the Spanish General Directorate of Foreign Trade (*Director General de Comercio Exterior* or DGCE) is commonly known as NOPI (Prior Import Notification or *Notificación Previa de Importación*). The DGCE verifies the document within five working days and it remains valid for six months after verification.

¶905 Administrative authorisation

The countries of origin from which goods require administrative authorisation are set out in ministerial orders dated 21 February and 23 April 1986, and 16 April and 3 July 1987.

Examples of goods which require authorisation before being imported into Spain are those imported without consideration, or goods which are exchanged for exported goods, oil, oil derivatives, and oil processing machinery. Imports from Andorra and imports which are essential to national security and which are exempted from the general system pursuant to Article 36 of the Treaty of Rome and Article XXI of the GATT also require authorisation.

Goods requiring authorisation may be imported into Spain only after such authorisation is obtained from the DGCE. Authorisation is granted for a period of six months.

¶906 Other import documents

The necessary forms are available directly from the Ministry of Economy and Finance. Many importers, however, prefer to minimise administrative detail and paperwork and appoint a licensed customs agent (*agente aduanero*) who obtains and completes the relevant forms on behalf of the importer. Customs agents advise on and carry out the necessary procedures in relation to the handling of imports, and the maximum commission they may charge is regulated by law. Customs agents must be members of a professional association.

(1) The Single Administrative Document
With a view to simplifying import and export procedures within the EEC, all import documents were merged into the Single Administrative Document (*Documento Unico Aduanero* or DUA), which must be used by all EEC member States.

(2) The Value Declaration at Customs
Customs clearance requires the completion of an additional Customs document known as the Value Declaration at Customs. All goods, with some minor exceptions, should be valued at Customs. The Value Declaration must be presented at Customs with the invoice and any transport documents.

¶907 Other restrictions

(1) Quantitative restrictions
Spain may apply these volume restrictions provisionally, in respect of those items covered by the Accession Treaty, or permanently, in respect of those products not covered by the Accession Treaty and which were subject to import restrictions before Spain's entry into the EEC. Permanent quantitative import restrictions may only be applied to countries listed in Zones C and D.

(2) Safeguard measures
Specific economic sectors or regions may benefit from protective safeguard measures which are intended to offset serious economic harm to a given region or sector. Spain may take advantage of these trade remedies whenever the protective trade measures of Article 115 of the Treaty of Rome are insufficient and until 31 December 1992. After this date, Article 115 will be applied in full.

(3) Article 115 of the Treaty of Rome
Article 115 grants the EEC Commission the power to authorise a member State to apply a variety of protective trade measures. In urgent situations, however, provisional protective policies may be applied directly by member States, in which case all other member States must be duly notified. The unilateral imposition of protective trade measures by a member State is subject to the subsequent approval of the EEC Commission.

(4) Unfair trade practices
An EEC industry may file a complaint before the EEC Commission and request protective trade measures whenever a third country engages in trade practices that are incompatible with generally accepted rules of international

trade law. Such practices must harm, or be capable of harming, an economic sector of the EEC.

(5) Anti-dumping and countervailing duties

Dumping is the practice of selling goods in one national market at a lower price than in another. EEC anti-dumping regulations are designed to protect companies or economic sectors against that unfair practice by imposing anti-dumping duties at such levels as to offset the economic harm caused to companies or sectors affected.

Some types of government subsidies granted to an industrial sector of a country may give rise to lower prices when goods are exported within the EEC. This may cause economic harm to a company or to an economic sector in the receiving country. Protective measures exist to combat this practice, which impose a countervailing duty to compensate the aggrieved party.

(6) The removal of tariffs

The transition period under the Accession Treaty allows for the graduated reduction of customs tariffs in Spain in respect of specific items.

(a) *Agricultural products.* In the agricultural sector, the transition period is anticipated to be ten years from the date of Spain's entry into the EEC, the greatest reductions being in the fourth and fifth years. Reductions are fixed at 25 per cent for each year up to 1990; 15 per cent by 1991; and a 4 per cent reduction annually in the five remaining years. Since 31 December 1989 Spain has been unable to fix a maximum import quota in the EEC for fresh milk, butter, beef, cheese, and soft wheat for bread. Spain has until 31 December 1990 to remove controls for oil seeds (*semillas grasas*) and seed oil (*aceites de semillas*).

(b) *Industrial products.* In the industrial sector, the removal of tariffs is to be completed after a seven-year transition period, with reductions of 15 per cent in 1989, 12.5 per cent in 1990, 1991 and 1992; and 10 per cent in 1993.

PAYMENTS

¶908 Customs duties

Customs duties are paid by the importer before or at the time goods are imported. In order to determine the customs duties applicable to a given product, the importer must refer to the zone of origin of the goods and the customs duty table. The duty table is arranged according to the type of merchandise and includes an index reference. All payments of duties may be made either to the Ministry of Economy and Finance or, if the importer gives prior notice, directly at Customs. Normally payment is made through a Spanish bank, and evidence thereof is presented to Customs. A tariff schedule reflecting internal economic policy and bilateral and multilateral international agreements is published every year by Spanish Customs.

¶909 Tariff quotas

A tariff quota gives preferential treatment to certain types of imports within a given period of time and up to a specific limit. Once the quota is reached, normal customs duties apply. Spain applies two types of tariff quotas: automatic (*contingentes arancelarios*) and conditional (*límite máximo arancelario*). Automatic tariff quotas result in the immediate application of regular import duties once the legal limit is reached. If the tariff quota is conditional, Customs must give notice that the legal limit has been reached before they can impose normal import duties.

In order to obtain preferential treatment under tariff quota regulations, an importer must file an application at the DGCE. If the application is accepted, a certificate is issued which must be presented at Customs, together with the relevant import documentation.

¶910 Payment for imported goods

The amount to be paid for the imported goods is stated in the relevant import documents. Exchange control regulations, discussed in Chapter 2 (Exchange Control and Foreign Investments), should be taken into account.

¶911 Time of payment

Payment for imported goods may be made up to six months before Customs clearance. If payment is made before clearance, the importer may advance up to 15 per cent of the total amount of the transaction to the seller without prior administrative authorisation. Advance payment of more than 15 per cent of the total amount of the goods requires prior authorisation from the Spanish government.

The imported goods must be paid for fully within 30 days of Customs clearance. Payments made after that period will be treated as financing of the imported goods, which has exchange control implications (see Chapter 2).

¶912 Payment procedure

Payment of the imported goods must be made through the international department of an authorised bank (*entidad delegada*), unless the total value of the imported goods does not exceed 500,000 pesetas payable in a one-year period as from the date of import. In that case, payments to the foreign seller may be made by whatever means the buyer wishes.

The authorised bank opens a file with all relevant import documents and conducts all financial operations arising from a particular transaction. The bank proceeds to pay the foreign seller once it has been provided with the relevant import documentation and the documents evidencing the clearance of the merchandise through Customs, or the bill of lading in case of advance payments.

¶913 Ancillary expenses and commissions

Ancillary expenses include transport, storage and insurance. These expenses may be paid in Spain, or they may be paid abroad through authorised banks. Under exchange control regulations they are deemed to be invisible transactions and thus deregulated. The bank transfer requirements discussed above must also be observed.

Commissions to foreign agents or brokers are not deemed to be expenses, and they should be paid through authorised banks. Such payments are also deregulated as invisible transactions for exchange control purposes.

SPECIAL IMPORT SITUATIONS

¶914 Products in transit

Goods originating from an EEC member State, or imported into an EEC member State from a non-EEC member State after paying all appropriate import duties, may circulate freely within the EEC, Austria and Switzerland. These last countries are included in this special treatment pursuant to special treaties ratified by them and the EEC.

¶915 Temporary imports

Goods imported into an EEC member State which are classified as temporary imports may not circulate freely within the EEC. Temporary imports are goods which may be brought into the EEC on a temporary basis, receiving a total or partial exemption of import duties. Goods imported for presentation at exhibitions, fairs, congresses or similar events, and/or imports of educative or scientific material may be included within this category. These types of goods may be allowed into Spain for periods of between six months and two years.

¶916 Internal processing and re-export

Goods imported for internal processing and re-export may be imported free of duty. Prior authorisation must be obtained from Customs, and authorisation is granted if the goods to be imported are deemed to contribute to the creation of favourable export conditions and do not harm the economic interests of national producers. The term 'internal processing' includes the elaboration, adaptation, assembly, transformation, repair and restoration of goods. Most kinds of goods may be imported for processing and re-export, although energy sources, lubricants and equipment used in processing are excluded.

¶917 Bonded warehouses and duty-free zones

Goods imported from EEC and third countries may be stored in bonded warehouses without incurring import duties or political economic measures. There are no time limits for the storage of goods, although Customs may fix a term at their discretion.

Similar regulations exist for duty-free zones and depositaries. Generally, goods imported into duty-free zones and depositaries are not subject to import duties and political economic measures.

10 Sales and Distribution

COMMERCIAL INTERMEDIARIES

¶1001 Introduction

Spanish law provides for various ways of conducting business in Spain without setting up an office or branch. Doing business in Spain through sales representatives, independent agents and brokers minimises capital investment risks and circumvents the potential labour issues involved in setting up an office or branch. Company sales representation in Spain is usually done through an '*agente comercial*', a licensed professional who undertakes to promote the business of, or act on behalf of, another. Commercial agents may act under short-term contracts or contracts to perform a specific act, in which case they are called '*comisionistas*', or under long-term contracts (*contrato de agencia*) within a territory. They may also act as brokers.

¶1002 Commercial agents

Commercial agents must belong to a professional association, and their performance is governed by the Commercial Code. They are to be distinguished from non-commercial intermediaries (*mandatarios*) who are governed by the Civil Code.

Spanish law uses the terms agent (*agente*) and intermediary (*intermediario*) broadly, and it is important not to associate these terms too closely with the legal implications attributed to them under English or American law.

A commercial agent in Spain has those agency powers and responsibilities set out by contract and may or may not be authorised to bind the principal. Any such authority must be expressly given in the contract. Moreover, the Civil Code provides that powers granted to another to enter into any act which precedes or requires a notarised deed, or which may be detrimental to the interests of another, must be granted in a notarised power of attorney (*poder de representación*).

The commercial agent becomes personally liable to the principal for any losses arising from the non-performance of his duty, and the principal undertakes to cover all reasonable expenses incurred by the agent in the performance of this duty. The underlying principle is that the commercial agency agreement is a contract based on results. This means that a commercial agent is remunerated only when the contract is fully performed.

As a general rule, the commercial agent is deemed to be independent from the principal, which means that no employment relationship exists between them. However, there has been a general trend in Spain to expand the scope of labour law. The trend is for labour courts to focus on the actual relationship between the parties, rather than on the form of the contract, in determining the rights and liabilities of the parties. There is a rebuttable presumption that a labour relationship between principal and agent exists wherever one individual attends to the business of another. The presumption may be rebutted if the agent assumes the risks and benefits (*riesgo y ventura*) of the operations in question, or if the agent is an independent business entity. Therefore, care should be taken not only in drafting the contract but also in its performance, so that the relationship between the parties is accurately reflected by its terms.

¶1003 Commissioned agents

A commissioned agent (*comisionista*) is normally engaged to perform a specific act or assignment and, on the instructions of the principal, may enter into contractual agreements either in his own name or on behalf of the principal. Unless otherwise agreed, there is no exclusivity between agent and principal, and the principal can revoke the contract at any time.

The commissioned agent must perform under the terms and conditions of the agreement, keeping the principal informed at all times. He may not delegate his duties and must attend personally to the assigned matters. He must take reasonable care and use that degree of discretion commensurate with the matters entrusted to him.

The principal is normally obliged to cover all costs and expenses necessary for the commissioned agent to perform under the contract. Unless otherwise agreed, the principal must pay such costs and expenses in advance, and the commissioned agent can refuse to perform if advance payment is not made.

Payment is due to the commissioned agent once performance has been rendered. It is usually a percentage of the underlying transaction or a fixed fee. The terms of payment should be clearly set out in the commission contract.

Transport agents (*agentes de transportes*), travel agents (*agentes de viaje*), shipping agents (*consignatarios de buques*), commercial notaries (*corredores de comercio*), banks which perform direct payment or other types of services, and factoring agents (*sociedades de factoring*) are all deemed to be commissioned agents under the Commercial Code.

Names and addresses of commissioned agents can be found in reference guides for specialised services, in the yellow pages of telephone directories, where it is common to advertise, and in lists available in the professional association of the area.

¶1004 Agency agreements

Generally speaking, the agency agreement implies a long-term relationship between agent and principal. Under the agency agreement (*contrato de agencia*) the agent undertakes to represent a given business in a particular geographic area. In the typical agency relationship, the agent is given the authority to sign contracts on behalf of the principal. There is an 'exclusivity clause' in favour of the agent, and the agent agrees, in return, to act exclusively on behalf of the principal. Neither party may unilaterally revoke the contract unless the contract so provides. Unless otherwise agreed, the agent is paid when the third party performs or executes the contract negotiated by the agent.

In addition to clauses incorporating the typical characteristics of the agency agreement, the following terms should be included when negotiating the agreement:

(1) the agent's obligations;
(2) financing and the method of payment to be offered to customers;
(3) the types of contracts which require prior approval by the principal;
(4) the agent's remuneration, which is usually a percentage of the amount actually paid by the customer;
(5) method of accounting; and
(6) the duration of the contract.

The Commercial Code specifically provides for this kind of contract in connection with commercial agents, insurance agents (*agentes de seguros*), advertising agencies (*agencias de publicidad*), and banking agents (*agentes o corresponsales bancarios*).

¶1005 Brokers

A broker is an intermediary who brings parties together with a view to entering into a contractual relationship. A broker is necessarily independent of both parties and may not be a dependent, a subordinate or an agent of either. The basic characteristic of a brokerage agreement (*contrato de mediación o corretaje*) is that it involves a legal relationship based on results obtained, which means that a broker will only be entitled to be paid when the contract between the two parties is concluded or the desired results are achieved.

A broker is obliged to maintain the confidentiality of his client's instructions, keep his client informed, and advise the client in the client's best interest. He is required to act impartially when acting for both parties. The client's obligations are to provide the broker with the information necessary to perform the job and to pay the brokerage fee.

Real estate brokers or estate agents (*agentes de la propiedad inmobiliaria*), insurance brokers (*corredores de seguros*) and advertising brokers (*corredores de publicidad*) are deemed to come within this category.

¶1006 EEC Council Directive

The EEC Council Directive of 18 December 1986 (86/633/EEC) applies to the co-ordination of the laws of member States relating to self-employed commercial agents. The Directive defines the term 'commercial agent' as a self-employed intermediary who has continuing authority to negotiate the sale or purchase of goods on behalf of another person, called the principal, or to negotiate and conclude such transactions on behalf of and in the name of that principal. The Directive expressly excludes from this definition persons who, in their capacity as officers, are empowered to enter into commitments binding on a company or an association, a partner who is lawfully authorised to enter into commitments binding on his partners, and receivers and managers, liquidators or trustees in bankruptcy.

Commercial agency contracts must be in writing and may include a non-competition clause. A non-competition clause is defined as any agreement contemplating a restriction of the business activities of a commercial agent after the termination of a contract, and it sets out the territory, persons and type of goods covered. A non-competition clause may be valid for a maximum term of two years.

The Directive should be incorporated into the laws of EEC member States before 1 January 1990, and be applicable to all contracts at the latest by 1 January 1994. If the Directive is not included in the internal laws within the term mentioned above, it will apply directly.

DISTRIBUTION

¶1007 Distribution methods

A distribution network may be set up by supplying companies or individuals, who in turn resell the goods in Spain. There is no legal formula for these arrangements other than basic contract law. A supply or sales contract may stand alone or be combined with franchising or licensing agreements.

Alternatively, a supplier and distributor may enter into a consignment agreement (*contrato estimatorio*) under which a supplier consigns his goods to a retailer (consignee) to be sold. The retailer never receives title to the goods, but assumes all risks of custody. If the goods are sold or lost, the retailer must pay the supplier a fixed price, otherwise the goods are returned to the supplier.

Consignment contracts are not expressly governed by either the Civil or Commercial Code. They are, therefore, governed by the general provisions applicable to commercial sales contracts. The Spanish Supreme Court has described consignment contracts as being a combination of sales on commission (*venta a comisión*) and a deposit of merchandise (*depósito de mercancía*).

¶1008 Franchising

Under a franchising agreement (*contrato de franquicia*) the franchisor allows the franchisee to use trade marks, designs and other products peculiar to the business to sell a given product or service in accordance with the franchisor's methods. Franchise agreements often include a clause exclusively assigning rights to the franchisee within a given geographical area and non-competition clauses. These non-competition clauses are regulated by EEC and Spanish competition law, which is discussed in more detail in Chapter 15 (Competition Law).

Typical terms and conditions of a franchise agreement are as follows:

(1) *Exclusive assignment of territory.* As noted above, such an exclusive assignment will trigger the application of EEC competition law.

(2) *Fees or royalties.* Unlike the supplier in a distribution agreement, a franchisor does not necessarily sell goods to the franchisee. Instead, the franchisor provides certain know-how and a recognised trade mark. The franchisee is often required to make a down payment (*pago de entrada*) and/or pay annually a percentage of profits or income.

(3) *Trade name and trade mark.* The franchisor allows the franchisee to use the trade name and trade mark in the specified territory.

(4) *Business methods, designs, know-how, etc.* The franchisor normally provides the franchisee with all necessary manuals, designs and training. Within the bounds set by competition law, the franchisee undertakes to keep this information confidential and to observe those methods and procedures.

(5) *Franchise transfer and sub-franchising.* The franchise agreement may allow for the franchisee to sub-franchise within the specified territory, although sub-franchising and transfer of the franchise is not usually permitted.

(6) *Non-competition clauses.* Most often the franchisee is required not to

participate in competing operations or own shares in competing companies.

The Spanish Association for Franchising (*Asociación Española de Franquicia*) is the trade association which looks after the interests of franchisors and franchisees.

¶1009 Licensing

Spanish law provides that both patents pending registration and registered patents may be licensed to another party. This topic is discussed further in Chapter 12 (Intellectual Property). Licensing agreements (*contratos de licencia*) are governed by the provisions discussed in that chapter and by the general principles governing commercial contracts.

The terms and conditions of a licensing agreement usually cover the following:

(1) *Royalties*. Licensing agreements often provide for a royalty to the licensor in the form of a percentage of profits or income. Some agreements also include a minimum or maximum level of royalties; others may include a down payment to be paid either in addition to, or in lieu of, royalties.

(2) *Goodwill*. The licensee is often required to insure and protect the goodwill of the trade mark or the marketability of the licensed product. This may include confidentiality, advertising, minimum production and sales levels, quality control, and accounting and reporting requirements. In addition, the licensor will often determine the labelling of the product used and have control over advertising.

(3) *Assignability*. Licences may be assignable to third parties under the terms and conditions of the agreement.

(4) *Warranty of title*. The licensor will normally ensure title over intellectual property rights and undertake to oversee and cover any litigation costs arising therefrom.

(5) *Merchantability*. Warranties of merchantability or fitness are governed by general contract law and consumer protection law, as appropriate.

11 Labour Law

INTRODUCTION

¶1101 The foundations of labour law

The Workers' Statute (*Estatuto de los Trabajadores*) is the foundation of Spanish labour law. It defines and regulates the relationship between individual employees and their employers. Special statutes and decrees complement the basic statute and govern the employment of senior executive officers, domestic staff, and other so-called 'special' cases. Some other types of services are excluded from the Workers' Statute, and are therefore not considered to be labour relationships (e.g. civil servants and independent contractors).

In addition to the above, other regulations govern the organisation and representation of workers. Generally speaking, under Spanish law all workers are given the opportunity to organise, electing delegates or representatives at plant or company level. These delegates and representatives must be employees of the company or workplace (workplace is used to describe any place of business or manufacturing where there are employees) but they do not necessarily belong to a bigger union or other labour organisation. Although they do not receive any additional pay, they are entitled to take a given number of hours from their regular work schedule to perform their representational duties.

There are also trade unions which operate at regional or national level, and their membership is comprised of employees from different companies or workplaces. Membership of a union is voluntary. The legal capacity of a union to participate in the bargaining process is determined by the number of union members within the industry or geographical area. A union which has met the minimum membership requirements to participate in the bargaining process is known as a representative union.

¶1102 Exclusions from the Workers' Statute

Certain types of activities or employment are covered by other statutes or provisions of law which do not form part of Spanish labour law, and which are specifically excluded from the Workers' Statute, including:

- civil service employment (*funcionarios*);
- mandatory performance of personal obligations, for example military service;
- directors of a company or corporation in the performance of their duties;
- services performed as a family member or friend;
- independent contractors (persons engaged to perform a job or service who personally assume the risks and benefits of an undertaking and are responsible for the ultimate outcome).

¶1103 Special labour relations

(1) In general

Regulations that complement the Workers' Statute cover special employment relationships; specifically, domestic help, professional athletes, senior executive officers, performing artists, agents and intermediaries, disabled persons working in special workplaces, and longshoremen (stevedores). For these workers, the provisions of the Workers' Statute apply in the absence of any other applicable regulation.

(2) Senior executive officers

(a) Definition of 'senior executive officer'

An employee is deemed to be a senior executive officer (*alto directivo*) if he has the power and authority to manage and represent the company and he reports directly to the board of directors and shareholders. The general manager (*director general*) normally qualifies, although it is not the job description or title but the powers and true nature of his work which must be considered.

In a recent Supreme Court decision, the court used the position of Chief Machine Operator on a ship to illustrate that which is deemed not to be a senior executive officer. The court stated that such a job was a vital technical function necessary to ensure the proper operation and maintenance of the vessel's machinery, and no matter how important or indispensable the job itself may be, it was only one job amongst many which make up the 'business' (i.e. the vessel). Moreover, the employee always acted under the orders of the captain, and was therefore not a senior executive officer within the context of Spanish labour law.

(b) Employment

The terms and conditions of a senior executive's employment are governed by specific regulations and a freely negotiated employment contract, which must be in writing and must set out remuneration, duration (if a fixed-term contract) and any other minimum requirements of a contract.

The relationship between a senior executive officer and his employer is based on mutual trust and good faith. A senior executive officer may not take on other employment at the same time, unless specifically authorised to do so or by virtue of a written agreement to the contrary. If the business has given the executive officer professional training, it may be agreed that the employer has a right to compensation for damages if the senior executive officer leaves his post before the end of the term of the contract.

(c) Termination at will

The treatment of senior executive officers differs substantially from the treatment of ordinary employees, in that the employer may terminate the employment contract of the former at will. If dismissed under the procedure of removal (*disistimiento*), which is provided by law and applies only to senior executive officers, an employer may remove the officer by giving three months' notice (or paying three months' salary) and paying minimum compensation of an amount equal to seven days' salary per year of service, or six months' salary, whichever is less. There is no equivalent procedure for ordinary employees, allowing an employer to discharge an employee without cause (see ¶1111 and ¶1112).

Because of this, it is very common in Spain to include a clause in these kinds of contracts covering the amount of compensation to be received by the senior executive officer if the employer terminates the contract without cause. It is not unusual to agree to compensation of up to two years' salary, although it may be more or less. The legal minimum is seven days' salary for each year of service.

Non-competition agreements with the employer upon termination of the special employment contract are allowed, with certain limitations. The non-competition period may not exceed two years, and such a clause is valid only if the employer has an effective business or commercial interest and the senior executive officer receives adequate compensation.

INDIVIDUAL EMPLOYMENT RELATIONS

¶1104 General conditions for hiring

(1) Hiring

An employment relationship is presumed to exist whenever a person provides a service to another for payment and is subject to the other's supervision or management, whether or not there is a written agreement. Under the Workers' Statute, the relationship is closely regulated. The Workers' Statute sets out minimum requirements for contract terms, fills in any gaps, and may replace less favourable terms agreed upon once an employment relationship is deemed to exist.

The minimum working age is 16. Persons between the ages of 16 and 18 may not work at night or engage in any other work which the Government determines to be harmful to the health or personal or professional development of young people.

An employer seeking to hire new employees must first contact the local employment office. An employer is not required to hire the unemployed persons listed there, although they must at least be considered. If a person is hired through an employment office, termination of the contract must also be reported to that office.

The employer may hire direct if there is no local employment office; he may also do so if the local employment office fails to respond within three days, or if the employer decides not to employ those persons referred by the employment office after appropriate consideration or, finally, if the employer offers an open examination to the public for the selection of employees. In order to use this last type of selection process, the employer must give prior notice to the National Employment Institute (*Instituto Nacional de Empleo* or INEM) and subsequently report the names of the persons hired in this way to the local employment office.

(2) Standard contract

Spain has historically had a strong preference for indefinite term contracts as a means of maintaining employment stability. The standard employment contract is for an indefinite term and can be terminated by the employer only under the limited circumstances specified by statute. However, circumstances may permit the parties to enter into any of the types of contracts – temporary, special or incentive – set out in ¶1105 and ¶1106 below, and includes provisions for a trial period.

(3) Trial period

The employer and employee may agree to provide for a trial period in any employment contract. The trial period may range from 15 days to six months, depending on the qualifications of the new employee. During this period either party may terminate the contract. The trial period is particularly important because it allows an employer to terminate the employment contract without cause and without having to compensate the employee.

¶1105 Temporary contracts

Contracts may be for an indefinite duration or for a fixed term. The characteristic of fixed-term contracts is that the parties recognise at the outset the finite nature of their working relationship.

Temporary contracts are defined as contracts of terms of three years or less. They are considered appropriate where there are specific limited tasks or services to be performed, where the business is subject to market or seasonal fluctuations or any other conditions resulting in the accumulation of work or production orders, which call for contracts for periods of not more than six months out of every 12, where a need arises to substitute workers on authorised leaves of absence with a right to return to their job, e.g. leave for military service, where there is a requirement for defined tasks arising on a periodic basis, or where a company is starting up a new project or venture.

Indefinite term contracts have been used traditionally to maintain employment stability. However, this has been significantly undermined by technological developments and economic factors. Political concern to contain unemployment and create jobs even on a short-term basis has produced government incentives which encourage employers to engage staff on temporary contracts.

In Spain the normal practice is to hire initially on the basis of one of the temporary contracts permitted by law. This not only takes advantage of the incentives and subsidies offered by the Government, but also gives the employer an effective trial period. Thus, if he is not completely satisfied with an employee's performance, the employer may allow the temporary contract to expire at the end of its term without any further liability on his part.

¶1106 Other special contracts and incentive contracts

In addition to temporary contracts, the Workers' Statute provides for certain other types of special employment contracts with additional features. Some contracts are allowed to accommodate peculiar aspects of the labour relationship, such as joint or group contracts. These resemble individual employment contracts, but allow the employer to have a single labour relationship with a group of workers. This is enforceable as a contract and is not a collective bargaining agreement. Another special contractual relationship takes the form of a cottage labour agreement. This functions on a basis similar to the normal employment contract, but allows the work to be performed at the place of choice of the employee and without the direct supervision of the employer.

The purpose of many special contracts is to promote the Government's policy of containing and reducing unemployment by giving employers an incentive to take on new workers. In exchange for subsidies, tax benefits, grants or other forms of aid, employers offer to employees working conditions that meet government requirements.

(1) Training and development contracts

These contracts may be offered to young persons between the ages of 16 and 20. The employer undertakes to provide training for between 25 per cent and 50 per cent of the working day. The employer is permitted to pay the employee only for time spent working, as opposed to training. Upon granting a full-time training and development contract (*formación*), the company receives:

(a) a 100 per cent exemption from social security payments, if the company employs less than 25 persons, and a 90 per cent deduction if it employs 25 or more; and

(b) a subsidy for each hour of training provided, paid by the National Employment Institute (*Instituto Nacional de Empleo*). In 1989 this subsidy amounted to 90 pesetas per hour.

(2) Apprenticeship contracts and subsidies

Those with appropriate academic qualifications and seeking to develop their skills and expertise may within four years of obtaining an academic degree be hired under special apprenticeship (*en prácticas*) contracts of between three months and three years. Businesses which offer employment on a full-time basis will be able to reduce social security contributions. Spouses of employees, or blood relatives of the first or second degree, and senior executive officers do not qualify for these benefits.

Companies which hire persons who have been registered as unemployed for at least two years, and who either hold a technical degree or have never held a job before, are eligible to receive a lump sum payment, the amount of which depends on the term of the contract. Benefits currently consist of a lump-sum payment of 120,000 pesetas if the internship contract is for a minimum initial term of between six and 12 months, a lump-sum payment of 240,000 pesetas if the minimum initial term is of between 12 and 24 months, and a lump-sum payment of 280,000 pesetas if the minimum initial term is of at least 24 months.

(3) Relay contracts

A relay occurs when an older employee, who is eligible for semi-retirement under social security, continues to work 50 per cent of his normal work schedule and the employer hires a previously unemployed person to cover the remaining 50 per cent of the working week. This relay arrangement may take place during the three years preceding the date of full retirement of the older employee. If the employer grants permanent employment to the new employee, he pays reduced social security contributions for that employee.

(4) Part-time contracts

Part-time means that the employee works for less than two-thirds of a normal work schedule, whether calculated by the year, month, or week. The employer pays reduced social security contributions in proportion to the number of hours worked by the employee.

(5) Employment of persons over 45 who have been unemployed for at least one year

Businesses which employ such persons receive a lump-sum payment and pay reduced Social Security contributions in respect of those employees. If requested by the employer, free training is also provided.

(6) Employment of disabled persons

Companies may receive a lump-sum payment for each disabled person they employ, a 70 per cent reduction in the employer's Social Security contributions for disabled employees under 45 years of age, and a 90 per cent reduction in the employer's contributions for those employees over 45 years of age. If requested by the employer, free training is also given.

(7) Permanent employment of a person under 26

If they give permanent employment to persons under 26 years of age, employers pay reduced social security contributions throughout the term of the employment contract.

(8) Tax benefits

A tax allowance of 500,000 pesetas is given to employers for each increase in the average number of staff during the fiscal year, as compared to the previous year.

¶1107 Rights and duties of employees

(1) Rights
Workers in Spain have the following fundamental rights:

- employment in the trade or profession of their choice;
- unionisation;
- collective bargaining;
- the exercise of fair labour practices in the case of disputes;
- to strike;
- association;
- participation in the company (e.g. in the representation of workers or unions or in the bargaining process);
- meaningful employment;
- professional training and development;
- equal treatment without discrimination on the basis of sex, civil status, age (within the limits of the Workers' Statute), race, social status, religious or political ideas, affiliation with a union, or language, or on the basis of a disability, whether physical or mental, as long as the person has the necessary aptitude to perform the tasks required;
- personal safety and health and safety practices in the workplace;
- respect of privacy and personal dignity;
- remuneration in accordance with the terms of the employment contract or as otherwise provided by law;
- the exercise of individual actions or claims arising from the employment contract;
- any other rights arising from the employment contract.

(2) Duties
Workers in Spain have the following fundamental duties:

- to perform the job assigned with diligence and in good faith;
- to observe all health and safety measures adopted by the employer;
- to comply with the orders and instructions of the employer issued in the normal course of business;
- not to compete with their present employer (as provided by Workers' Statute);
- to contribute to increased productivity;

- to perform any other duties which may arise from their employment contract.

¶1108 Salary and wages

(1) General

'Salary' is a general term which includes wages and all economic benefits received by an employee in return for services rendered. It includes monetary remuneration and benefits in kind, but excludes Social Security contributions, reimbursement for expenses incurred in the course of employment (including relocation expenses) and payments made on the dismissal or suspension of an employee. Salary must be paid regularly and at least once a month. Collective bargaining agreements must include the agreed annual salary and the number of hours to be worked. Total salary is divided into three parts: basic salary, supplements, and bonuses.

(a) *Basic salary*. This is usually determined in the employment contract or collective bargaining agreement, with due consideration paid to the law regarding minimum wages.

(b) *Supplements*. These are calculated according to basic salary and include any increases resulting from seniority or length of service adjustments, supplements for a particular job or function, and production incentives.

(c) *Bonus and extraordinary payments*. Spanish workers are usually paid monthly. Bonus and extraordinary payments include all additions to basic salary which are paid other than on a monthly basis. Spanish law provides for two compulsory extra monthly payments to be made at Christmas and in the summer, unless otherwise agreed between the parties. The average Spanish worker is therefore paid 14 times a year.

(2) Minimum wage

The minimum wage (*salario mínimo interprofesional*) is set by the Government and applies to all employees. The minimum wage is reviewed annually, in consultation with the major unions and management organisations, and the revised minimum wage is usually published in April each year. However, by law the minimum wage may be adjusted every six months if there are sharp fluctuations in the consumer price index. The minimum wage is only a legal minimum, and has no effect on employment contracts which provide for a higher level of remuneration. The 1989 minimum wage was 46,680 pesetas per month. As indicated in (1) above, the minimum monthly wage is paid 14 times per year.

¶1109 Work schedule

(1) Regular hours

(a) *Maximum working week.* The regular working week consists of a maximum of 40 hours. An employee may not work for more than nine hours in a single day, and there must normally be a period of at least 12 hours between one day's work shift and the next.

(b) *Continuous and split schedules.* The working day may be split (*partida*) or continuous. It is deemed to be split if there is a break in the working day of at least one hour. If the working day is continuous, a 15-minute 'sandwich' break must be provided, which is counted as working time.

(c) *Rotating shifts.* Work may be performed in shifts, if necessary.

(d) *Night shifts.* Night shifts generally begin at 10 p.m. and finish before 6 a.m. Workers are entitled to a 25 per cent salary supplement, unless salary is previously agreed taking into account this special circumstance.

(2) Overtime

Overtime (*horas extras*) includes all hours worked over and above regular hours. Unless agreed otherwise, it is voluntary, and must be paid by increasing the employee's basic hourly wage by at least 75 per cent. An employee may not work more than 80 hours of overtime in the course of one year, save in exceptional circumstances, such as a business collapse. Workers on the night shift and workers under 18 years of age may not work overtime. Overtime provided for in a collective bargaining agreement is referred to as 'structural'. Structural overtime is subject to preferential social security treatment. It is therefore usually in the interest of both the employer and the employee to agree to it at the bargaining table.

(3) Breaks

(a) *Weekly.* A consecutive day and a half is the minimum weekly rest period provided by law. Time off may be calculated and adjusted, based on a four-week period for shift schedules.

(b) *Public holidays.* There are 14 public holidays per year; 12 are set by the national government and the remaining two by each autonomous region.

(4) Vacations

Spanish law lays down a minimum requirement of at least 30 calendar days' vacation, although longer vacations may be agreed through collective bargaining agreements. The timing of vacations is agreed by the employer and employee, or in accordance with the terms of the collective bargaining agreement. However, in seasonal businesses the employer may refuse requests for vacations during the busiest times of the year. Employees with families have priority during school vacations, and employees are entitled to be informed of their vacation schedule at least two months in advance.

(5) Leave

An employee is entitled to the following leaves of absence with pay for the following events, upon giving proper notice. These are the legal minimum periods of leave, although collective bargaining agreements may provide for longer periods.

(a) Marriage – 15 days.

(b) Birth of a child (to be distinguished from maternity leave), or the serious illness or death of a first or second degree relative – two days. This period may be extended for up to four days if travel is necessary.

(c) Moving house – one day.

(d) Mothers of children of less than nine months of age have the right to leave work for one hour in the middle of the regular working day, or, alternatively, to shorten their working day by half an hour.

(e) Any person with legal guardianship of a child less than six years of age, or of a mentally or physically handicapped person, is entitled to reduce his working day by one-third, or by one-half, with a proportional reduction in pay.

(6) Maternity leave

In 1989 changes were introduced in Spain with regard to maternity and paternity leave. The mother is entitled to 16 uninterrupted weeks' paid leave, and 18 weeks if it is a multiple birth (twins, triplets, etc.). The only condition imposed is that at least six weeks' leave must be taken after the birth. If the mother dies, the right to take leave passes to the father. If both the father and mother work, the mother may choose to allow the last four weeks of leave to be taken by the father. Notice of this choice must be given at the beginning of her absence from work and may only be taken if it is not detrimental to her health when the time arrives.

In the case of an adopted child, if the child is less than nine months old on the legal adoption date, the mother is entitled to eight weeks' paid leave as from that date. If the child is more than nine months, but less than five years old, then she is entitled to six weeks' leave.

In addition to the above, the mother or the father may request a period of up to three years of unpaid absence from work, technically a suspension of the employment contract, in order to look after the child. If the parent returns during the first year, he/she is entitled to have his/her job back on the same terms as before. After the first year, he/she is entitled to return to a job of equal or similar status as the one held before.

¶1110 Modification or suspension of the employment contract

(1) Changes to the employment contract

(a) *Substantial changes.* Substantial changes affecting the work schedule, opening and closing times, rotation or shift schedules, the system of pay or production must be justified by the employer. Such changes must have the agreement of the workers' representatives or be approved by the labour authorities. If an employee is adversely affected by such changes, he may rescind his employment contract the following month and receive compensation (*indemnización*).

(b) *Change of function.* An employee may be assigned a different function if it does not adversely affect him financially or professionally.

(c) *Relocation.* If justified by organisational needs or special production contracts, the employer may temporarily relocate an employee away from his usual residence for a period of up to one year, provided that the employer pays all transport and relocation expenses. This is referred to as '*desplazamiento temporal*', and the employee is required to comply with the order, even though he may appeal the basis for it thereafter.

Transfers requiring a change of residence for a period of over one year or indefinitely are called '*traslados*' and are not allowed unless justified by the employer and approved by the labour authorities. Even if so approved, the employee may opt either to accept the move with all expenses paid or rescind the employment contract and receive compensation. The option must be exercised within 30 days of the approval of the move by labour authorities. It is therefore advisable to include a transfer clause in the employment contract if it is likely that the employer will require the employee to move at some point.

(2) Suspension of the contract

Throughout the period of suspension, the parties are relieved of their respective obligations under the contract. A contract may be suspended by mutual agreement, by its terms, by reason of temporary incapacity or disability, lay-off, maternity leave, military service or substitute social service, election to public office, arrest (until convicted or absolved), for disciplinary reasons, reasons out of the control of the parties which make performance of the contract temporarily impossible, economic or technological reasons, forced leave of absence, and strikes or lock-outs.

Once the legal justification for the suspension no longer exists, the worker has the right to return to his former position, unless otherwise provided in the employment contract or, in the case of temporary disability, the employee is found to have a more serious disability. Once military service, substitute social service, public office or union service has ended, the worker must return to work within 30 days.

¶1111 Dismissals

The indefinite term contract is still the standard form of contract used for workers in Spain, although temporary contracts are becoming increasingly common. An indefinite term contract can originate as such or become one, if either party fails to give notice of termination of a fixed-term contract or fails to convert it into another form of contract. In any case, dismissal of an employee before the natural termination of the contract can be a difficult and often costly matter.

(1) Terminating the employment contract

The law recognises that under the circumstances mentioned below an employment contract may be terminated. However, most contracts provide for compensation to be paid to an employee if the employer chooses to terminate the relationship. Grounds for termination recognised in the Workers' Statute are:

(a) mutual agreement;

(b) under the terms of the employment contract;

(c) termination of the employment contract or full performance thereof;

(d) resignation, retirement, or dismissal of the employee;

(e) death, major disability, permanent or absolute disability of the employee (as defined by social security);

(f) death, retirement or disability of the employer or dissolution of the company;

(g) *force majeure*;

(h) where a business, trade, or service goes out of business for technological or financial reasons;

(i) voluntary termination of the employee due to non-performance by the employer;

(j) any other reason from time to time permitted by law.

(2) Disciplinary dismissal

The employer may unilaterally terminate the employment contract and dismiss the employee for failure to do his job in accordance with the provisions of the Workers' Statute. Notice of dismissal must be given in writing, stating the reasons for dismissal and the date on which it is to take effect.

(3) Other grounds

An employer may unilaterally terminate the employment contract for 'objective' cause (*causas objetivas*), based on incompetence on the part of the employee discovered after granting him permanent employment, failure of the employee to adapt to reasonable technical changes in his job within two months, a demonstrated need to reduce jobs on a one-by-one basis in businesses having less than 50 workers, or repeated absenteeism (with certain exceptions) whether justified or not, if the employee has been absent for 20 per cent or more of working hours in two consecutive months, or if he has been absent for 25 per cent of the working hours in four non-consecutive months within a 12-month period.

In order to terminate the employment contract for objective causes the employer must pay the employee compensation (*indemnización*) equal to 20 days' salary per year of service, up to a maximum of 12 months' salary, and allow for a minimum period of grace during which the employee remains in the job. The period of grace required is one month for those who have been employed for less than one year with the company, two months for those who have been employed for between one and two years, and three months for those who have been employed for two or more years. During this period of grace, an employee may leave work for up to six hours a week in order to look for a new job without losing pay. The employer does, however, have the option to pay the employee his salary for the period of grace in lieu of having him report for work.

¶1112 Challenging the dismissal

An employee has the right to contest a dismissal in the labour courts, which may declare the dismissal to be valid (*procedente*), unjustified (*improcedente*), void (*nulo*) or radically void (*radicalmente nulo*). A dismissal will be deemed to be *valid* if it is shown to be justified, and will result in the termination of the employment contract without any right to compensation. The dismissal will be declared to be *unjustified* if there is insufficient proof of the reasons for the dismissal. The employer then may choose to reinstate the employee or pay compensation equal to 45 days' salary for each year of service, up to a maximum of 42 months' salary (reduced by the amount of any other compensation or payment received for a non-disciplinary dismissal), and compensate the employee for wages lost during the period between the dismissal and the labour court decision, of which the employer pays the employee two months' accumulated back-pay, any excess being paid by the State out of the salary guarantee fund to which an employer makes monthly mandatory contributions.

A dismissal is *void* if the employer fails to comply with formal procedural requirements. This results in the employee's immediate reinstatement to his former position and the payment to him of any lost wages. The employer may dismiss the employee again, using the proper procedures, within seven days of the court order.

A dismissal is *radically void* if the employer violates the employee's constitutional rights or dismisses him fraudulently or maliciously. When a labour court finds a dismissal to be radically void, the employee must be immediately reinstated to his former position and compensated for any lost wages. These measures were introduced to prevent employers from abusing the dismissal procedure or dismissing employees for invented or unjust reasons, and for cases where the employer may be willing to pay compensation but not observe the procedural requirements. The result may be extreme, in that there are cases in which employers have been prevented from closing down a workplace and forced to reinstate employees until a negotiated settlement is reached with the employee. Tables 11.1 and 11.2 summarise the various forms of dismissals and their consequences, and refer to the removal (*desistimiento*) of a senior executive officer for the purposes of comparison.

¶1113 Negotiating a dismissal

The dismissal of an employee, except in cases which are clearly justified, is very expensive for an employer, especially if the employee has worked for that employer for a long time. This is particularly true in those cases in which the courts can order the employer to reinstate the employee to his former post and pay lost wages. Because of this, in Spain it is very common to negotiate the terms of dismissal directly with the employee, using the amount of 45 days' salary for each year of service (the legally mandated amount for unjustified dismissals) as a basis for discussions. Negotiating with an employee may be the only way to terminate employment without cause, given the ability of the courts to require the employer to reinstate an employee for void or radically void dismissals.

Table 11.1: Dismissal of ordinary workers

Dismissals	*For cause (disciplinary)*	*For cause (objective)*
Justified	No compensation.	20 days' salary/year worked. Maximum of 12 months.
Unjustified	45 days' salary/year worked. Maximum of 42 months.	45 days' salary/year worked. Maximum of 42 months.
Void	Rehire with the possibility of compensation.	Rehire with the possibility of compensation.
Radically void	Immediate rehire.	Immediate rehire.

Table 11.2: Dismissal of senior executive officers

Dismissals	*Consequences*
Justified Unjustified	No compensation. 29 days' salary/year worked. Maximum of 12 months.
Removal (*desistimiento*)	• Compensation agreed in contract or, if none, 7 days' salary/year worked. Maximum of 6 months. • 3 months' notice (or equivalent pay).

Negotiation of a dismissal offers a number of distinct advantages. Decisions regarding the dismissal of the employee do not fall into the hands of a third party, it is normally cheaper for the business, since the costs of a hearing and other legal costs are avoided, the employee's dismissal will not appear in his curriculum vitae, which would otherwise be to his disadvantage, and the employee is likely to receive greater compensation and sooner than he would otherwise.

¶1114 Collective dismissals and staff reductions

Dismissal of a number of employees at the same time (*regulación de empleo*) must be made by way of a special procedure and must be approved by the workers representatives or, if not, by the labour authorities. Reasons for the dismissal must be based on sound technological or financial reasons or a *force majeure*. Workers' representatives generally negotiate the agreement, and the employer is required to report it to the labour authorities. Labour inspectors and a certified public accountant must also submit a report if more than 50 employees are affected. Workers' representatives and employees with large families are given priority over other employees in keeping their jobs. Employees receive compensation of the equivalent of 20 days' salary per year of service, up to a maximum of 12 months' salary.

The labour authorities accept this type of application only if the employer can adequately substantiate the reasons given for the dismissals. Accordingly, it is common to negotiate dismissals individually if the employer wishes to restructure the business and reduce staff.

COLLECTIVE LABOUR RELATIONS

¶1115 Labour representation

In Spain, employees of a business with six or more employees have a right to elect from among them one or more representatives. They do not form official representative bodies such as unions, but they do represent the employees when negotiating with the employer and generally look after the employees' interests within the company or at the workplace.

(1) Workers' representatives

Personnel delegates (*delegados de personal*) exist in businesses of between six and 50 employees. If the company has from six to 30 employees, one delegate may be elected by a majority vote. If there are 31 to 49 employees, there may be up to three delegates.

Company committees (*comités de empresa*) exist in companies of 50 or more employees. The size of the committee depends on the number of employees and may vary from five, for a company of 50 to 100 employees, to 21, for companies with 751 to 1,000 employees, with two additional representatives for every further thousand employees or part thereof.

Inter-workplace committees may be formed pursuant to a collective bargaining agreement, so that a number of workplaces may be jointly represented.

(2) Functions

Although the authority of workers' representatives may be expanded by a collective bargaining agreement, the basic functions of personnel delegates and company committees are to protect employees' rights, keep informed as to how the business is doing, and participate in decisions affecting certain significant changes to the company, its structure, or the workforce.

(3) Privileges

Although a workers' representative is not paid directly for the time he dedicates to representational activities, depending on the number of workers he represents, he can devote up to 40 hours per month with pay to attend to such duties.

If a representative is disciplined for alleged negligence in the performance of his job, a period is required to allow him to defend himself before the sanction is imposed, otherwise it is void and unenforceable. Workers' representatives stand a greater chance of keeping their jobs when staff reductions are being made, and cannot be disciplined for any action taken in the course of their duties as representatives, during the time served or for one year thereafter. They may also freely express opinions on matters related to their duties, as long as they give prior notice to management and do not disrupt the normal course of business.

(4) Election and terms

Workers' representatives are elected by all employees of the company over 16 years of age and employed with the company for at least one month. Any employee having reached the age of 18 who has been employed with the company for at least six months is eligible to stand for office. Senior executive officers may neither vote nor present themselves as a candidate to represent the workers.

A workers' representative is elected for a term of four years, which is automatically extended if new elections are not held before the term runs out. He may be removed by a simple majority vote at a meeting called by at least one-third of the workers.

¶1116 Union representatives

Since 1985, Spanish law has encouraged union representation at the company level through the creation of company-wide union sections and union delegates. Employees affiliated with a union within a given company may form or join a union section, if so provided by the union's by-laws. They then have the right to participate in collective bargaining, to have a bulletin board on the premises, and to have an office in businesses with more than 250 employees.

If a business has 250 or more employees, union sections may appoint one union representative. They may have up to four seats in companies with over 5,000 employees. Union representatives enjoy the same rights and privileges as the members of the company committee, but if a union representative is also a member of the company committee, his rights and privileges are not doubled; the representative may enjoy those of one or the other position.

¶1117 The collective bargaining process

Collective bargaining may be confined to a single business or workplace. Alternatively, several employers or an entire sector in a province, autonomous region or the nation may be involved.

(1) Bargaining committee

For agreements covering one workplace the bargaining committee is made up of up to 12 representatives of the workforce and 12 from management. If the collective bargaining agreement has a wider scope, the negotiating committee may have up to 15 representatives from each side. A chairman of the bargaining committee is jointly appointed. Advisers may be present at the meetings and may be heard, but may not vote.

If the collective bargaining agreement is limited to a single company, the employees may be represented by their workers' representatives (company committee or personnel delegates). In the case of bargaining agreements relating to more than one company, workers may also be represented by major unions deemed by law to be the most representative, either at national level or autonomous regional level, or having a substantial representation on the company committee or among the personnel delegates.

(2) Procedure

The party initiating the negotiations must provide written notice to the other party, setting out, *inter alia*, the matters to be negotiated. Once notice has been received, a party may refuse to negotiate only under specified conditions established by law or practice, or when negotiations are called for a purpose other than the renegotiation of an expired collective bargaining agreement. Within one month after receipt of written notice, the agenda is agreed and a timetable set. The negotiators must act in good faith and the committee may appoint a mediator at any point. Negotiations may be suspended if violence ensues.

¶1118 Collective bargaining agreements

So far commentary has been confined to the minimum requirements laid down by Spanish law in labour matters. Collective bargaining agreements negotiated between the employer and employees are usually more advantageous to the employee; therefore, it is not surprising that nearly all sectors have a national collective bargaining agreement. This means that in any business set up in Spain, the terms of any applicable sector-wide agreement will automatically apply to the employees. For example, for a number of years the national collective agreement for office-workers has included a clause providing for a continuous working day (8 a.m. to 3 p.m. without a lunch break) for 11 weeks during the summer. This would, therefore, automatically apply to the employees of a newly-formed office in Spain covered by the agreement, even if the employer had not negotiated at all. Changes can only be effected by negotiating a special agreement (this would be difficult), or going before the labour authorities to effect the change by showing adequate justification. Thus, collective bargaining agreements are highly important, even to a newly set-up business, since they have force of law and are far-reaching.

Agreements reached by management and labour representatives concerning the terms and conditions of employment are published in the appropriate Official Bulletin and become law. Collective bargaining agreements regulate any matters relating to the terms and conditions of employment and must include at least a description of the parties affected, the scope of application (geographic area, business or sector affected, duration, type of personnel covered), the appointment of a joint committee to oversee the implementation of the new agreement, and termination notice provisions.

The parties determine the duration of the agreement, but if no agreement is subsequently negotiated, it runs from year to year, until notice to terminate is given by one of the parties. Upon termination of a collective bargaining agreement, and until a new agreement is reached, all non-essential terms and conditions lapse. Other terms and conditions, such as wage levels and work schedule, remain valid and apply until a new agreement is reached.

The agreement reached by the bargaining committee must be in writing and approved by at least 60 per cent of the representatives of each side. It must be registered with the labour authorities within 15 days and subsequently filed with the Institute for Mediation, Arbitration and Conciliation.

¶1119 Strikes and lock-outs

(1) Strikes

Article 28 of the Spanish Constitution guarantees workers the right to strike, subject to the continuation of essential services. A 1977 law governs the right to strike, forbidding, *inter alia*, rotational strikes (when employees take turns in abstaining from work), strikes in strategic sectors and slowdowns.

Each workplace must decide, by majority vote of its representatives, whether to call a strike. At least five days' notice must be given to the labour authorities and to the employer; and at least ten days' notice if the strike affects public services. A strike committee must promise to provide the necessary services for the safety of persons and property and the reopening of the business after the strike.

Once a strike is called, the dispute may be submitted to mediation by the labour authorities. The parties may also agree to submit the matter to arbitration. Any mediation agreement or arbitration award has the legal status of a collective bargaining agreement.

(2) Lock-outs

Lock-outs are allowed only in case of a strike or other labour practice which threatens violence against persons, damage to property or illegal occupation of the premises, or where the level of absenteeism or work stoppages severely interrupts production. The labour authorities must be notified and the company may remain closed for the minimum time necessary.

SOCIAL SECURITY

¶1120 Scope

Social Security is a nationwide programme designed to provide certain benefits to a variety of individuals. Participation is mandatory for all employees, independent contractors, members of production co-operatives, domestic employees, students, civil servants, and military personnel.

¶1121 General provisions

(1) Registration of employer

Employers must register at the regional bureau of Social Security before starting up business. There is an official registration form which the employer must update periodically. In particular, if a place of business is closed, this fact must be reported within ten calendar days. A company must also indicate whether insurance for accidents at work will be provided by Social Security or by an Employers' Insurance Mutual (*Mutualidad Patronal*).

(2) Employee registration and deductions

All eligible employees must be registered with Social Security. An employee is registered only once, and this is done by the employer, who is also responsible for updating the employee's status (employed, disabled, unemployed, etc.). Employers must report to Social Security the hiring of new employees or the termination of any employee's contract within five calendar days. All employee records must be retained by the company for a period of at least five years.

Both the employer and the employee make contributions to Social Security, although the employer is responsible for collecting and paying the employee's contribution through wage deductions. If the employer fails to make the deduction, there is no recourse against the employee.

In addition to joint Social Security contributions, employers make a separate contribution for insurance for work-related accidents and illnesses and to the salary guarantee fund (*Fondo de Garantía Salarial*).

(3) Contributions

(a) Contribution base

Social security contributions are calculated on the total monthly basic pay received by the employee, excluding per diems (*dieta*) and travel expenses, distance and transport supplements, petty cash allowances, the value of work clothing or uniforms, death indemnities, relocation expenses, suspension or dismissal compensation, and supplemental payments on marriage. Bonuses or extraordinary pay not accruing on a monthly basis must be allocated in equal parts throughout the year.

The legislation sets out a minimum and maximum contribution base for each occupational or professional category (see Tables 11.3 and 11.4).

(b) Contribution rates

Social Security contributions are collected and allocated to five funds. The amount of contribution payable is calculated by multiplying the employee's contribution base by the contribution rates (*tipos de cotización*) shown in Table 11.5.

(c) When payable

Contributions are payable monthly in arrears. There is a 10 per cent penalty charge (*recargo*) for late payments made within one month after their due date. The penalty rises to 20 per cent if the employer fails to register or report the current status of the employee or payments are over one month late.

¶1122 Services provided

(1) Health care

To those who make the necessary contributions, the health care (*asistencia sanitaria*) programme makes available medical and pharmaceutical services for common illnesses, maternity and non work-related accidents to employed persons, persons collecting pensions or other types of fixed income, and their relatives and other dependants.

Table 11.3: Social security contribution base (monthly)

Contribution group	*Category*	*Minimum monthly base (in pesetas)*	*Maximum monthly base (in pesetas)*
1	Engineers and licensed professionals	81,330	275,820
2	Technical engineers, experts, assistants with a degree	67,440	275,820
3	Supervisory personnel	58,620	275,820
4	Assistants with no degree	54,480	175,800
5	Administrative officers	54,480	175,800
6	Subordinates	54,480	155,520
7	Administrative assistants	54,480	155,520

Table 11.4: Social security contribution base (daily)

Contribution group	*Category*	*Minimum daily base (in pesetas)*	*Maximum daily base (in pesetas)*
8	First and second degree officers	1,816	5,312
9	Third degree officers and specialists	1,816	5,184
10	Office boy	1,816	5,184
11	Workers 17 years of age	1,114	3,031
12	Workers under 17 years of age	701	1,910

Table 11.5: Social security contribution rates (%)

Funds	*Employer*	*Worker*	*Total*
General benefits fund (*contingencias comunes*)	24.00	4.80	28.80
Overtime:			
Structural or due to *force majeur*	12.00	2.00	14.00
Non-structural	24.00	4.80	28.80
Unemployment	5.20	1.10	6.30
Salary guarantee fund (to cover back-pay and compensation (*indemnización*) risks	0.50	–	0.50
Training fund	0.60	0.10	0.70

(2) Temporary incapacity benefits

An employee is deemed to be temporarily incapacitated if, because of illness or any kind of accident, he is unable to work for up to 12 months (extendable by another six months). In such a case, he may be able to claim temporary incapacity benefits (*incapacidad laboral transitoria* or ILT). Observation periods for work-related illnesses are covered for up to six months (extendable to one year).

Eligible employees are those covered by Social Security who are employed or qualify for unemployment benefits, and who have paid in to Social Security contributions for a minimum period. A woman registering for maternity benefits must have become eligible at least nine months before the birth. There is no minimum contribution period required for incapacity due to an accident.

(3) Disability benefits

With regard to disability benefits (*invalidez*), the law distinguishes between temporary and permanent disabilities.

(a) *Temporary disability*. A temporary disability occurs when a worker requires continued health care and is unable to work after having exhausted temporary incapacity benefits.

(b) *Permanent disability*. Employees are eligible to receive benefits if they are employed or qualify for unemployment benefits and have contributed to Social Security for the minimum periods required by law (this does not apply to accidents). Permanent disabilities are further classified as follows:

   (i) *Partial disability*. This causes a person to perform at less than two-thirds the normal level of performance in his job or profession, but does not completely prohibit him from performing the required tasks. This type of disability entitles the employee to a lump-sum payment.

   (ii) *Total permanent disability*. This occurs when a person is completely unable to perform his job, but it does not preclude him from engaging in another form of employment. The Social Security provides a tax-free pension for life of monthly payments, or a lump-sum payment if the employee is under 60 years of age.

   (iii) *Absolute permanent disability*. This occurs when a person is unable to carry out any job or profession. He is entitled to receive a tax-free pension equal to 100 per cent of net salary.

   (iv) *Major disability*. This occurs when a person is also dependent on a personal help to attend to his essential needs. He is entitled to a tax-free pension equal to 100 per cent of net salary, plus an additional 50 per cent increase to cover the expense of hiring a help.

(4) Unemployment benefits

If an individual becomes unemployed for reasons beyond his control, he may collect unemployment benefit for a maximum of 24 months after four years of contribution, and proportionately less for shorter contribution periods (see Table 11.6).

Table 11.6: Unemployment benefits

Period of contribution (in months)	*Period of benefit (in months)*
6 to 12	3
12 to 18	6
18 to 24	9
24 to 30	12
30 to 36	15
36 to 42	18
42 to 48	21
48 and over	24

The amount of monthly benefits varies, and the employee receives 80 per cent of the contribution base monthly during the first six months, 70 per cent of the contribution base monthly from the sixth to the twelfth month, and 60 per cent of the base monthly after the twelfth month.

Under no circumstances may the monthly benefits exceed 170 per cent of the minimum wage, unless the worker has dependent children, in which case this limit rises to 220 per cent.

(5) Retirement benefits

Employees who have reached the age of 65 and who have contributed to Social Security for at least 15 years, including at least two of the eight years immediately before retirement, have the right to collect retirement pension benefits. Employees belonging to a Labour Mutual before 1967 may retire upon reaching the age of 60 and receive a percentage of their total pension benefits, ranging from 60 per cent at age 60 to 92 per cent at age 64.

Pension benefits are calculated by multiplying the employee's contribution base by a percentage varying according to the number of years of contribution. Employees who have contributed for 15 years receive 60 per cent of contribution base, which increases thereafter by 2 per cent for each year of contribution, until it reaches 100 per cent after 35 years. Except in the case of partial retirement, the person may not collect pension benefits while still working. However, it is possible to receive pension benefits at the same time as other Social Security benefits.

(6) Death benefits

Survivorship benefits arise upon the death of an employee or a recipient of retirement benefits, temporary or permanent disability benefits and, except for death by accident or work-related illness, require a minimum contribution period.

Benefits include a small subsidy for funeral expenses and a pension for the legitimate spouse, an orphan's pension payable to children under 18 years of age, a pension to other qualifying family members' and a temporary subsidy to qualifying relatives.

¶1123 Special provisions

There are special provisions relating to contributions and benefits for those working in agriculture, coal mining or the armed forces, and civil servants, seamen, domestic employees or independent contractors. Employees covered under the special provisions usually contribute to Social Security at the same rate as ordinary employees; however, contributions to Social Security are made directly, taking into account the manner in which income is earned, so that in some instances a fixed monthly amount is contributed, independent of the actual remuneration received.

SETTING UP A WORKPLACE IN SPAIN

¶1124 Labour report

A report must be filed with the provincial Labour Authorities (in Madrid this is the *Dirección Provincial de Trabajo*, Calle de la Princesa, N° 3) within 30 days of opening an office, plant or workplace in Spain. There is a set form which must be submitted in quadruplicate, providing the information set out below. One copy is dated and stamped by the Labour Authorities and returned to the company.

(1) *Employer:*
   - (a) name, registered office, city, province, postal or zip code, and telephone number;
   - (b) national identification card or tax number or, in the case of a foreigner, exile or refugee, a passport or equivalent document;
   - (c) whether the employer is a newly set up or existing business;
   - (d) business activity;

   (e) name of the entity managing the company's accident and sickness insurance scheme.

(2) *Workplace:*
   (a) name, registered office, city, province, postal or zip code, and telephone number. The exact location of the new place of business must be clearly described;
   (b) Social Security registration number, type of workplace, reason for the application (e.g. if a new workplace or change of workplace), and the date business began;
   (c) business activity;
   (d) total number of male and total number of female employees;
   (e) size of the workplace in square metres;
   (f) building safety and health approvals required under Royal Decree 555/1986 of 21 February 1986;
   (g) descriptive report of the technical aspects of the project, citing all types of activities which are disagreeable, unhealthy or dangerous pursuant to Article 29 of Decree 2414/1961 of 30 December 1961.

(3) *Production and storage information:*
   (a) electrical power source (kw or cv);
   (b) list of the machinery and other apparatus installed.
   (c) a statement as to whether certain dangerous materials are used, stored or produced, or whether workers are exposed to chemical agents.

¶1125 Social Security registrations

The employer opening the office must also register with Social Security (General Treasury) and apply for a separate identification number for each workplace set up by the same employer in Spain.

¶1126 Foreign workers

(1) Reciprocity

Foreign workers are required to obtain work and residence permits before they may carry on any lucrative activity in Spain. This is further discussed in Chapter 17 (Personal Business).

Foreign workers in Spain enjoy the same rights and privileges as their Spanish counterparts in respect of labour relations and Social Security benefits and obligations. They may vote in elections for workers' representatives and run for office, subject to the principle of reciprocity in respect of citizens of non-EEC countries.

(2) Treaties
Great Britain, Portugal, Andorra, the Philippines, Brazil, and most Latin-American countries have reciprocity treaties with Spain. There is also a 1988 Treaty with the United States, which allows Spanish employees working in the United States and US employees working in Spain to receive credit in their home country for Social Security contributions made while abroad for periods of up to five years. The treaty refers to the contribution periods required to qualify for retirement pensions and death and disability benefits (but not health care).

¶1127 Workplace inventions and intellectual property rights

(1) Inventions in the course of employment
The 1986 Patent Law (discussed in detail in Chapter 12) provides for the protection of intellectual property developed in the course of employment.

The 1986 Law distinguishes between the following three types of workplace inventions:

(a) *Job-related.* This term refers to all inventions made by an employee which result from research closely related to the performance of the job. These inventions belong to the employer. However, depending on the benefit derived therefrom by the employer, and the degree of personal effort invested by the employee, the employee may be entitled to some form of compensation, either as agreed by the parties or as determined by the courts.

(b) *Exploitation.* This term refers to inventions made by the employee with knowledge acquired mainly from the employer, or with tools and equipment provided by the employer. These inventions belong to the employee. However, the employer has the right to assume title over the invention or obtain rights to use it upon payment of fair compensation to the employee.

(c) *Unrelated.* This term refers to inventions not included in either of the above, which are predominantly the result of the creative activity of the employee and belong to him exclusively.

(2) Copyright
The employee is deemed to be the author of any work created in the course of employment. Unless the employment contract expressly provides otherwise, the employer has the right to market the work, although it may not be used for any purpose other than that for which it was created.

12 Intellectual Property

¶1201 Introduction

The law governing patents in Spain consists of the Spanish Patent Law of 20 March 1986 ('the 1986 Law'), and the European Patent Convention, in force in Spain since 1 October 1986. Subsequent regulations dated 10 October 1986 also form part of Spanish patents law.

There are two ways to obtain patent rights in Spain, by domestic application or by a European application designating Spain, invoking the provisions of the European Patent Convention. A Spanish application is filed in the Spanish Patent and Trade Mark Office and is subject to, and, if approved, granted in accordance with, the applicable provisions and procedures of Spanish law. A European application designating Spain is filed in the European Patent Office and is subject to, and, if approved, granted pursuant to, European Patent Convention procedure. This patent becomes a Spanish patent after its Spanish translation is filed at the Spanish Patent and Trade Mark Office. The rights obtained by both types of patents are the same as those provided under Spanish law.

In general, a Spanish patent is applied for when exploitation is anticipated to take place in Spain only, or when a first patent giving a priority right is sought (this is normally the case for Spanish inventors). A European patent designating Spain is normally applied for when exploitation is planned for several European countries, including Spain.

Spain is a member of the 1883 Paris Union Convention, and since 1974 has applied the Stockholm version. This Convention governs the rights of citizens of signatory States if they apply for intellectual property rights in Spain. Spain is also a signatory of many of the major international treaties on patents, with the exception of the Patent Co-operation Treaty. However, it is likely Spain will become a signatory in the near future. The Luxembourg Convention on the Patent for the Common Market of 1975 will be effective in Spain when it comes into force, but this is not likely to happen in the near future.

¶1202 Scope of protection

Spanish law provides for the grant of patents in order to protect inventions, and further provides for the issue of certificates in order to protect utility models (see ¶1210 below). Protection may be obtained by Spanish individuals or companies, persons habitually resident or who have set up business in Spain, or any person entitled to the rights and benefits granted under the Paris Union Convention. Spanish citizens, citizens of the signatory countries, and any person domiciled or who has set up business in those countries, may invoke the provisions of the Paris Union Convention.

¶1203 Domestic patents

(1) Grant of patent

An invention may be patented if it is novel, innovative and capable of industrial application. An invention is deemed to be novel when it is not considered part of the current 'state of the art' (*estado de la técnica*). 'State of the art' includes all technology generally available before the date of the patent application. An invention is deemed to be innovative when the invention is not obviously derived from the 'state of the art' according to expert opinion. An invention is deemed to be capable of industrial application when it may be manufactured or used in any type of industry.

Patent rights belong to the inventor and can be assigned to third parties. If several persons independently invent the same product, then patent rights will belong to the person who first files the patent application in Spain.

Inventions by persons in the course of their employment are dealt with separately in Chapter 11 (Labour Law).

(2) Exclusions of patentability

The 1986 Law does *not* deem any of the following to be patentable:

(a) discoveries, scientific theories or mathematical methods;

(b) intellectual works (they are protected by copyright law);

(c) plans, rules and procedures for intellectual activities, games or business activities;

(d) reproduction of information, such as tables, forms, writing patterns;

(e) computer software (this is protected by copyright law), although an invention including a computer program can be patented;

(f) forms and methods of medical treatment, although medical equipment and chemicals or pharmaceuticals for medical treatment can be patented;

(g) inventions which are contrary to public order or morality;

(h) plants, which are protected by a special law of 12 March 1975;

(i) animals;

(j) essentially biological processes to obtain plants and animals (microbiological processes and products obtained by these processes can be patented).

Although they are not listed in the 1986 Law as unpatentable, chemical and pharmaceutical products will not in fact be patentable in Spain until 7 October 1992. This allows Spain time to adapt to EEC requirements. However, processes for these products are already patentable in Spain.

¶1204 Filing a patent application

The 1986 Law establishes three procedures to apply for a patent:

(1) the current provisional procedure;

(2) a general procedure to come into force no later than 26 March 1991 (however, as of 26 March 1989, the Government has the authority to implement this procedure for particular technical fields); and

(3) a procedure with prior examination to come into force by government decision after 26 September 1991.

(1) The application

All procedures begin with the filing of the patent application in the Spanish Patent and Trade Mark Office (*Registro de Propiedad Industrial*), although all foreign applicants are required to act through Spanish patent agents. The application must include a form supplied by the Spanish Patent and Trade Mark Office, a description of the invention, the claims (*reivindicaciones*) (i.e. the technical description of that for which protection is sought and which is to be the subject of the patent), and drawings, if necessary to understand the description. The Patent and Trade Mark Office may require additional documents, such as a certificate of priority or a power of attorney. All documents must be submitted in Spanish.

(2) Secret patents

Secret patent applications are kept confidential for two months after submission, unless the Spanish Patent and Trade Mark Office decides otherwise. The initial two-month period may be extended to up to five months if the Spanish Patent and Trade Mark Office considers the invention to be of interest to national security. If the Ministry of Defence then decides that national security interests are affected, the Spanish Patent and Trade Mark Office will be notified, before the confidentiality period expires, that the patent application must be processed in confidence. The patent will then be registered in the Secret Registry. It will remain there throughout the first year after the patent is granted, and the Ministry of Defence may request on a yearly basis that it remain in the Secret Registry. The patent holder may demand compensation for the period in which the patent is kept secret. If the patent holder and the Government fail to reach an agreement, the amount of compensation is determined by the courts.

Such inventions developed in Spain may not therefore be patented outside Spain until two months after the initial application is made in Spain, unless authorised by the Spanish Patent and Trade Mark Office. Furthermore, if national security is affected, applications for patents outside Spain must also be expressly authorised by the Ministry of Defence.

(3) Provisional procedure

During the provisional procedure, the Spanish Patent and Trade Mark Office only checks that all formal requirements have been complied with and whether the subject of the application is patentable *per se.*

During this period any objections to the applications may be raised, and requests for additions to or amendment of the applications be made. If this is accomplished satisfactorily, the patent is granted. If not, the application is deemed to be withdrawn. The whole patent document is published at the same time as the grant is announced in the Official Gazette.

(4) General procedure

The main steps in the general procedure are as follows:

(a) a preliminary examination of formalities and patentability *per se* is made, as in the provisional procedure;

(b) the application is published (not before 18 months after filing, except in particular cases);

(c) a state of the art report must be requested by the applicant no later than 15 months after the filing date of the application (the clarity and sufficiency of the description is examined in order to draw up the report);

(d) once the state of the art report is published, third parties may make written observations with respect to the report, which may be made available in court in the event of a challenge to the validity of a patent;

(e) the patent is granted and published.

In the course of the general procedure, the applicant can make restricted modifications to the application in order to avoid patentability problems raised by the state of the art report or the third parties' observations.

(5) Procedure with prior examination

In the procedure with prior examination, after the publication of the state of the art report, a substantive examination of the patentability requirements is required before granting the patent.

(6) Summary

In the provisional procedure, patents are granted without checking substantive patentability requirements; the validity of a patent may be challenged in the ordinary courts.

In the general procedure, patents are also granted without checking substantive patentability requirements; nevertheless, any challenge of the validity of a patent in the ordinary courts is clarified to a great extent by the documents published in the course of the procedure, in particular, the state of the art report and third parties' observations.

In the procedure with prior examination, patents are granted after checking substantive patentability requirements; nevertheless, a challenge of the validity of a patent in the ordinary courts remains possible.

(7) Fees

The Spanish Patent and Trade Mark Office publishes an annual list of minimum fees for filing, for the issue of patents, for a state of the art report, and for miscellaneous applications made in the course of the procedure.

¶1205 Duration and contents

Patent rights are granted for a non-renewable period of 20 years from the date on which the patent application is filed. The patent becomes effective when notice that the patent has been granted is published. A patent may expire before this if the annual fee is not paid or if the patent holder renounces his right by written notice to the Spanish Patent and Trade Mark Office.

The patent entitles its holder to prevent a third party from making use of the patented invention in any of the following ways:

(1) manufacturing, marketing, importing or using the patented product, or possessing such product for any of those purposes;

(2) using or offering the use of patented procedures without the patent holder's consent, when the third party knows or should know from the circumstances that the use of such procedures is prohibited;

(3) marketing, importing or using a product obtained directly through the

patented procedure, or possessing such a product for any of the above purposes.

The patent does not provide protection to the patent holder against claims for infringement of other patents pre-dating that of the holder. Patented products and procedures may not be used in a way which is immoral or inconsistent with the law, public order or public health.

Once the patent application has been published, the patent holder has the right retroactively to claim reasonable damages from a third party which used the invention in the period between the date of filing and the date the patent grant was published, if such use would have been considered an infringement of the patent, once granted.

¶1206 Infringement actions

All patent infringement claims are currently within the jurisdiction of the ordinary courts, although specialised courts within each autonomous region may be created in the near future. Damages and equitable relief are available.

A patent holder is entitled to damages for infringement amounting to the actual loss incurred, as well as lost profits. Lost profits are those which:

(1) the patent holder could have reasonably earned but for the infringement;

(2) are earned by the infringing party through the use of the patented invention;

(3) are equivalent to the fee that the infringing party should have paid to the patent holder for a licence permitting use of the invention.

The limitation period for bringing claims in respect of patent infringements is five years from the time the claim becomes actionable, which is normally when the patent holder has reasonable notice of the infringement.

The 1986 Law offers greater protection than previous legislation for patents, both in terms of the number of rights protected and the types of actions and remedies available – in particular, injunctive relief. In the case of patents of manufacturing processes, the burden of proof is on the defendant rather than on the plaintiff. The 1986 Law also reinforces the rules of evidence and provides for judicial notice and the use of pre-trial hearings. The measures available to ensure enforcement of a final judgment have been strengthened.

Jurisdiction and other procedural aspects are all applicable to patent claims, as well as to any other claims regarding intellectual property rights.

¶1207 Property rights pertaining to a patent

(1) Co-ownership

A patent application may be made and a patent may be held jointly by two or more persons on whatever terms they agree. In the absence of any agreement the provisions of the 1986 Law or the Civil Code regarding joint ownership of intellectual property will apply. The licensing of a patent to a third party must be granted jointly by all co-owners, unless the courts decide otherwise.

(2) Expropriation

A patent or patent application may be expropriated if fair compensation is paid. A patent may be expropriated in order to put it in the public domain, where anyone may use it without a licence, or be reserved for exclusive use by the State, which then becomes the patent holder. If an expropriation is made it is published as a law, which must define the public interest served by the expropriation and specify whether the patent is to be put into the public domain or reserved for the exclusive use of the State.

(3) Transfer and licensing

Patents and patent applications are transferable and may be the subject of licensing and other agreements. They may also be used as security. Licences may cover all or part of the rights and privileges of the patent, be exclusive or non-exclusive, and have effect throughout Spain or in certain regions only. Unless agreed otherwise, it will be presumed that the licence is non-exclusive, allowing the licensor to grant other licences in the future or to use the patented invention himself. Licensees may not transfer their licences to third parties, nor grant sub-licences without the consent of the patent holder. As a general rule, the transfer of a patent or the grant of a licence, or any other acts affecting a patent, will be binding on third parties only after they have been registered at the Spanish Patent and Trade Mark Office.

(4) Licences of rights

Patent holders may notify the Spanish Patent and Trade Mark Office in writing that they are prepared to offer a non-exclusive licence to third parties. This offer is noted in the Spanish Patent and Trade Mark Office and the Office publishes notice of the offer. The offer may be withdrawn by written notice to the Office, provided that it has not already been accepted by a third party. A patent holder may not make an offer if an exclusive licence of the patent already exists.

A licence of right (*licencia de pleno derecho*) is treated as a contract, but if the parties cannot agree on the consideration to be paid, then it will be determined by the Spanish Patent and Trade Mark Office.

(5) Use requirements and mandatory licences

The patent holder must use his patent rights, either by personally exploiting the invention or by granting a licence to a third party within four years of the date of the patent application or three years of the date the patent grant is published in the Official Gazette for Patents, whichever is later. The Government may require mandatory licences to be granted for a patent or a patent application if there is insufficient exploitation of the patented invention, the need to export, dependence or interdependence of separate patents, or if it is in the public interest.

Mandatory licences are not exclusive, unless exclusivity is found to be in the public interest.

¶1208 Additions to patents

The holder of an unexpired patent may protect further inventions which perfect or develop the original patent by applying for an addition to the patent which may be fully incorporated into the original one. Such additions do not need to be innovative if they relate to the original invention. The priority date for an addition is the date of application for the addition, and this addition will expire on the same date as the original patent. If the Spanish Patent and Trade Mark Office considers the proposed additions not to be sufficiently related to the original patent, or the patent holder relinquishes his rights to the original patent, the application for an addition may be converted into a separate patent application. All regulations regarding patents will also usually apply to additions.

¶1209 European patents

The European Patent Convention, currently in force in 13 European countries, provides for a simple procedure for granting patents in those signatory countries.

A patent is granted by the European Patent Office. Thereafter the patent is divided into a 'bundle of national patents', governed by the applicable national laws for all purposes. When applying, the applicant decides the countries ('designated States') for which he wants the patent. The application for a European patent, taking into account procedural costs, is cost-effective if the number of designated States is at least four.

The main features of Spanish law concerning European patents designating Spain are the following:

(1) The European patents granted for Spain need to be published in Spanish by the Spanish Patent and Trade Mark Office to be valid in Spain. The applicant must pay a fee and provide a Spanish translation of the patent to the Spanish Patent and Trade Mark Office within a three-month period after the date of publication of the original grant.

(2) European published applications may obtain the same provisional protection in Spain as enjoyed by Spanish applications (see ¶1204(3)). The applicant must pay a fee and provide a Spanish translation of the claims and the drawings to the Spanish Patent and Trade Mark Office so they can be published.

(3) The European Patent Convention admits full patentability of chemical and pharmaceutical products. Nevertheless these patents will be not valid in Spain until 7 October 1992. If the European patent covers both a process and a product, the process is protected in Spain.

¶1210 Utility models

Utility models, similar to utility patents in other countries, are inventions which are both novel and innovative and lend shape and structure to an object, which results in a measureable improvement in its use or manufacture. The novelty requirement is restricted to previous inventions known in Spain. This is the main difference between a utility model and a patent with respect to the criteria for patentability. Utility models frequently take the form of utensils, instruments, fixtures, devices, gadgets or tools.

Protection, evidenced by a certificate, lasts for a period of ten years, and no extensions to that period are permitted. Otherwise utility models are protected in much the same way as ordinary patents.

(1) Application procedure

The main features of the utility model application procedure are as follows:

- The application is similar to a patent application.
- A preliminary examination of the formal requirements is carried out by the Spanish Patent and Trade Mark Office.
- Claims and drawings are published.
- Third parties may challenge the validity of the utility model by written oppositions.
- The Spanish Patent and Trade Mark Office grants the utility model, taking into account any oppositions filed and the applicant's replies.
- There is no utility model search procedure.

(2) Fees
Fees for utility models are generally the same as for patents at each procedural step (see ¶1204(7)).

TRADE MARKS

¶1211 Spanish and EEC laws

The 1988 Trade Mark Law, which came into force in Spain on 12 May 1989, has brought Spanish law into line with EEC regulations.

EEC policy on trade mark legislation has two main aims:

(1) to create an EEC trade mark to be registered by a Community Office (which will probably be situated in Madrid) according to a uniform Community law and to be valid throughout the EEC. A draft EEC regulation is expected in the near future;

(2) to harmonise national laws in order to minimise competition distortions arising from different national trade marks. The 89/104/EEC Directive of 21 December 1988 has been promulgated, dictating the harmonisation of national trade mark laws. National laws should be adapted in line with this Directive by no later than 1 January 1993. Although the new 1988 Spanish Trade Mark Law was passed before the Directive, it follows its main principles.

The main changes introduced by the 1988 Trade Mark Law are:

(a) the duration of a trade mark is now ten years instead of 20 years;

(b) to keep the trade mark in force will require actual use (the renewal procedure includes a declaration of actual use);

(c) it is now clear that the risk of confusion between trade marks as a criterion for registration is restricted to trade marks relating to the same category of goods or services (with the exception of well-known trade marks); and

(d) the 1988 Trade Mark Law provides effective legal remedies for trade mark infringements.

¶1212 The concept of the trade mark in Spanish law

A trade mark is any symbol, word or distinctive mark used to distinguish the products or services of a particular supplier from identical or similar products or services in the marketplace.

In particular, the following may constitute a trade mark:

(1) words or a combination of words, including those used to identify persons;
(2) images, figures, symbols and graphics;
(3) letters, numbers or combinations;
(4) packaging, containers, the form of the product or its presentation; and
(5) any combination of the symbols, words and distinctive marks mentioned above.

¶1213 The registration procedure

(1) Application

Application for the registration of a trade mark may be made by Spanish nationals or companies, by foreign individuals or companies habitually resident in Spain, or which have set up business in Spain, or which enjoy the benefits of the Paris Union Convention, and by any other foreign individuals or companies whose country of origin allows reciprocal registration of trade marks to Spanish individuals or companies.

Spanish individuals or companies, as well as nationals of the signatories to the Paris Union Convention or those domiciled or running a business in any of the signatory countries to this Convention, may invoke the provisions of the Convention whenever they are more favourable to them than Spanish law. In particular, the six-month priority right of the Paris Union Convention may be invoked.

The application must include:

(a) a form provided by the Spanish Trade Mark Office;
(b) a description of the trade mark;
(c) two-dimensional reproductions of graphic elements;
(d) the list of products or services to be covered.

(2) Procedure

Once the application is filed, the Spanish Patent and Trade Mark Office carries out a preliminary check on the formal requirements. The applicant is notified of any lack of information or oppositions filed, and he is given the opportunity to amend or supplement the application.

The publication opens a two-month period for challenging the trade mark by interested third parties (by way of written oppositions).

The Spanish Patent and Trade Mark Office conducts a full examination of the application in order to determine whether it is the subject of any exclusion from registration (see ¶1214).

Oppositions arising from interested third parties and/or the examination mentioned above are notified to the applicant, and the applicant has a period of one month to reply to the oppositions.

The Spanish Patent and Trade Mark Office then makes a decision. This administrative decision may be appealed within the Spanish Patent and Trade Mark Office and subsequently to the courts.

(3) Fees

The Spanish Patent and Trade Mark Office publishes an annual list of minimum fees for filing, registration, oppositions, replies, renewals, and quinquennial fees for maintenance.

¶1214 Exclusions from registration

Patent law defines the conditions for patentability in positive terms. An invention will be patentable if it complies with the legal patentability requirements: novelty, innovation, and industrial application.

For trade marks, conditions for registration are defined in negative terms. A mark may be a registered trade mark if there are no legal causes for exclusion from registration.

The essence of the registration procedure, as outlined in ¶1213(2), is to examine the application in the light of the causes for exclusion. Both the examination conducted by the Spanish Patent and Trade Mark Office and any oppositions raised by third parties make reference to them.

There are three types of exclusions from registration: absolute exclusions, relative exclusions, and miscellaneous exclusions. Apart from the different nature of the exclusion categories, the type of exclusion invoked gives rise to different legal effects. Relative and miscellaneous exclusions may be invoked in annulment actions within a period of five years after the date of the registration publication. This limitation period does not apply to absolute exclusions.

Due to the great importance of exclusions, they are dealt with in detail below.

(1) Absolute exclusions

In addition to those symbols, words or distinctive marks which do not constitute a trade mark, the following may not be registered:

(a) generic terms;

(b) commonly used descriptions of the products or services, or descriptive terms or symbols which are customarily or regularly employed in the trade or business;

(c) symbols or terms which are used within the trade or business to designate the type, quality, quantity, purpose, value, geographical source, period of production or service or other features, unless the trade mark has acquired its own distinctive character as a result of its use (as an exception to this, however, it should be noted that symbols, words or distinctive marks in (a), (b) and (c) above, which otherwise would not be individually subject to registration, may be combined and registered as a trade mark if such combination meets the legal definition of a trade mark);

(d) technical designs which affect the intrinsic value of the product;

(e) symbols, words or distinctive marks which are contrary to the law, public order or custom;

(f) symbols, words or distinctive marks which are misleading as to the nature, quality, characteristics or geographical source of the products or services;

(g) a colour by itself (although registration may be possible if used in a specific shape);

(h) symbols, words or distinctive marks which reproduce or copy the titles, coat of arms, flag or other emblems of Spain, its autonomous regions, municipalities, provinces or other local bodies, unless prior consent is obtained. Such symbols may only be ancillary to the main trade mark;

(i) unauthorised symbols, words or distinctive marks which contravene Article 6 of the Paris Union Convention;

(j) symbols, words or distinctive marks which reproduce or copy the official seal or stamp of the Spanish government or any other State without prior authority.

(2) Relative exclusions

The following symbols, words or distinctive marks may not be registered as trade marks:

(a) those which may create confusion in the marketplace, either because they are so similar in concept, or because they look or sound so similar to a trade mark which has already been applied for or is already registered and which relates to similar or identical products or services;

(b) those which may create confusion in the marketplace, either because they are so similar in concept, or because they look or sound so similar to a trade name (*nombre comercial*) which has already been applied for or is already registered in connection with business activities related to the products or services which are the subject of an application;

(c) those which are identical to the title of establishment (*rótulo*) used by a company or individual, which has already been applied for or registered and is used in connection with the same business as the products or services related to the trade mark.

(3) Miscellaneous exclusions

The following symbols, words or distinctive marks may not be registered as trade marks:

(a) the name, surname, pseudonym or other term or symbol which identifies the applicant and which falls into any of the above categories;

(b) the name or image of a person other than the applicant, or the name, surname, pseudonym or any other term or symbol which would identify a person other than the applicant, without prior authority. The general provisions of law apply to these as well;

(c) those which unlawfully make use of the reputation or prestige of other registered trade marks;

(d) those which copy inventions protected by the patent, trade mark or copyright laws, without prior authority.

¶1215 Duration and contents

A trade mark is registered for a period of ten years from the date of the application and may be renewed every ten years indefinitely. The registration of a trade mark remains effective, provided that the owner pays the fees which must be paid in advance every five years. Non-payment leads to forfeiture of the trade mark.

Rights to a trade mark are acquired by registration. However, the user of a trade mark which is already well-known in relevant sectors of the Spanish market but not registered has the right, within five years of the date of publication of the grant of a newly-registered trade mark, to demand through the courts the cancellation of the registration of the new trade mark if it is used in conjunction with identical or similar products and creates confusion with that well-known trade mark. If the application for the new trade mark was made in bad faith, this limitation period does not apply. The prior user must file a trade mark application at the same time, but the application will not be processed until a final decision is reached by the courts.

If a trade mark application affects the rights of third parties or any other legal or contractual obligation, the aggrieved party may claim ownership of the trade mark in a legal action, either before the trade mark is granted or within five years of the date of publication of the grant of the trade mark.

A trade mark will be deemed to have expired if it has not been used in Spain within five years of the date of publication of the registration of the trade mark, or if the use of the trade mark is suspended for a continuous period of five years.

Registration confers on the owner the exclusive right to use the trade mark for commercial purposes. The registered owner may display the trade mark in conjunction with the marketing of the products or services to which it relates. He may also use the trade mark in advertising. He can protect his rights through the courts as against third parties using an identical or a similar trade mark or other symbols, words or distinctive marks without consent, whenever such resemblance may lead to confusion. The infringing party may be specifically prohibited from:

(1) using the mark on the product or its packaging;
(2) selling, marketing or otherwise stocking the products, or offering or providing services using the mark;
(3) importing or exporting or engaging in any other related activity (such as transit and deposit) using the mark; or
(4) using the symbol or mark in any business documents or marketing material.

The registered owner may forbid businesses or suppliers removing the trade mark without express consent, although he may not stop them from also using their own trade marks or distinctive symbols or marks. No prior consent is required for third parties who act in good faith to use the full name and address of the registered owner or other information regarding type, quality, quantity, purpose, value, geographical source, time of production of the products or services or other characteristics of the products, provided that they do not use the trade mark. The registered owner may not prohibit third parties from using it when it is required to show the purpose of a product or service, particularly in the case of accessories or spare parts, or whenever it is used in good faith for industrial or commercial purposes.

When an owner makes his application for registration he had the right to the provisional protection of the trade mark, and he will be entitled to reasonable compensation from any third party who uses the trade mark during the application period if its use would have been prohibited if the trade mark had already been registered.

¶1216 Remedies

Both civil and criminal remedies are available to a registered owner of a trade mark. Civil remedies include injunctions, damages, measures to put a stop to the infringement, such as withdrawing from the market all products, packages, containers, marketing material, stickers or other documents which infringe the trade mark, and publishing the court decision at the expense of the defendant by way of announcements and notice to the parties involved, if the court so requires.

Damages may comprise actual losses or lost profits due to the trade mark infringement. Lost profits may be calculated with regard to the profits the owner could have earned had the infringement not occurred; those which are obtained wrongly by the infringing party; or those which are equivalent to the price which the infringing party should have paid to the owner for a licence to use the trade mark legally.

The limitation period for trade mark actions in the civil courts is five years from the date the owner has the right to bring a claim, which runs from the date he has knowledge, or ought to have had knowledge, of the infringement. Recoverable damages include only those incurred during the five-year period before the date the claim is made. Therefore, it is up to the owner to take timely action within the given period in order to ensure that any damage suffered before exercising the claim is included. This may have particular importance in cases where a substantial period of time exists between the beginning of the infringement and the moment the owner has, or can reasonably be expected to have, knowledge of it. Trade mark actions are subject to all the usual requirements regarding jurisdiction and procedure set out in the 1986 Patent Law.

¶1217 Trade mark property rights

Independently of any transfer of all or part of a company's assets, trade marks and trade mark applications are freely transferable by any means permitted by law. In respect of transfers or liens, trade mark applications and the resulting registered trade marks cannot be separated, although they may be owned by two or more persons jointly. Trade marks may be licensed for the whole or part of the products or services covered by them and may apply throughout Spain or in certain regions only. Licences may be exclusive or non-exclusive.

A trade mark may be given as a guarantee or be mortgaged. It may also be attached or charged in the execution of a court judgment.

In order for a transfer or licence or other dealing in the trade mark to be effective *vis-à-vis* third parties, they must be in writing, registered in the Spanish Patent and Trade Mark Office, and published in the Official Gazette for Patents and Trade Marks. In 1988 Trade Mark Law sets out all the necessary requirements for applications to register dealings, and the procedure and notice requirements for third parties, and provisions for annulment, expiry and waiver of trade mark rights.

¶1218 Collective, warranty and international trade marks

(1) Collective trade marks

Trade associations for producers, manufacturers, businesses or persons providing services may apply for a collective trade mark. The application must include its proposed use, the persons authorised to use it, the requirements for membership of the association, the terms and conditions for using the trade mark, and the reasons for refusing its use to any member of the association. A collective trade mark may not be transferred to third parties.

(2) Warranty trade marks

A warranty trade mark is the symbol or distinctive mark which guarantees certain basic standards, such as quality, component parts and the source of the products manufactured or distributed, or services rendered by persons under the control of the owner of the trade mark. The trade mark application must set the standards established for the product or services, including quality, components, source and any other relevant aspects, as well as methods of quality control and penalties for non-compliance.

Warranty trade marks do not include references to the origin of wines and other alcoholic beverages.

(3) International trade marks

Spain is a signatory country of the 1891 Madrid Convention (*Arreglo de Madrid*) concerning the international registration of trade marks. This Convention provides a simplified filing procedure for trade mark applications. Registration and the effects of these trade marks continues to be governed by national law.

According to the Convention, a national trade mark application may be expanded into an international application for various countries, provided such countries are signatories to the Convention. The international procedure is carried out by the World Organisation for the Intellectual Property (WIPO). WIPO receives the international application and publishes it in an official gazette ('*Les Marques Internationales*'), and thereafter each designated country for an international trade mark employs the registration procedure provided under its national law.

¶1219 Trade names and titles of establishment

A trade name is the name by which an individual or company is identified as a business, and which distinguishes it from identical or similar businesses. A trade name may be a family name, a firm name, a corporate name, an imaginary name, a name referring to the corporate purpose, an anagram, or any unusual or distinctive combination of the signs, words or names mentioned above.

Trade names are protected under the Paris Union Convention. When the trade name is also used as a trade mark of the product or service, separate registration is required. A trade name may only be transferred if it is part of a transfer of the whole of the business and assets to which it relates.

A title of establishment (*rótulo*) is one which is normally displayed outside the place of business, showing the location of the establishment and distinguishing it from other identical or similar businesses. A title of establishment may consist of the same names, imaginary or real, anagrams or combination of trade names as mentioned above. Titles of establishment are registered in the municipality stated in the original application. Only one title of establishment may be registered for any one business, and a fresh application must be filed for any subsequent registrations. The specific regulations for trade names and titles of establishment are supplemented by trade mark law.

¶1220 Unfair competition

The 1988 Spanish Trade Mark Act also governs unfair competition, recognising that some of its effects are similar to trade mark infringements. The legal definition of unfair competition is stated in general terms as 'all acts which are contrary to the fair regulation of business or trade custom', and cites the following as examples of unfair competition:

(1) all acts capable of creating confusion on the part of the public regarding the business, the products or the commercial activities of a competitor;

(2) false statements made in the course of business to discredit a competitor, its products or business;

(3) all false or untrue statements regarding the nature, the manufacturing procedures, the characteristics, the use or quantity of the products;

(4) the direct or indirect use of a false or misleading statement regarding the source of a product or a service, or regarding the identity of a producer, manufacturer or trader;

(5) the direct or indirect use of a false or misleading statement of origin, or an imitation statement of origin, even if it is the true origin of the

product, using a translated statement of origin or using it together with expressions such as 'type', 'form', 'copy' or the like.

The same legal actions applicable to infringement of a trade mark apply to unfair competition.

¶1221 Industrial models and designs

Industrial models and designs are intellectual property rights granted to protect the industrial exploitation of the aesthetic form of a product. Industrial models apply to three-dimensional designs, and industrial designs apply to two-dimensional designs.

Until the 1986 Patent Law and the 1988 Trade Mark Law came into force, the 1929 Industrial Property Law governed all aspects of intellectual property rights. The 1929 Law remains in force in respect of industrial models and designs only. The procedure is very similar to the procedure relating to utility models. The rights, however, are similar to those accorded to trade marks. The rights to industrial models and designs last for ten years and may be renewed every ten years indefinitely. Quinquennial fees must be paid in order to keep those rights in force.

COPYRIGHT

¶1222 Works protected by copyright

The 1987 Copyright Law protects all original literary, artistic, or scientific creations published through any transitory or intransitory means. Protection is also given to the original title of a piece of work, if that also is original. Computer software may also be protected (see Chapter 13 (Computer Law)).

The rights of creators of original works, translations, adaptations, revisions, up-dates, annotations, compendia, summaries, extracts, musical arrangements and other variations of and additions to a literary, scientific or artistic work may all be protected. Collections of works of other authors, such as anthologies, or compilations of certain subject matter or information requiring some intellectual effort in the selection or organisation of material, are also protected. Expressly excluded from protection are all laws, legal decisions, statutes, bills at any stage of their legislative history, rules and regulations, rulings, and all other Acts, agreements, and deliberations, including official translations, issued by public institutions.

Any original work enjoys the protection of copyright law as soon as it is created and published. There is no need for it to be registered. The Spanish National Copyright Office (*Registro de Propiedad Intelectual*) created under the previous law still exists, but registration is entirely optional.

¶1223 Authors

A copyright is held by the author of the work. The law defines an author as an individual who creates a literary, artistic or scientific work. Only under exceptional circumstances may a company be deemed to be an author. Unless proved otherwise, the author is deemed to be the person appearing as such in the work. If the work is published anonymously or under a pseudonym, the copyright is attributed to the person who publishes the work until the author reveals his identity.

(1) Co-authors

Co-authors are those persons who collaborate in the creation of a work. The consent of all co-authors of a work must be obtained before it may be published or modified. Co-authors may individually profit from their respective contributions to the work, provided that this is not to the detriment of the other co-authors in respect of the work as a whole.

(2) Collective works

A collective work is one created through the initiative and co-operation of an individual or company, and which is edited and published under that individual's or company's name. It is composed of the combined contributions of a number of authors, all of which together make a single edition, with no individual contributor having any claim or right over the overall work. Rights over a collective work, unless agreed otherwise, are exercised by the individual or company which edits or publishes it.

(3) Compound works

A compound work is a work which incorporates a pre-existing work. A compound work does not necessarily imply the collaboration of the first author, but his consent is required.

Works created by persons in the course of their employment give rise to special circumstances, dealt with separately in Chapter 11 (Labour Law).

¶1224 Content of rights

An author will generally have moral rights and exploitation rights over his work.

(1) Moral rights

Moral rights are personal and may not be transferred or waived, except as set out below. The author may:

(a) decide whether the work is to be published and in what form, or decide if such publication should be made under his real name, a pseudonym or anonymously;

(b) demand recognition as the author of the work;

(c) demand that the integrity of the work be respected, preventing any modification, alteration, or any other attempt to change or distort the work, his legitimate interests or his reputation;

(d) modify the work, having regard to any rights acquired by third parties, as well as withdraw it from the market in the event of a change in his intellectual or ethical convictions, indemnifying holders of any rights to profits;

(e) obtain access to a unique or rare copy in the possession of a third party in order to exercise the right to publish or any other right related to the work.

Upon death of the author, those appointed by him or, if none, his heirs may continue to exercise the rights listed under items (b) and (c) above for an indefinite period of time, and exercise the publishing rights to the work for 60 years after his death.

(2) Exploitation rights

Exploitation rights include, *inter alia*, the rights to reproduce, distribute, publish and broadcast the work. Exploitation rights are exclusively the author's, although in practice they are usually assigned to third parties. Nevertheless, the author maintains the right to publish his works as part of a selected or complete collection. Any assignment of some or all of the exploitation rights must be made in writing. The author or his assignees may protect their rights through the courts.

Rights of exploitation may be mortgaged, although they may not be attached; earnings and profits may be garnisheed.

¶1225 Duration of exploitation rights

Exploitation rights are enforceable throughout the life of the author and for 60 years after death, or declaration of death if the author is anonymous. If a work is published for the first time posthumously, exploitation rights will survive for a total of 60 years from the date the work is first published, provided that publication occurs within 60 years of the author's death. In the case of co-authors, the 60-year period begins upon the death of the last co-author. In the case of a collective work, this period commences upon publication. If the work is published anonymously or under a pseudonym, or if the identity of the author is unknown, rights will last for a total of 60 years from the date of first publication.

¶1226 Limitations of rights

A work may be reproduced without the prior authority of its author if this is done during judicial or administrative proceedings, for private use (as long as the copy is not for collective use or profit-making purposes), or for use by the blind when the work is reproduced into Braille or a similar language. The law allows for fragments or quotations from other works to be incorporated into a work, if done solely for analytical, critical, educational or academic purposes. Articles and other works concerning current affairs which appear in the media may be reproduced, distributed and published by similar means, citing the source and author, provided that no express reservation of rights has been made and that this does not preclude the author's right to compensation. The author or his assignee may not object to reproductions made by museums, libraries, record libraries, newspaper libraries or public archives, if they are made for research purposes.

Authority to broadcast includes simultaneous transmission by cable within the authorised geographical zone, but it does not include transmission via satellite without the express consent of the author.

¶1227 Other related rights

(1) Actors, musicians and other performers

Prior written authority from actors, musicians and other performers, and stage or orchestra directors is necessary for the publication or reproduction of their performances. If the performer is under contract, this right is deemed to belong to the producer, unless agreed otherwise. This right is enforceable for 40 years after the date of publication, broadcast or recording of the performance.

The right to oppose any change or rearrangement of the performance which may be detrimental to the prestige or reputation of the performer is retained throughout the life of the performer. Upon the performer's death, his successors retain this right for a further period of 20 years. Prior authority must be given by the actors or performers in order to dub a performance given by them in their native language.

(2) Sound recordings

The producer of a sound recording is the individual or company which has taken the initiative and responsibility to make such a recording for the first time. The producer has the exclusive right to authorise the reproduction of the recording, to distribute copies, and to authorise any broadcast thereof. This right is enforceable for 40 years from the date of broadcast, or production, if never broadcast.

(3) Audio-visual recordings

The producer of an audio-visual recording is the individual or company who has taken the initiative and responsibility to record a sequence or series of images, with or without sound, whether or not it may actually be classified as an audio-visual work.

The consent of the producer is required for the reproduction, distribution or broadcast of an audio-visual recording. The producer also has the right to use photographs made during the filming or recording. These rights are enforceable for 40 years from the date the recording is first broadcast, or produced, if never broadcast.

(4) Radio stations

Radio stations have the exclusive right to authorise the retransmission, the recording, or the visual or sound reproduction of their broadcasts or transmissions. This right is enforceable for 40 years.

(5) Still photographs

The photographer has the exclusive right to authorise the reproduction, distribution and publication of a photograph, even if the photograph does not meet copyright requirements. This right is enforceable for 25 years after the date the photograph was taken.

(6) Editorial works

Editors of unpublished works have the same rights as an author, except that such rights last for only ten years after the date of publication.

¶1228 Protection of copyrights

Infringement of copyrights may result in criminal prosecution, with penalties varying from a fine to imprisonment, depending on the circumstances of the case. A claim may also be made through the civil courts, where proceedings may be expedited and injunctions are available.

¶1229 Protection of foreign authors' rights

Foreigners who are entitled to the same protection as Spanish citizens include:

(1) those habitually resident in Spain; and

(2) those who, although not habitually resident in Spain, publish the work

in Spain before publishing it abroad, or publish the work in Spain within 30 days of its first being published abroad. This notwithstanding, the Government may limit the protection afforded to citizens of countries which do not provide sufficient protection to Spanish authors in similar circumstances.

In any event, rights established by international treaties and conventions to which Spain is a signatory are protected; in the absence of such treaties, foreign authors are entitled to the same rights as Spanish authors on the basis of reciprocity. The moral rights of all authors, regardless of their nationality, are recognised in Spain.

13 Computer Law

¶1301 Protection of computer programs

Spanish legislation providing protection of intellectual property is still in its infancy. The 1987 Copyright Law, the 1988 Trade Mark Law and the 1986 Patent Law replace nineteenth-century codes, which through time and technological progress had become completely outdated.

The 1987 Copyright Law dedicates a series of articles to computer programs. The general provisions of the 1987 Copyright Law apply to those aspects not expressly covered in these articles.

The definition of a computer program under the 1987 Copyright Law is substantially the same as found in other countries. A computer program includes all sequences of instructions or indications used, directly or indirectly, in a computer system to perform a function or to obtain a given result, irrespective of its form of expression or fixed support. By definition, therefore, program codes are covered by the Copyright Law. The 1987 Copyright Law goes on expressly to give technical documentation and users' manuals the same protection it gives to computer programs. Subsequent versions of a program, as well as derivative programs, are also protected.

Exploitation rights of a program are protected for 50 years from 1 January of the year following its publication, or creation, if no publication was made.

An author may not prevent a licensee holding the exploitation rights from making or authorising the making of subsequent versions or derivative programs, unless otherwise agreed. Assignment of the right to use the program is understood to mean that the holder of the exploitation rights over a computer program authorises another to use it, but reserves all proprietary rights over it.

Unless proven otherwise, the right to use a program is non-exclusive and non-transferable, and it is presumed that the intention is solely to meet the needs of the user. Copying a program, including for personal use, requires the authorisation of the holder of the exploitation rights, with the exception of the back-up copy.

Passing the program into the internal memory of the computer by the user for his own purposes is not deemed to be copying. This provision of law, however, does not override any agreement between the parties to provide notification thereof to the holder of the exploitation rights. For the purposes of the 1987 Copyright Law, a user may adapt a program for his exclusive use without that being considered a transformation (translation or other modification which results in a different work). Rights to a computer program, as well as to subsequent versions, may be registered, if so desired, in the Intellectual Property Registry.

Due to the relative newness of the legislation, Spain has little or no case law, doctrine, or other legal commentary on the subject of the legal protection of computer programs. Protection of specific aspects of computer programs which give rise to issues which have not yet been directly dealt with in Spain, such as the concept of 'look and feel', computer screens and sequence, structure and organisation, must be argued on interpretations of the law as yet untested. Precisely because of this, the reaction of the Spanish courts to the new legislation and in light of ever-evolving modern technology should prove to be of great interest. Early court decisions will give guidance to judges and lawyers and allow those directly concerned, both software owners and copiers, a clearer view of the legal parameters.

¶1302 'Look and feel'

'Look and feel' infringement occurs when the infringer captures the overall 'concept and feel' of the owner's program. In other words, 'look and feel' refers to the perception of the program from the user's standpoint. The 'look and feel' would consist of the windows, pull-down menus and, in general, the user-friendliness of the program itself. It includes audiovisual components such as display windows, text and pictures on the screen, and functional components such as the performance of a specified function when the user presses a specific key on the keyboard.

In order to proceed with the analysis of the potential protection of the 'look and feel' in programs, it should be noted that different program codes (the program code is the various sets of instructions which together perform the desired function or obtain the desired result) may create the same 'look and feel' of a program. Because of this the justification and test for the protection of 'look and feel' cannot go through the traditional channels of the copyright laws, i.e. through the test of substantial similarity in the program codes. Protection must therefore be looked upon from a different perspective.

'Look and feel' is more an idea than the expression of an idea. It is a general principle in copyright law that ideas are not protectable, although the 1987 Copyright Act does not expressly state, in contrast with, for example, the United States Copyright Act of 1980, that copyright protection does not extend to ideas, concepts or methods of operation.

The result of copying, for instance, the audio-visual or functional components of a program, without copying the actual code, is no more than the creation of a derivative work without the consent of the owner of the original program. However, a definite answer to the protectability of 'look and feel' has not yet been given. In all likelihood, a uniform policy will be difficult to establish, and decisions and reasoning may vary substantially on protectability of 'look and feel', just as has occurred in the United States. The following should be considered when evaluating the chances of securing protection for the 'look and feel' of a computer program:

(1) Ideas are not protectable, only the expression of ideas. Copyright infringement cannot be claimed just because one program performs the same function as another, i.e. it expresses the same idea although by different means.
(2) Whether the ideas behind the expression are inseparable from the expression. If there are limited ways of expressing one idea, then such expression is not protected by copyright.
(3) A study of the parts of the program which are similar or identical, in order to establish whether the expressions used are necessary to achieve the specific purpose of the program and, if so, are not protectable. Therefore, if similarities of two programs are found in the necessary expressions, infringement cannot be claimed.
(4) A study of the user interfaces of the original and similar or allegedly identical computer programs, in order to establish whether slavish copying has occurred.
(5) If the copy bears substantial enhancements, then a claim for infringement weakens considerably.

'Look and feel' has traditionally been excluded from copyright protection, although there are some signs that an effort is being made to bring it within the scope of legal protection. Limiting protection to the literal copying of the program code, thus ignoring 'look and feel' questions, would permit a copier to benefit unfairly from the intellectual work of a copyright owner. On the other hand, granting copyright protection to the 'look and feel' of the program would result in granting copyright owners monopoly rights over ideas and methods, an area which has been traditionally reserved to patents and subject to a different set of criteria.

'Look and feel' and other similar issues bring to light the continuing debate as to whether computer programs should be included at all under copyright law as literary works. As in many countries where the controversy as to which area of law is most appropriate for the protection of computer programs (e.g. patents, trade secrets, copyright or unfair competition) has been dealt with, the solution may be to address specific issues applicable to computer programs in a separate law. Even though copyright law satisfies to a greater degree the needs of computer programs, when compared to all other alternatives, a specific law on the subject would plug the loopholes, thereby eliminating the need and difficulty of stretching the more traditional copyright principles in order to offer protection to computer programs.

¶1303 Sequence, structure and organisation

'Sequence, structure and organisation' was defined in the United States case, *Whelan & Jaslow* [3rd Circuit, 1986], as 'the manner in which the program operates, controls and regulates the computer in receiving, assembling, calculating, retaining, correlating and producing useful information, either on a screen, print-out or by audio communication'.

Sequence, structure and organisation take up a substantial part of the time required to create a computer program, much of which is identifiable in charts, designs, and logistical material. From a technical point of view, this part of the creation of a program, together with flowcharts, designs and notes, forms a part of a package of technical information. In this respect, the 1987 Copyright Law, when defining the subject matter of the computer programs protected, includes the program codes, the package of technical information, and the user's manual, thus arguing in favour of protection.

However, looking at already-tested laws of other jurisdictions with more experience in this area of the law, such as the United States, 'look and feel' and the issue of sequence, structure and organisation tend to be handled together in an interrelated context, applying the same underlying legal considerations.

¶1304 Computer screens

As in the case of 'look and feel', different codes can result in very similar, if not identical, screens. The 1987 Copyright Law does not, therefore, afford protection to screens.

Once again, copyright protection will have to be based on non-traditional grounds. A primary consideration is the originality of the screen. If the computer screen only shows functional and utilitarian ways to achieve a given result, copyright protection is not available. On the other hand, protection can be given to computer screens as a graphic or design where the display shows graphic elements, or as a compilation where the display shows information arranged in a particular way.

In order to protect the design or information contained in the computer screen, at least one of following conditions must be met:

(1) the design or information must not be vital to obtaining the general result of the program (necessary expression of an idea is not protectable);

(2) the screen must contain enhancements to software standards; or

(3) the screen must contain original arrangements of symbols and/or data.

¶1305 Microcodes

A microcode is the interface between software written in machine language and the hardware operation. It controls the data flow into the hardware. Microcodes are contained in the memory device of the machines, known as ROM.

For reasons of convenience, microcodes are stored in a fixed device and consequently defined by many authors in various countries as 'firmware' and not software, thus excluding them from copyright protection. Although this particular approach has been seen elsewhere, this does not prevent microcodes from falling within the legal definition of computer programs under Spanish law. Microcodes are therefore legally protectable in Spain.

¶1306 Databases

Databases are capable of protection under Spanish law. Technically, databases are nothing more than compilations of data, namely the selection, arrangement and systematisation of data electronically stored, all of which constitute an intellectual work and are subject to the protection granted to all literary works.

Databases, however, also involve an additional problem, namely the rights of the authors, if any, of the various works contained in the databases. The information contained in databases may be divided in three broad categories:

(a) standard bibliographical data, such as the name of the author, title, year and place of publication;

(b) complete texts of copyrighted works;

(c) analytical summaries or extracts of copyrighted works.

Consequently, with the exception of the first category, databases require, upon their creation, consent from the authors of the works for potential users to retrieve all or part of the information stored in the database.

¶1307 Ownership of programs

The author of a program may be an employee or an independent consultant. In either case, the question of ownership of a given development is governed by the terms of the contract between the author and the entity engaging the author's services.

In Spain the terms of a contract cannot govern the moral rights of the author (see also ¶1224(1)). Moral rights, such as the recognition of authorship and the prohibition of any modification, deformation or change to the detriment of the author's interests and reputation, are not, as a matter of law, subject to negotiation between the parties. Moral rights always remain with the author. Thus, all references to ownership made in this paragraph refer only to the exploitation rights of the software.

In the absence of contractual provisions where the author is an employee, ownership of the software passes to the employer. By law, the employer may only use such software in the course of the employer's regular business. The use of software created by the employee for purposes other than the employer's regular business will require the employee's prior consent.

Where the software has been created by a consultant and there is no governing contractual provision, the software is deemed to be owned by the person or entity engaging the services of the consultant.

¶1308 Computer programs and patents

The 1986 Patent Law expressly excludes computer programs from the scope of patent law. None the less, the 1987 Copyright Law permits the patentability of computer programs if they form part of a product that is patentable or otherwise protected as a utility model. In this way, computer programs are increasingly being protected. Computer screens and icons, however, cannot be patented, either as an industrial design or as a utility model.

¶1309 Trade secrets

A computer program may be deemed to be a trade secret. Protection of trade secrets in Spain is currently afforded only by contractual agreement between the parties, although it is envisaged that in the near future legislation dealing with unfair competition will be introduced in Spain, which will provide greater protection of trade secrets.

¶1310 Software and criminal law

At the same time as the 1987 Copyright Law was passed, the Spanish Criminal Code was modified, making copyright infringement a crime.

A copyright infringement occurs when the reproduction, copying, distribution, public disclosure or transformation of software or databases is both intentional and done without the prior consent of the copyright owner. Importation, exportation and storage of software without the consent of the author or the holder of the copyright is also deemed to be a crime. The penalty is a fine of 30,000 to 600,000 pesetas.

In the event that copyright infringement is done for profit, the fine imposed on the infringement of the author's right of disclosure of the work or the usurpation of the author's recognition as author varies from 50,000 to

1,500,000 pesetas, together with imprisonment for a term of between one month and a day, and six months.

Furthermore, if the copyright infringement is carried out for a profit, and the number of illicit copies produces severe economic harm and/or the damages caused are otherwise significant, the penalty may reach a fine varying from 50,000 to 3,000,000 pesetas, imprisonment of between six months and a day and six years, plus the inability to engage in activities related to the crime for a period of two to five years. The court may also order that the business involved in the illicit activity be temporarily or permanently closed down. Bringing a criminal action does not prevent the owner of a copyright from bringing a civil action simultaneously or subsequently.

14 Advertising and Consumer Protection

ADVERTISING

¶1401 The General Advertising Law

Advertising in Spain is governed by the 1988 General Advertising Law ('the Advertising Law'), which replaced legislation dating back to 1964 which had fallen into disuse. The Advertising Law is intended to harmonise Spanish legislation with EEC advertising law. In addition to the provisions of the Advertising Law which govern all advertising in Spain, radio or television advertising must be specially authorised and is subject to statutory provisions which incorporate the standards set by the Spanish Radio and Television Council.

The Advertising Law sets out those measures the media and advertisers must take to protect the public. The media must distinguish between advertisements and other information transmitted to the public, and advertisers must unequivocally make known the advertising nature of the message. Nevertheless, advertisers have the right to control how their advertising campaigns are carried out, and the advertising industry is largely self-regulated.

¶1402 Restrictions on advertising

Advertisements which are detrimental to the dignity of the individual, to constitutionally recognised values and rights (especially those relating to children, young people and women), or which are misleading, unfair or subliminal are unlawful. It is also unlawful to use subliminal advertising with techniques intended to influence the public subconsciously, and there are also restrictions on advertising certain products, goods, activities or services.

¶1403 Misleading advertising

(1) Spanish law

Advertising is deemed to be misleading if it in any way misinforms the consumer and causes him to modify his spending pattern, or if it withholds basic information about goods, activities or services, if such an omission misleads the consumer. Advertising which injures, or is capable of injuring, a competitor is also misleading. An advertisement is looked at as a whole, with particular attention given to the characteristics of the goods, activities or services (which are set out in the Advertising Law in great detail); the full price, estimated price, or way of determining the price; the terms and conditions of purchase, use and delivery of goods or services; the basis of the offer; the advertiser's background, qualifications and rights; and after-sale services.

(2) EEC Directive

The Advertising Law has harmonised Spanish law with EEC Directive 84/450, which mainly governs advertising which distorts competition and which is against the interests of consumers. The EEC Directive refers to misleading advertising only; the harmonisation of unfair advertising laws is to be dealt with at a future date. The EEC Directive is short. After setting out its terms of reference, it defines advertising as 'the making of a representation in any form in connection with a trade, business, craft or profession in order to promote the supply of goods or services, including immovable property, rights and obligations'.

'Misleading advertising' is defined as 'any advertising which in any way, including its presentation, deceives or is likely to deceive the persons to whom it is addressed or whom it reaches and which, by reason of its deceptive nature, is likely to affect their economic behaviour or which, for those reasons, injures or is likely to injure a competitor'.

The EEC Directive requires member States to provide legal provisions under national law, allowing a party with a legitimate interest to take legal action against misleading advertising or bring the advertiser before a competent and impartial administrative authority to resolve the complaint or initiate legal proceedings. The administrative authority or the courts must have the power to order cessation of the advertising or to institute appropriate legal action to order the cessation of the misleading advertising, or, if imminent but not yet published, order the prohibition of, or institute proceedings for the prohibition of, the misleading advertising.

Member States must also provide for an expedited administrative or legal procedure with an interim or definitive effect. The EEC Directive sets out penalties which may be imposed on an advertiser who has produced a misleading advertisement, for example the text of the decision must be published or broadcast in whole or in part or it may order the publication or broadcast of an advertisement correcting the misinformation.

¶1404 Unfair advertising

Advertising may be considered unfair if, by its content, presentation or distribution, it discredits, denigrates or directly or indirectly disparages a person or a company, its products, services, or activities. Advertising is unfair if it leads to confusion with other businesses, occupations, products, names, trade marks or other distinctive marks of competitors. This would include the unlawful use of the name, acronym, or trade mark or distinctive mark of another company or institution. It may also be deemed to be unfair if it is generally contrary to acceptable practice in the trade.

Comparative advertising is allowed in Spain, provided that products or services are truthfully compared on the basis of essential, similar and objective characteristics. Products or services may not be compared with others which are dissimilar, unknown, or which have only a limited share of the market.

¶1405 Restrictions on advertising certain products

Advertisements for health products and other products, goods or services which may endanger the health and safety of persons or property are subject to special regulations. Advertisements for gambling, games of chance or card games are also subject to specific regulations and/or subject to prior authorisation. The principles of fair competition and possible harm to competitors are taken into account in the authorisation process. Refusal of an application for authorisation must be soundly based on reason. The rule of silent approval applies, which means that if no refusal or other form of notice is given by the Government within the specified period, the authorisation is deemed to have been granted. Non-compliance with these special regulations is deemed to be a violation under the General Consumer Law (*Ley General para la Defensa de los Consumidores y Usuarios*) and the General Law Relating to Health (*Ley General de Sanidad*).

Tobacco advertising and advertising alcoholic drinks with more than 20 per cent alcohol content (10° proof) on television is prohibited. The Government has the authority to extend the television ban on advertising alcoholic drinks to drinks of less than 20 per cent alcohol content. Tobacco and alcohol may not be advertised in places where their sale and consumption are banned. Other forms of tobacco and alcohol advertising are regulated, and strict regulations govern the advertising of tranquillisers, drugs and medications for the use of persons and animals.

¶1406 Agreements

The Advertising Law governs all advertising agreements and lays down standard terms. If the Advertising Law is silent on a particular point, then EEC law applies. Typically, contracts are made between a client and an advertising agency (either or both of which may be called the 'advertiser'), and between advertisers and the media, which sell units of advertising space or time. In general, advertising agreements must not include clauses which limit the liability of, exonerate or impute liability to, a third party. Clauses which directly or indirectly guarantee the effectiveness of any advertisement or a specific result are void.

(1) Advertising agencies

An advertising agency contracted to create, prepare, plan or execute advertisements on behalf of a client incurs certain liabilities under the law. Any ideas, information or material supplied by the client may only be used for the purpose stated in the contract. If an advertisement does not meet the terms and conditions of the agreement or comply with the client's instructions, the client may demand a reduction in the fee, a total or partial repeat of the advertisement under the terms agreed, or a rescission of the contract and the return of all fees paid, and compensation (*indemnización*).

Similarly, if the client unilaterally and without good reason rescinds the contract or fails to perform in full his part of the contract, the agency may demand compensation.

(2) The media

The Advertising Law regulates the dissemination of the advertisement through the media. If the publisher or broadcaster publishes or broadcasts the advertisement with alterations or defects and it is not possible to repeat it, the advertiser may demand a fee reduction and compensation for damages. Except in the case of an act of God (*force majeure*), if the advertisement is not broadcast or published, the advertiser may either demand that it is broadcast or published at a later date on the same terms agreed, or rescind the contract and demand a refund. In either case compensation must be paid to the advertiser.

If the failure to advertise is caused by the advertiser, then the advertiser is liable to pay compensation to the advertising medium and to pay the fee in full, unless the units of time or space have already been filled, wholly or in part, with other advertisements.

(3) Sponsorship
Agreements between the sponsored person and the sponsor regarding participation in the sponsor's advertising are governed by the same statutory provisions as those governing media agreements.

¶1407 Remedies

Government agencies, consumer groups, individuals or companies demonstrating a right or legitimate interest may require the advertiser to retract or rectify an unlawful advertisement. A written demand for retraction must be made before legal action is taken and may be made at any time while the advertisement is being shown. The demand must be in such form as to prove the date, receipt and content thereof, either by certified letter, return receipt requested, or through a notary. If the advertiser agrees to retract the advertisement, he must formally notify the requesting party within three days and proceed to withdraw the same within seven days. If the advertiser refuses or does not rectify the advertisement within the specified time, the applicant may take the advertiser to court, showing that he has demanded retraction or rectification in the above form.

Disputes resulting from unlawful advertising are settled in the ordinary civil courts using a simple and quick procedure called '*menor cuantía*', with certain distinct features laid down by Spanish law. For example, the court may make provisional orders, such as a temporary withdrawal or ban of the unlawful advertisement. The judgment may include remedies, such as allowing the advertiser a specified period of time to delete the unlawful parts of the advertisement, ordering the retraction of the advertisement, definitively banning the unlawful advertisement, publishing the judgment, in whole or in part, at the cost of the advertiser, or requiring an amendment or correction of the unlawful material. These specific provisions do not exclude the possibility of taking other civil, penal or administrative action, including an action for fraud or misleading advertising brought by a government agency or consumer group.

¶1408 Self-regulation

The International Chamber of Commerce approved an International Code of Fair Practice in Marketing, which regulates advertising, market research and sales promotion. In addition, the Spanish advertising industry has adopted a code of professional conduct.

In 1977 a corporation/limited company, 'Autocontrol, S.A.', was set up in Spain. Its shareholders are advertising agencies, advertisers and the media. Membership is entirely voluntary, but once one becomes a member, the standards and penalties imposed by the Legal Committee and the Advisory

Council must be observed. In addition to the internal structure, consisting of the shareholders and a board of directors, it is supervised by a General Board (*Dirección General*), a Legal Committee, and an Advisory Council.

The Legal Committee examines cases and issues rulings, and may impose penalties for violations or failure to act. It may also make recommendations and is available for consultations. The Legal Committee investigates numerous individual cases each year and publishes 'Autocontrol News' (*Noticias de Autocontrol*), summarising its main rulings. It may also issue opinions on advertising campaigns which have not yet been launched and draw up guidelines for professional, ethical and fair practice in advertising.

An action before the Legal Committee may be initiated at the instance of the injured party or on the initiative of the Director General, who also investigates cases brought before the Legal Committee. The advertiser is informed of the claim and has 15 days in which to prepare his defence. The Director General gathers evidence and puts the case before the Legal Committee to be decided. The board of directors is then informed of the outcome, notifies the parties and supervises the enforcement of the judgment. Decisions are appealed to the board of directors within a period of ten days from the date of notification. The board of directors then has 15 days to decide the appeal. Actions may be initiated against non-members, and although the decisions are not binding on the non-member advertiser, the members of Autocontrol, S.A. are obliged not to do business with that party.

In addition to these functions, the board of directors approves advertising standards such as the General Regulations (1979), which set out the functions of Autocontrol, S.A., regulations for advertising relating to children (1979), alcoholic drinks (1979), cosmetics and perfumes (1981), and others.

CONSUMER PROTECTION

¶1409 The General Consumer Protection Law

In 1984, a General Consumer Protection Law ('the Consumer Law') was passed for the first time in Spain in response to the provisions of the 1978 Spanish Constitution. The Consumer Law evidences the growth of consumerism in Spain and the interest of the Government in establishing minimum standards and guarantees for goods sold. Until the Consumer Law was passed, consumers enjoyed protection only in certain specific sectors of the economy. The only laws which existed in Spain applied to anti-competitive practices, unfair competition, market domination, hire purchase (instalment sales), and construction and insurance contracts. Consumers in Spain now have a greater assurance of obtaining the goods and services they need in the best possible condition and, if necessary, the legal machinery to obtain redress. The Consumer Law also serves to prevent fraud and to prevent sellers from imposing excessively burdensome conditions on the consumer.

The Spanish Constitution obliges the Government to guarantee the health, safety and economic welfare of consumers, to promote consumer information and education, and to encourage the creation of consumer groups or associations in order to allow consumers to play a greater part in consumer affairs.

The Consumer Law defines a consumer as any individual or company who is the ultimate buyer or user of personal or real property, products, services or activities, regardless of whether the seller, supplier or producer is a public or private entity, acting alone or collectively. The consumer, therefore, not only has rights in respect of goods bought or services rendered, but also in respect of public services which do not provide him with the quality of service he may expect.

Products, activities and services available to consumers must not involve any risk to health and safety, except those which are generally accepted as normal and foreseeable. The manufacturer or distributor of the product or service must inform the consumer of any foreseeable risks in the normal use of a product or service, their implications and how to avoid them. It then becomes the responsibility of the consumer to avoid those risks. In particular, the Consumer Law:

(1) prohibits the use of any additive which is not expressly authorised by the Ministry of Health and Consumer Affairs;

(2) prohibits stocking and storing prohibited products in places where food or drink is produced, processed, stored or transported;

(3) sets out requirements regarding the control of toxic or poisonous substances. All products which contain toxic or caustic substances must be safely packaged and must visibly display appropriate warnings concerning the risks of handling;

(4) prohibits door-to-door sales of food and beverages, although this does not affect delivery, distribution or supply of goods purchased or ordered by consumers in commercial establishments authorised to sell direct to the public;

(5) prohibits the sale or supply of packaged goods which do not display a food hygiene registration number on their packaging, labels, bottle stoppers or seals.

(6) requires the effective withdrawal or suspension of any product or service which does not comply with current regulations, or which involves a foreseeable risk to health and safety;

(7) prohibits the use of materials in housing or public buildings likely to involve a risk to health and safety;

(8) requires the proper packaging and sealing of all pharmaceutical products. Packaging and information sheets must list the ingredients, indicate appropriate uses and any adverse effects, give directions for use and the date of expiry of the product. The intention is to improve information for medical practitioners and to promote the health of the general public and, in particular, the safety of children.

Other regulations designed to protect the health and safety of consumers include the Spanish Code of Foodstuffs (*Código Alimentario Español*), standards for the labelling of packaged foods, chemical products, textiles and pharmaceutical products, and regulations governing the advertising and consumption of tobacco and alcohol.

¶1410 Basic consumer rights

The Consumer Law attempts to correct the unequal bargaining power of companies in the marketplace in respect of individual consumers.

(1) The contract

The offer, promotion and advertising of products, activities or services must not be misleading. Companies must also ensure that any clauses, conditions or stipulations made in connection with the offer, promotion or sale of goods and services are expressed clearly and simply, so that they are easily understood without the need to refer to other material not made available to the consumer at the time of entering into the contract. At the same time the seller must give the consumer a receipt or other proof of sale.

The contract must be made in good faith and consideration must be fair. Abusive clauses or conditions imposed on the consumer are void. These include those which treat the consumer in a disproportionate or inequitable manner by increasing prices for additional related services or other financing terms, deferment of payment or surcharges, or indemnities or penalties which do not relate to the services provided; provide an absolute limit on the liability of the seller; force the consumer to waive any of his legal rights; or force him to purchase complementary goods or merchandise, or unsolicited accessories. Clauses which are valid but nevertheless put the parties in an inequitable bargaining position may render the contract void. The Consumer Law also provides that the consumer should be given the opportunity to satisfy himself of the nature, condition and use of the goods or services, and allows him to make a claim for any defects or deterioration and/or request his money back.

(2) Guarantees

All consumer contracts must contain a guarantee in favour of the consumer, containing the subject matter of the guarantee, the company giving the guarantee, the person who is to enjoy the benefit of the guarantee and his rights, the length of the guarantee period, and an express statement that during the guarantee period the consumer has the right to:

(a) have the product repaired so that it is totally free from the original flaws or defects and damage incurred by such defects; or

(b) a replacement if the original is not satisfactorily repaired; or

(c) a refund.

In the case of durable goods, in addition to the guarantee, the consumer has the right to a repair service (*servicio técnico*) and replacement parts for a specified period of time.

(3) Consumer affairs offices

All consumers have the right to information. On the one hand, the consumer has a right to be provided with information about the essential characteristics of goods, products and services. At minimum this means information regarding origin, nature, composition and use, quality, quantity, common name, full or estimated price, date of production, supply, recommended 'sell by' date or date of expiry, as well as instructions for correct use or consumption and warnings as to foreseeable risks.

On the other hand, the consumer also has a right to be informed and advised on consumer affairs. To this end the Consumer Law provides for the creation of information offices and services. These offices may be public or private entities and offer information, assistance and guidance to consumers for the proper exercise of their rights. They also receive and register complaints or claims, or direct parties to the place where their problems can be resolved. They provide consumers with information on research, reports, analyses or quality control testing done on goods and services, as well as information regarding government authorisations or goods which have been withdrawn from the market because of possible risk and danger to public health and safety.

(4) Consumer groups

Consumers have the right of assocation. The Consumer Law provides for consumer groups or associations to represent the interests of their members. These groups may concern themselves generally with consumer affairs or limit their focus to certain products and services. In order to enjoy the powers allowed by law, these consumer groups must be registered at the Registry of the Ministry of Health and Consumer Affairs (*Registro del Ministerio de Sanidad y Consumo*). They have the right to be heard in any proceedings relating to draft legislation directly affecting consumers.

(5) Government agencies

Consumers have a right to be protected. The Consumer Law imposes a direct obligation on the Government to protect the consumer, and therefore the Government is required to adopt and establish appropriate means of placing the consumer in a stronger position. In addition to consumer affairs offices and information services, public agencies organise public information campaigns, carry out quality control testing, and give the consumer the opportunity to compare terms, conditions, availability of replacement parts, and repair and maintenance services. They also investigate consumer complaints.

In cases of serious harm to the consumer, the Spanish government may delegate its administrative powers to a special agency to work with representatives of the autonomous regions in order to guarantee public health and safety, serve the interests of affected parties, and redress damages.

¶1411 The most important consumer regulations

(1) Retail advertising and marketing

Retailers must put individual price stickers on all merchandise offered for sale, or otherwise communicate the price to the consumer. The sale price must state the total amount payable, including all taxes and duties (e.g. VAT). It is an administrative violation to charge more for an item than advertised or to charge the higher price when more than one price has been advertised.

(2) Textiles, labelling, and composition

Textiles which are offered for sale must bear a label clearly identifying the seller, manufacturer or importer, his tax identity number, and the composition and origin of the material. The label must be sewn on the garment, stamped on the product, or appear on the packaging. Non-compliance with these requirements constitutes an administrative violation.

(3) Invoicing

Businesses and professionals must issue an invoice for all transactions. Invoices also serve the purpose of correctly recording income and deductions to the tax authorities. Failure to comply with this requirement is deemed to be a minor violation.

(4) Household appliances

The Consumer Law requires that whenever household appliances are sold, a repair service and replacement or spare parts must be made available. A written estimate must be given for all repair services, unless expressly waived by the customer. Repairs carried out are guaranteed for a minimum period of three months. Claim forms must be made available to customers, as well as basic information in respect of services rendered.

(5) Dry cleaning and leather goods

All establishments which provide dry cleaning, laundry and services for repairing and dyeing textiles, leather, furs and synthetic fabrics must give the customer a receipt when the garment or garments are handed in. This receipt should give as much information as possible concerning the company, the customer and the garment in question. Those providing such services will be liable for any damage caused to the goods whilst in their care, with certain exceptions.

(6) Jewellery and precious metals

All products made with precious metals sold in Spain must meet certain standards directly related to the proportion of the weight of the pure precious metal to the alloy. As a guarantee that such standards have been met, the products must bear hallmarks, unless this is impossible because of the size or design of the article.

(7) Spanish Foodstuffs Code

The Spanish Foodstuffs Code (*Código Alimentario Español*) sets minimum standards in respect of food for human consumption, such as basic standards of preparation, preservation, packaging, distribution, transport, advertising, and consumption.

(8) Labelling, presentation and advertising of packaged foodstuffs

Packaged foodstuffs sold direct to the public must be labelled, advertised and presented in such a way that leaves no doubt as to the nature, composition, quality, quantity, origin, general treatment to which it has been subjected, or any other essential information. The Consumer Law prohibits anything being printed on the inside of the packaging which comes in contact with the food.

(9) Tobacco

The rights of non-smokers are considered more important than the rights of smokers in those places or under those circumstances where non-smokers are affected. Smoking is thus restricted in certain places. Current legislation also regulates points of sale and sales to persons under 16 years of age. In addition to administrative actions, violations may give rise to civil and penal liability.

¶1412 Remedies

The consumer has a right to be compensated for damage arising from the use of goods, products or services, as long as such damage is not due solely to his own negligence. The manufacturer, importer, vendor or supplier of goods and services is usually liable for damage suffered by a consumer due to original defects or lack of fitness of the product or service.

In the case of bulk goods, the liable party is the last holder of the goods or services. In the case of packaged goods, labelled or sealed goods, the liable party is the one mentioned on the label or packaging or in the advertising.

Liability for damages caused by defects also includes those actions where the standards or representations of purity, efficiency and safety which the consumer may reasonably expect are not met; this in particular applies to foodstuffs, hygiene and cleaning products, cosmetics, pharmaceutical products and medicines, health services, gas and electricity, household electrical goods, lifts, means of transport, motor vehicles, toys, and other products designed for children.

Producers or sellers of consumer goods which cause damage or injury will be discharged from liability if they can show that they have fulfilled with due care and diligence all the conditions and requirements set out in the regulations.

(1) Violations

In addition to the remedies available in the civil or penal courts, all violations of the Consumer Law may be subject to administrative sanctions and fines. The Law sets out four major groups of administrative violations in consumer affairs:

(a) *Health-related*. This group includes, *inter alia*, non-compliance with health requirements, and acts or omissions which involve real risk of injury to the health of consumers, whether done knowingly or through neglect or failure to take the necessary precautions. It also includes non-compliance with or deviation from specific preventative measures issued by health authorities.

(b) *Violations affecting specific consumer protection laws*. This group covers alteration, adulteration or fraud relating to goods or services for consumption. This includes adding or extracting any substance or ingredient, or otherwise changing the composition or quality of the product. Also included is non-compliance with requirements relating to the nature of goods, warranties, mending or repairing durable goods, which misleads or confuses the consumer or hides the true nature or condition of the product or service. This heading also includes non-compliance with the rules of registration, labelling, packaging and advertising of goods and services, and violations regarding business transactions, conditions of sale and retail prices, and charging higher prices than authorised by law for services rendered or failing to comply with the specifications or regulations relating to prices and profits margins.

(c) *Violations affecting non-meat foodstuffs*. This group specifically includes violations in respect of food and agricultural products, such as lack of documentation or authorisation, and failure to comply with other instructions issued by the Government.

(d) *Other violations*. This group includes violations relating to consumers, including acts of resistance or reprisals which impede or delay inspections by government agencies.

(2) Penalties and fines

Violations are classified as minor, serious and very serious, depending on such factors as risk to health, the seller's position in the marketplace, the amount of benefit obtained, whether or not the violation was intentional, the negative effect, type and purpose of the violation, and whether it is the first or only violation.

The Government may impose fines ranging from 500,000 pesetas for minor violations to 100 million pesetas for very serious violations. For serious and very serious violations, the penalty may exceed the maximum and be up to five times the value of the goods or services involved. In cases of very serious violations, the Council of Ministers may close the business for a period of up to five years. Additionally, the adulterated, spoiled, falsified, fraudulent or unidentified merchandise may be confiscated.

¶1413 Complaints and claims procedure

If the consumer comes across situations which may affect his health or safety, or if he has reason to believe he has been defrauded or misled or goods or services supplied to him do not reach the standards set by health and safety regulations, then he may invoke the complaints procedure provided by the Consumer Law. There are a number of specific legal procedures set out in the Consumer Law, some of which complement each other and may be instituted simultaneously, and others which are exclusive.

If the claim is for monetary compensation, the action should be brought in a civil court in ordinary proceedings (*procedimientos ordinarios*). Criminal offences are dealt with direct by the criminal courts.

Administrative recourse may be taken either alone or at the same time as another civil action. These actions are brought to request the Government to take the measures necessary to redress wrongs, protect the rights of the injured party, and/or penalise the offender. A claim must be brought within five years after the violation is committed and should be made to the branch of the municipality or regional government where the consumer lives. A claim may also be brought to consumer groups or associations, the National Institute for Consumer Affairs (*Instituto Nacional de Consumo*), and/or any other authorised consumer agency or body in the regional governments. If a claim requests a penalty or other measures and redress of injury, such a request must be brought before an agency authorised to make inspections and issue penalties.

There is no specified form or method of bringing a claim, which can be made in person, in writing, or by telephone to any authorised agency. Usually the claim is in writing and includes the identity of the claimant, the basis of the claim and the specific request of the claimant, together with photocopies of all supporting documentation. Normally, a copy will be stamped and returned to the claimant as evidence that he has presented his claim, together with the relevant documents.

A consumer may include his evidence in the original claim or make a separate request for an inspector to intervene. The function of the inspectors is to investigate, gather facts, and file a report which can be used as the basis of proceedings. The inspectors may take samples and conduct expert analyses which will determinate whether violations have occurred, and may confiscate the merchandise if it is likely that such a penalty would ultimately be imposed on the seller.

The Consumer Law also provides for mediation or arbitration. This is an attempt to bring the parties together to try to reach some form of amicable agreement. Any settlement reached by means of this informal arbitration procedure is binding on the parties. Arbitration is not available in cases of poisoning, injury or death, or where there is evidence of a criminal offence. Arbiters may be sector representatives or come from consumer organisations and authorised public agencies. An arbitration award does not prejudice any punitive measures which the Government may impose on the seller.

15 Competition Law

¶1501 Introduction

The 1989 Competition Law ('the 1989 Law') embodies the general spirit of the Spanish Constitution concerning protection and defence of competition, and harmonises Spanish law with EEC regulations regarding restrictive trade practices and unfair competition.

The 1989 Law addresses three different types of market practices: prohibited practices, mergers and acquisitions, and state subsidies.

¶1502 Administrative bodies

The 1989 Law authorises three bodies under the Ministry of Economy and Finance:

(1) The Court for the Protection of Competition (*Tribunal de Defensa de la Competencia*) ('the Court'). The Court has exclusive jurisdiction over matters governed by the 1989 Law. It is strictly an administrative court, and all its decisions are subject to review by the Chamber for Administrative Matters of the Supreme Court.

(2) The Bureau for the Protection of Competition (*Servicio de Defensa de la Competencia*) ('the Bureau'). The Bureau brings cases before the Court, ensures that the decisions of the Court are enforced, and maintains the Registry of Restrictive Practices. It also studies and researches the level of competition in the economic sectors and co-operates with foreign and international institutions.

(3) The Registry of Restrictive Practices (*Registro de Defensa de la Competencia*) ('the Registry'). The Registry is maintained by the Bureau and is where the decisions, agreements, recommendations or practices which are authorised by the Court, and mergers and acquisitions which might be deemed to be restrictive to trade, must be registered.

¶1503 Prohibited practices

(1) In general

Any agreement, decision or collective proposal is prohibited which impedes, restricts, distorts, or is intended to impede, restrict or distort, competition in the national market or in a particular sector thereof.

Certain practices are specifically prohibited and are deemed to be null and void, and the agreements, decisions or collective proposals relating to them are therefore invalid.

A parent company is held liable for any activities of its subsidiaries which are deemed to be prohibited practices. These prohibited practices include:

- (a) direct or indirect price fixing, or imposing commercial or service terms and conditions;
- (b) restricting or controlling production, distribution, technical development or investments;
- (c) dividing up the market or supply sources between two or more businesses;
- (d) applying different conditions to the same type of business or service transactions to the detriment of competitors;
- (e) requiring that a party to a contract accept additional goods or services which are not related to the subject of the contract, either by their nature or by trade custom.

(2) Abuse of dominant position

The 1989 Law prohibits any abusive exploitation of a dominant market position in the national market or in a sector thereof by one or more businesses.

Any of the following acts will be deemed to be abuse of a dominant position:

- (a) directly or indirectly imposing unfair prices or any other commercial or service terms and conditions;
- (b) limiting production, distribution or technological development to the detriment of consumers and industry;
- (c) unjustified refusal to satisfy demand for either goods or services;
- (d) applying different conditions to the same type of business or service transactions to the detriment of competitors;
- (e) subjecting the performance of a contract to the acceptance of supplementary services which are not related to the subject matter of such contracts, either *per se* or by trade custom.

Even if a company or group of companies has been authorised by law to hold a dominant position in the market, the provisions of the 1989 Law will nevertheless prevail and apply to them.

(3) Unfair competition

In certain cases where freedom of competition is exercised abusively and the public interest is affected, the Court may intervene. Unfair competition legislation is expected to be enacted in 1990.

¶1504 Mergers and acquisitions

(1) Voluntary notification

The parties involved may voluntarily notify the Bureau before the merger or acquisition occurs or within three months of the date of the merger or acquisition.

Voluntary notification before the merger or acquisition does not postpone the merger or acquisition, unless it is opposed by the Government. Proposed legislation exists to ensure that any notification remains confidential.

The authorities must be given notice of the nature and effect of the transaction, in particular:

(a) information identifying the business concerned;

(b) balance sheets of the company or group of companies concerned, and their respective market shares.

(2) Government approval

Details of any proposed or actual merger or take-over bid (OPA) of one or more businesses by an individual, company or group of companies must be sent by the Minister of Economy and Finance to the Court, if it affects the Spanish market and creates or reinforces a dominant position, whenever a market share of up to 25 per cent of the Spanish market of specific goods or services is being acquired or increased, or whenever the total amount of sales in Spain of the parties involved together exceeds 20 billion pesetas in the previous accounting years. Details must also be given of the form and development of the transaction and the legal and financial situation as a result of the transaction.

The Court will issue an opinion to Ministry of Economy and Finance, paying particular attention to the definition of the relevant market and its structure, the possibility of choosing suppliers, distributors and consumers, the economic and financial power of the parties, supply and demand, and competition from abroad.

The Court must consider the positive contribution which the proposed merger or acquisition may make to improve production or distribution, to increase the international competitiveness of national industry or to benefit the consumer.

After due consideration by the Ministry of Economy and Finance, the case is presented by the Ministry to the Government, which has a three-month period to decide whether or not to oppose the operation, or to impose additional conditions on the transaction.

¶1505 State subsidies

The Court may examine any subsidies from public resources given to companies, and their effect on competition, if so requested by the Ministry of Economy and Finance. Once the Court has issued its opinion, the Ministry may propose the withdrawal or modification of a subsidy and the adoption of measures to re-establish competition.

During the period in which the Court is reviewing the matter, it may ask the companies for any additional information about any state subsidies or financial benefits which have already been granted.

¶1506 Authorised practices

(1) Authorisation of prohibited practices

Prohibited practices may be authorised under certain circumstances. In general, any agreements, decisions or proposals will not be deemed to be prohibited practices if specifically allowed by law. Similarly, the Court may propose that such laws permitting prohibited practices be eliminated or amended.

Prohibited practices arising from any decision, proposal or agreement may be authorised by the Court if they fall into the following broad categories:

(a) practices which contribute to improve production or distribution of goods and services or which promote technical and economic progress, provided that consumers reap adequate benefit, the restrictions are essential to the above objectives, and the practices do not allow any party to eliminate competition in a substantial part of the market in the goods or services in question;

(b) prohibited practices which can be justified by the general economic situation and public interest, and which fulfil one or more of the following requirements –

  (i) they defend or promote exports,

  (ii) they increase demand, in the event that there is a general downward trend in demand,

(iii) they improve the economic and social level of depressed geographical areas or economic sectors,
(iv) they do not significantly affect competition due to their size.

The Court authorisation sets out the date on which it takes effect, the term for which it is valid, and the obligations, modifications or changes to be made. The authorisation is renewable upon the request of the interested parties.

(2) Exemptions
The exemption rules (*reglamento de exención*) allow the Government to authorise any proposals, agreements or decisions if:

(a) only two companies impose restrictions on distribution or supply of goods for sale, or which relate to acquisition or use of intellectual or industrial property rights or industrial secrets;
(b) the purpose of the practice is the uniform production or application of a certain type of process or research and development; and
(c) the purpose of the practice is to improve the competitiveness of business, especially small and medium-sized businesses.

¶1507 Sanctions

(1) Injunction
Before imposing a penalty, the Court may issue an injunction (*requerimiento*), notifying those parties indulging in prohibited practices to cease the practices and eliminate the harmful effects thereof.

(2) Penalties
Sanctions (*multa coercitiva*) may consist of a fine of up to 150 million pesetas. A further penalty of up to 10 per cent of total sales volume, in the financial year immediately before the Court's decision, may also be imposed.

If the party at fault is a company, the Court may impose an additional fine of up to 5 million pesetas on its legal representatives or members of the board of directors participating in the agreement or decision. Any legal representative or director who voted against the decision or who did not attend the board meeting in which the decision was made will not be subject to this fine.

The facts the Court may consider when fixing the fine are the following:

(a) the form and extent of the restriction on competition;
(b) the size of the market affected;
(c) the market share of the party at fault;

(d) the effect on the competitors, other parties and consumers;
(e) the duration of the restriction on competition;
(f) whether the prohibited practices are repeated.

(3) Fines

In addition to the above, the Court may impose periodical fines of between 10,000 and 150,000 pesetas for the purpose of preventing a prohibited practice.

(4) Damages

No matter what penalty is imposed by the Court, damages may be claimed by those who have suffered damage by the unlawful practices. Applicable law and procedure are contained in the Civil Code and the Civil Procedure Law.

16 The Spanish Judicial System

JURISDICTION

¶1601 Overview

Jurisdiction and choice of law are primary questions in any litigation involving parties or subject matter from different countries. The first consideration is whether a Spanish court has jurisdiction or competence to hear the matter.

If the action is to be brought in Spain, the second consideration is to identify the subject matter of the claim. The courts are divided into four general areas of competence, based on subject matter: civil (including commercial), criminal, administrative, and labour. If the claim does not fall into a specific category, then the case will usually be referred to the civil courts.

The third consideration is to ascertain which court should hear the case at first instance. If a civil matter, this depends on the matter and amount of money involved.

The fourth question is where in Spain the case should be heard. This depends on the territorial jurisdiction of the courts and the agreement of the parties. In the absence of any agreement, the provisions of the Civil Procedure Law apply.

The final consideration concerns the court where pre-trial or post-trial proceedings, such as execution of the judgment, may be heard. As a general rule, the court which hears the main action will also hear pre-trial and post-trial proceedings.

¶1602 Jurisdiction of Spanish courts

(1) Civil law and contractual matters

The 1985 Judiciary Law ('the 1985 Law') sets out in detail the matters over which Spanish courts have jurisdiction. The general rule is that the defendant's country of residence has jurisdiction. Spanish courts have exclusive jurisdiction over the incorporation, validity and dissolution of Spanish companies, registrations at public registries, Spanish real property rights, and the recognition and enforcement in Spain of foreign judgments. Unless otherwise agreed between the parties, Spanish courts retain jurisdiction over such matters as contracts made in Spain (between Spaniards, between foreigners, or between Spaniards and foreigners) or to be performed in Spain and actions for torts which are committed in Spain.

In a contract which is valid under the law of the country where it is executed, the parties may agree to submit to the jurisdiction of Spanish courts or they may choose another jurisdiction having some relationship to the agreement, unless it is a matter in which the Spanish courts have exclusive jurisdiction. A valid jurisdiction clause must clearly specify one jurisdiction which is to govern the contract. If more than one jurisdiction is specified, the clause will be void. The clause must also expressly waive any rights or privileges entitling any of the parties to the protection of other jurisdictions. A jurisdiction clause specifying the Spanish courts is only enforceable if one of the parties is a Spanish citizen or entity or the underlying matter has some connection with Spain. If there is no jurisdiction clause, then the rules of the 1985 Law and of private international law, as set out in the Spanish Civil Code, are applied.

(2) Labour matters

Spain's labour laws are protective of the worker, and this affects the jurisdiction accorded to the labour courts, which differs from the norms applied to the civil courts acting in civil matters. Jurisdiction is decided on the basis of the place of execution of the employment contract and the place of performance.

The labour courts have jurisdiction if the employee is a Spaniard and the employment contract is executed in Spain, or, in the case of a seaman, if the offer to join ship is made in Spain. The Spanish labour courts also have jurisdiction if the employer and the employee are Spanish, even if the contract is executed and/or performed abroad. Moreover, if a foreign entity enters into an employment agreement with a Spaniard which is to be performed in Spain, the Spanish labour courts have jurisdiction.

¶1603 Choice of applicable law

Under certain circumstances, Spanish courts may apply foreign law to civil or commercial matters brought before them. Spanish courts will not apply foreign law unless requested by one of the parties, who then must prove to the court the applicable provisions. This issue arises most frequently in the following types of matters:

(1) *Contractual obligations*. Unless agreed otherwise, the national law common to both parties applies. If there is no common national law, then the law of the country where both parties habitually reside applies. In the last resort, the law of the country where the contract is to be performed governs the contract.

(2) *Employment contracts*. If there is no express agreement in the contract, it will be governed by the law of the country where the contract is to be performed.

(3) *Torts and similar non-contractual obligations*. The law of the country where the tort occurred applies.

(4) *Real and personal property*. Property rights are governed by the law of the country where the property is situated, although this does not apply to goods in transit, aircraft, vessels, or railways.

(5) *Trade marks and patents*. Trade marks and patents are protected in Spain by Spanish law.

(6) *Securities*. These are governed by the law of the country where the security is issued.

(7) *Execution proceedings*. If a judgment must be executed abroad, then the law of the country where the judgment is to be executed governs.

¶1604 Organisation of the courts

The 1985 Law and the implementation bill approved in December 1988, provide for the reorganisation of the Spanish court system.

(1) The Constitutional Court

The Constitutional Court is the guardian of the Constitution and a check on the actions of the executive and legislative branches.

(2) The Supreme Court

The Supreme Court (*Tribunal Supremo*) is the highest court in Spain in all but constitutional matters. The Supreme Court has four chambers: civil, criminal, administrative, and labour. It is an appellate court, although it may serve as a court of first instance in civil or criminal actions against the highest public officials for acts performed in their official capacity, and for challenges to decisions of the Council of Ministers.

(3) The National Court

The National Court (*Audiencia Nacional*) is a court of first instance with exclusive jurisdiction in matters of overriding national interest. The court has three chambers: (i) criminal, which hears such actions as crimes against the

Crown, currency counterfeit and extradition proceedings; (ii) administrative, where challenges to acts of ministers and secretaries of state are heard; and (iii) labour, where actions regarding nationwide collective bargaining agreements are heard.

(4) The Superior Court

The 1985 Law abolishes the former Territorial Courts and provides each autonomous region with a Superior Court (*Tribunal Superior*) to serve as a court of appeal. The Superior Court is divided into three chambers: one for both civil and criminal, administrative, and labour. It is the highest court for matters expressly reserved to the governments of the autonomous regions by the Constitution, such as local commerce, industry, agriculture, housing and welfare, roads and highways. Judgments of the Superior Court may only be appealed to the Supreme Court.

(5) Provincial courts

The 1985 Law provides for the existence of one provincial court in each provincial capital. Sections of this court may be opened in other provincial cities, as necessary.

(6) Courts of First Instance

Before the 1985 reforms, the Courts of First Instance (*Juzgados de Primera Instancia*) and Courts of Instruction (*Juzgados de Instrucción*), the District Courts (*Juzgados de Distrito*) and the Justice of the Peace Courts (*Juzgados de Paz*) heard civil and commercial matters at first instance. The 1985 Law abolishes the District Courts. The Courts of First Instance hear most civil cases, and the Courts of Instruction hear criminal cases only. The Justice of the Peace Courts are the lowest courts within the court system.

(7) Labour courts

Under the 1985 Law the separate labour courts and the Central Labour Court are phased out, and the Courts of First Instance for labour and social matters hear most labour disputes. Appeals are made to the Superior Court's labour chamber, and subsequently to the labour chamber of the Supreme Court.

(8) Administrative courts

In matters directly involving the State, administrative remedies must be exhausted before court action may be brought. Among the most important administrative courts in Spain are the Tax Courts, the Courts for the Protection of Competition, and the Administrative Claims Courts (*Tribunales Económico-Administrativo*). The Central Administrative Claims Court (*Tribunal Económico Central*) is the central administrative appeal court, which also sits in first instance for specific matters involving the Ministry of Economy and Finance, Social Security, and the autonomous regions.

¶1605 Choice of forum

Unless otherwise agreed, forum will be chosen in accordance with the provisions of the Civil Procedures Law. For example, in contractual claims, the case is heard in the court nearest to where the contract was to be performed; in personal property actions, the court nearest to the defendant's home or office address; and in real property actions, the court nearest to the place where the property is situated.

TYPES OF PROCEEDINGS

¶1606 Civil and commercial proceedings

Many different types of proceedings are available under Spanish law, depending on the type of claim and relief sought. The following is a summary of the general types of proceedings available, although the list is by no means exhaustive.

(1) Proceedings for provisional remedies

These types of proceedings are used in anticipation of a subsequent court action, either to maintain the status quo or to block an owner's right to dispose of or act upon property. These provisional measures are available in order to ensure that, in case of the positive outcome of the future action, the effective value of the remedy sought is not lessened or eliminated. The most common measures are:

(a) *Injunctions (interdictos)*. There are various kinds of injunctions to recover or retain possession, to prevent new construction, and injunctions against maintaining buildings in dangerously deteriorated conditions.

(b) *Attachment (embargo preventivo)*. This proceeding is used in respect of cash debts or debts in kind. Its purpose is to limit, to a greater or lesser extent, the right to dispose of or act upon all or part of the debtor's assets, or a particular asset, so that the outcome of declarative or executory proceedings is not frustrated.

A petition for attachment may be made prior to filing a complaint or thereafter. If made before proceedings have been initiated, the complaint must be filed within 20 days thereafter. In order to be granted, the following requirements must be met –

(i) the petition must include a document evidencing the debt;
(ii) the debtor must be a non-resident foreigner; or,
(iii) if a Spaniard or a resident foreigner, he has no known address, owns no real property or agricultural, industrial or commercial premises in the place where he can be sued for the payment of the debt; or
(iv) if there is a known address or he owns property, he has disappeared from his home address or office premises, leaving no one in charge; or
(v) if someone is left in charge, that person does not know his whereabouts, or conceals his whereabouts; or
(vi) there is reasonable cause to believe he will conceal or squander his assets to the detriment of his creditors.

If the document presented adequately proves the plaintiff's right, attachment is available.

(c) *Attachment of the property in litigation (aseguramiento de bienes litigiosos)*. Rather than independent proceedings, these are ancillary to proceedings in which the ownership of mines, mountains (*montes*), plantations, or industrial and manufacturing premises are claimed. The object is to request judicial intervention in the administration of the property in litigation.

(d) *Miscellaneous*. Other measures of this type include: those taken for missing persons (*ausentes*) or a request for temporary maintenance (*alimentos provisionales*).

(2) Ordinary declarative proceedings

Ordinary declarative proceedings (*procedimientos ordinarios declarativos*) are used to resolve most civil and commercial claims, and are classified according to the value of the claim.

(a) *Large claims (mayor cuantía)*. These are claims for 100 million pesetas or more and for actions for defamation and the protection of a person's dignity and honour. These claims must be brought before a Court of First Instance.

(b) *Lesser claims (menor cuantía)*. These are medium-sized claims between 500,001 and 100 million pesetas, and unliquidated claims. These claims must be brought before a Court of First Instance.

(c) *Claims of recognition (cognición)*. These are smaller claims between 50,001 and 500,000 pesetas. They must be brought before a Court of First Instance.

(d) *Oral claims (verbal)*. These involve small claims of 50,000 pesetas, and must be brought before a Court of First Instance. If the amount involved is 5,000 pesetas or less, the claim is heard by a Justice of the Peace (*Juez de Paz*).

(3) Special proceedings

Some of the most important types of special proceedings (*procedimientos especiales*) are:

(a) executory proceedings (*juicio ejecutivo*);
(b) those relating to urban and rural leases;
(c) those relating to the rights of the family, including divorce and judicial separation;
(d) those relating to the law of succession (*derecho sucesorio*).

(4) Universal executory proceedings

Universal executory proceedings (*juicios universales de ejecución*) include:

(a) proceedings to make arrangements with creditors (*quita y espera*);
(b) agreements for the suspension of payments;
(c) proceedings for a creditors' meeting (*concurso de acreedores*); and
(d) bankruptcy proceedings.

¶1607 Criminal proceedings

Criminal proceedings may be special or ordinary. Special proceedings are available for such matters as the impeachment of members of Parliament, judges, magistrates and police officers, actions for defamation, and crimes against a person's fundamental rights.

¶1608 Administrative proceedings

The Administrative Procedures Law sets out model proceedings, to be followed where there are no specific administrative proceedings applicable to a particular matter. Certain matters are referred to administrative courts with express jurisdiction, such as tax courts and competition courts.

Judgments in administrative proceedings may be appealed to a higher administrative court. Once all administrative channels have been exhausted, a party may appeal a civil court with jurisdiction in administrative matters by way of a contentious administrative appeal (*recurso contencioso-administrativo*).

¶1609 Labour proceedings

Labour matters also are subject to a variety of proceedings, relating to such matters as dismissal, work sanctions, and social security claims.

CIVIL LITIGATION

¶1610 Parties, lawyers and procurators

Any individual or company may be a party to a civil action, including minors and mentally disabled persons, if represented by a guardian. Every party to an action must instruct a duly licensed procurator (*procurador*) and a lawyer (*abogado*), who may not be the same person, to represent them. Procurators must be Spanish citizens and have a law degree. They are responsible for all the procedural or administrative aspects relating to a particular case, ensuring that all court procedures are followed and time limits met. They may represent the client in court at trial but they do not argue the client's case before the judge; that is the role of the lawyer. The client appoints the procurator and the lawyers by signing separate duly notarised powers of attorney (see Chapter 3 (Business Organisations) regarding powers of attorney executed abroad).

The parties may represent themselves before the court only in small claims cases (*juicios verbales y de cognición*) or in certain special proceedings.

¶1611 The foreign party

Nationals and foreigners are treated equally under Spanish law, with the following exceptions.

(1) Capacity

A foreigner only has capacity to act on his own behalf if deemed to have such capacity both under the law of his home country and under Spanish law. If the foreigner does not have capacity under the law of his home country, a guardian must be appointed in accordance with that law.

(2) Bond for court costs

If so requested by a Spanish defendant, a foreign plaintiff must pay a bond (*caución de arraigo*) into court to guarantee payment of any legal fees and court costs for which he may ultimately be liable. However, foreign companies with assets in Spain and foreign counterclaimants are not required to pay a bond, nor is a bond necessary for appeals and certain expedited proceedings. Bond provisions do not apply if there are overriding treaties or conventions, or reciprocity.

(3) Preventative seizure

A Spanish court may order the seizure of a foreign debtor's assets before trial, depending on potential liability. In determining the amount to be seized, the court will take into account any assets of the debtor in Spain.

(4) Free legal defence

The law is silent as to whether foreigners without means have a right to free legal defence (*abogado de oficio*) in criminal matters, although it is likely that this right does extend to foreigners since Spanish law states nothing to the contrary.

¶1612 Legal fees and costs

Legal fees and court costs are usually awarded against the losing party. Court costs and other expenses are subject to official fixed rates. Legal fees, expert's fees and other expenses not subject to official fixed rates may not exceed one-third of the total 'value' of the litigation, unless the court determines that the successful party conducted the litigation recklessly. If the 'value' of the litigation cannot be quantified, it is deemed to be 1 million pesetas. In the case of an appeal of a matter decided in declarative proceedings, the general rule is that the appellant may recover all costs and legal fees if all the issues are confirmed on appeal.

¶1613 Effects and enforcement of foreign judgments in Spain

There are a number of ways in which a foreign judgment may have effect in Spain. Orders issued pursuant to such a judgment may be enforceable through the Spanish courts, in which case the ruling is said to have executory force (*fuerza ejecutoria*). A foreign judgment may also have certain collateral effects. It may bar any future consideration of the matters decided in the foreign judgment as *res judicata*. A foreign judgment may also be used as evidence in other legal proceedings.

(1) Treaties

Spain has entered into treaties regarding the execution of foreign judgments with Austria, Czechoslovakia, Colombia, France, Germany, Italy, and Switzerland. Certain multilateral treaties – the most important being the New York Convention on The Recognition and Execution of Foreign Arbitral Rulings of 1958 ('the New York Convention') and the Geneva Convention of 1961 on private international arbitration – allow for arbitral awards to be treated as judgments and executed in the same way as other foreign judgments. All foreign judgments are executed by the Supreme Court.

(2) Exequatur

If there is no applicable treaty, a foreign civil judgment is binding in Spain with the same force and effect as a Spanish judgment only after being so deemed by the Supreme Court in expedited proceedings called '*exequatur*'. In order that a foreign judgment be executed in the same way as a Spanish judgment, the country of origin must give reciprocal treatment to Spanish judgments, and the judgment must have been given in a personal action, in adversarial proceedings in which the parties had the right to be heard. The judgment must be final, with no further right to appeal or retrial, and may not conflict with the principles of public order under Spanish Law. The judgment must have been rendered in accordance with the laws of the country of origin and meet all Spanish criteria regarding legalisation or placement of an apostille.

A quicker and more direct system for the execution of judgments in EEC member States will be implemented when the Lugano Convention of 1988 comes into effect.

ARBITRATION

¶1614 Choosing arbitration proceedings

The substantial increase in the volume of litigation, and the resulting burden placed on the courts, has led to the passing of the 1988 Arbitration Law ('the 1988 Law'). Although arbitration has existed in Spain for many years, the 1988 Law simplifies the arbitration process. It also expressly precludes from arbitration family disputes, matters of public interest, or matters concerning the Ministry of Economy and Finance (e.g. tax) and employment matters, which are submitted to special labour arbitration.

(1) Arbitrations clause

First, the parties must unequivocally express in writing their intent to submit the matter to arbitration. This is known as the arbitration agreement, whereby the parties agree to arbitrate any dispute which arises, to be bound by the arbitration award, and to waive the jurisdiction of the ordinary courts. The Arbitration Court of the Spanish Chamber of Commerce suggests a model arbitration clause along the following lines:

> 'Any litigation arising from the interpretation or execution of the present agreement will be definitively resolved through arbitration by (one or more) arbitrators within the framework of the Spanish Arbitration Court, its by-laws, and the Rules of the United Nations Arbitration Commission applicable to matters of International Commercial Law.'

(2) Legal and equitable arbitration

There are two different types of arbitration, legal and equitable. Legal arbitrations deal with points of law and must be decided by qualified lawyers, whereas equitable arbitrations may be decided by any persons exercising their civil rights. The majority of arbitrations are equitable, and if there is no express condition that an arbitration is to be the legal type it is presumed that it is equitable.

¶1615 Arbitration proceedings, appeals and annulments

Arbitration proceedings must follow the procedure as set out in the arbitration agreement, or as otherwise specified by the arbitrators. There must always be one, three or five arbitrators. Where the agreement does not specify a number, three are appointed. One is appointed as chairman, whose decision is decisive if there is a tie or an abstention impeding a majority vote.

The parties may agree how the arbitrators are selected or appoint a third party to do so. If there is no such agreement, the arbitrators are appointed by a judge of first instance. The proceedings must be consistent with the right to be heard, the right to confrontation and the right to equal treatment before the law. In all proceedings the initial pleadings and relevant admissible evidence must be presented and a final argument be heard.

Unless otherwise specified in the arbitration agreement, the arbitrators have six months from the date of accepting their appointment to resolve the matter. The arbitrators must issue a written opinion, explaining the legal basis of their finding. This opinion must be signed by the arbitrators and notarised. All computation errors or ambiguities must be resolved within five days.

The arbitration award has the effect of a court judgment. The only appeal a party may make is to have it set aside or reviewed by the Supreme Court. The Supreme Court will only review the award if there are found to be irregularities in the appointment of the arbitrators or in the performance of their duties, if the arbitration award was not given during the prescribed period, if the issues in dispute should not have gone to arbitration, or if the award is contrary to public order.

Legal fees and costs are normally shared by the parties, unless there is evidence of recklessness or bad faith on the part of one of the parties.

¶1616 Execution of an arbitration award

The parties must carry out the arbitration award within ten days. If this is not done, execution proceedings may be initiated before the local Court of First Instance. If there is no pending petition for annulment, the arbitration award will be executed in the same way as any other order. Foreign arbitration awards may be executed by Spanish courts through 'exequatur' proceedings, as discussed in ¶1613(2) above.

Since 1977 Spain has been a party to the New York Convention, and the Spanish Supreme Court has given its provisions a liberal interpretation. A Supreme Court judgment in 1981 made it clear that the execution in Spain of an arbitration award made in London could only be refused on the basis of the criteria laid down in the New York Convention. The Supreme Court has confirmed its position in various other judgments that the grounds for opposition to enforcement are limited to those provided for in Article V of the New York Convention. In particular, in 1984 a Spanish defendant attempted to invoke the provisions of the Spanish Civil Code, alleging that a foreign arbitration award awarded in default was not recognisable in Spain and therefore the award could not be enforced. The Supreme Court held that default was not included as a ground for refusal of enforcement in the New York Convention.

17 Personal Business

¶1701 Introduction

Under the Spanish Constitution foreigners enjoy the same civil liberties as Spaniards, with certain exceptions, such as the right to vote and eligibility for public office. Any person who does not have Spanish nationality is nevertheless deemed to be a foreigner, with certain exceptions made for diplomatic personnel and members of international organisations covered by international law.

All foreigners who wish to visit, reside or work in Spain must comply with requirements concerning visas and residence and work permits. Work permits are discussed later in this chapter (¶1704). It is important to note that if a person intends to work during his stay in Spain he must have all three documents.

¶1702 Passports and visas

As a general rule, a foreigner who wishes to enter Spain for any reason requires a valid passport and a visa. Nationals of certain countries are specifically exempted from the need for a visa if their visit to Spain does not exceed a certain period of time. Some of the most important examples are:

(a) US citizens, up to six months;

(c) EEC citizens, citizens of South American countries (excluding Cuba) and of various other European countries, up to 90 days;

(c) citizens of certain Middle Eastern countries, up to 30 days.

(1) Types of visas

There are different types of visas which may be issued, depending on the length of stay envisaged by the applicant, and whether or not he intends to work in Spain.

(a) *Short-term visas*. These are normally granted for up to seven days for those in transit through Spain, or up to 30 days for those in Spain on business or on holiday.

(b) *Ninety-day visas*. These are granted to those who wish to stay in Spain as visitors for up to 90 days, and they normally allow the holder to leave and enter Spain three times during that period.

(c) *Residence visas*. A residence visa is required if a person intends to stay in Spain to work or reside, and is valid for up to 90 days. The holder may leave and enter Spain three times during the term of his residence visa. The type of persons who might apply for a residence visa would be, for example, employees or self-employed persons who wish to work in Spain, and those who wish to live in Spain.

This type of visa is valid for the purpose of entering the country and in order to establish residence, and should not be confused with a residence permit, which provides resident status and the legal right to remain in the country.

(2) The application

Application should be made at the Spanish Embassy or Consulate in the applicant's home country on forms available there.

The application for a visa must include the visa application form duly completed, the applicant's passport together with a photocopy, three passport-size photographs, and evidence supporting the reason given for seeking a visa (such as an employment contract or school enrolment certificate). The applicant must also demonstrate proof of means and his or her potential ability to adapt to Spanish society if deemed necessary. There is no requirement to give reasons for the refusal of a visa.

Entry into Spain will normally be refused if a person has previously been expelled from Spain, or has previously been convicted of an offence which carries a penalty of imprisonment of more than one year, or if he is known to be involved in criminal activities.

(3) Extension of visas

A visa can be extended for up to 90 days, and normally the extension is given for the same period as the original visa. The applicant must personally present his application form to the Police Headquarters or Police Station (*Comisaría de Policía*), with his passport, three passport-size photographs and proof of means, before his original visa expires. In addition, producing a train or airline ticket showing the expected date of departure from Spain may be advisable. If the extension is not granted the applicant is given a period of time in which to leave the country.

¶1703 Residence permits

(1) Non-EEC citizens

All foreigners, including EEC citizens, may only reside in Spain if they have a valid residence permit. To become a resident, a foreigner other than an EEC citizen must obtain one of the following types of residence permits. Any person seeking a residence permit with the intention of carrying on any kind of work or business must also apply for a work permit.

(a) Types of permits

(i) *Initial residence permits*. These are granted to foreigners who have not legally resided in Spain within the previous two years but who wish to take up residence there. They are usually granted for a period of one year.

(ii) *Ordinary residence permits*. These may be granted for periods of up to five years to persons who can show that they have been legally residing in Spain for a continuous period of two years immediately before making the application.

(iii) *Special residence permits*. These may be granted for up to ten years, to foreigners who can prove that they have been legally residing in Spain for more than two years continuously and who fall within certain categories. This type of permit is required for persons such as retired foreigners, persons who, because they have worked in Spain or otherwise, are entitled to receive a pension from the Spanish government, persons married to and living with a Spanish national resident in Spain or who are responsible for close relatives of Spanish nationality, or who were born in Spain or Gibraltar. Any foreigner who can establish that he has legally resided in Spain for a continuous period of over ten years will also be eligible for a special residence permit.

Applicants for an initial residence permit must already have a valid residence visa (see ¶1702(1)). In the same way, applicants for ordinary residence permits must already have an initial permit, and until a person is in possession of an ordinary residence permit he may not apply for a special residence permit.

(b) Application requirements

The applicant must submit the following documents, together with a photocopy: an application form, passport, a residence visa or ordinary residence permit, as the case may be, together with a certificate of registration at the Consulate in Spain of the applicant's home country. In addition, he must submit three passport-size photographs, and adequate proof of means, accommodation, health insurance and a medical certificate, plus a certificate of good conduct from his home country if he is a first-time applicant, or from the Spanish police. If the applicant already holds a work permit he must also present copies of all the documentation pertaining to the work permit application, and the birth and school certificates of any children studying in Spain in order to prove their relationship with and economic dependence on their parents.

All documentation must be presented personally by the applicant to the local police station (*Jefatura Superior* or *Comisaría de Policía*), the local *Guardia Civil*, or the Spanish Embassy or Consulate in the applicant's home country.

(c) Extensions and renewals

An application for an extension or renewal of a residence permit must be made at least 45 days before the original permit expires. The same documentation must be presented as for the initial application, accompanied by proof that all taxes due in Spain have been paid.

(d) Expiry, revocation and annulment

A residence permit automatically expires at the end of its term.

Residence permits for dependants under 18, which are included in the permits of their parents or guardians, expire when those dependants attain the age of 18 or cease to be under the guardianship of those persons.

A residence permit may be revoked for lack of a valid passport, means of support, insurance or adequate accommodation, or if the permit holder changes or loses his nationality, is absent from Spain for more than six consecutive months in any 12-month period, or is deported or liable to be deported.

A residence permit may be annulled if any statement made by the holder in his application is materially inaccurate, or if any of the documents presented in support of his application prove to be false.

(2) EEC citizens

(a) Types of permits

Although EEC citizens do not require a visa to enter Spain for less than 90 days, in order to remain longer one of the following residence permits is required, depending on the length of stay envisaged:

(i) *a temporary residence permit*, which is valid for three to 12 months;

(ii) *a provisional residence permit*, which is valid for up to six months and is issued while an application for a full residence permit is being processed; or

(iii) *an EEC citizen's residence permit*, which is valid for five years and is renewable thereafter.

(b) Application requirements

An application for a residence permit must be made within 15 days of entry into Spain.

To obtain a residence permit, EEC nationals must apply to the local police station in the place where they wish to reside or work. They must provide proof of their identity and nationality, a medical certificate and, if appropriate, a copy of their employment contract. Self-employed people must provide proof that they have satisfied all the requirements and applied for all the licences necessary to carry on their business or trade in Spain.

Family members of EEC citizens must be able to prove their kinship and that the EEC citizen to whom they are related is willing and able to support and assume responsibility for them. If they are not themselves EEC citizens or otherwise exempted, they must be in possession of a valid visa.

(3) Renewals

In order to renew a residence permit, application must be made to the local police station. The documentation required for renewal of a residence permit is the same as for the original application. Certain applicants have the right to automatic renewal. For example, EEC citizens who have been employed or self-employed in Spain will be granted automatic renewal of their residence permit if:

(a) at the time they cease to be employed or self-employed they have reached pensionable retirement age under Spanish law, have carried on their employment or business during the 12 preceding months, and have lived in Spain for more than three years;

(b) they cease working because of a permanent disability, as long as they have lived in Spain continuously for more than two years. However, if the disability results from an accident at work or a professional illness, proof of period of residence is not necessary;

(c) they carry on their activities in another member State after three years of continuous employment or work and residence in Spain, maintaining residence in Spain and returning there at least once a week.

The residence permits of family members of EEC citizens who have been employed and who fulfil the relevant requirements will also be automatically renewed.

(4) Refusal

Except in emergencies, if a residence permit is refused, a report is required from the General Directorate of State Legal Services (*Dirección General de Servicios Jurídicos del Estado*), and the applicant is given at least 15 days, or one month, if he is already in possession of a valid residence permit, to leave Spain. Any appeal the applicant may wish to make against the decision must be made to the local government office (*Delegación del Gobierno*), and if such appeal is refused, the applicant may appeal to the courts. The applicant will not normally be expelled from Spain pending his appeal.

(5) Validity

Although it is assumed that the holder of a residence permit will remain in Spain throughout the term of the permit, the following breaks will not affect its validity:

(a) absences from Spain of less than six consecutive months;

(b) absences due to military obligations;

(c) if the holder leaves because of illness, accident or redundancy lay-off, which is confirmed by the National Employment Institute (*Instituto Nacional de Empleo*).

¶1704 Work permits

Any person who does not have Spanish nationality and carries on, or attempts to carry on, any economic activity as a professional or an employee or otherwise in Spain, will be deemed to be a foreign worker. All foreign workers must obtain a work permit in addition to their residence visa and residence permit. No employer in Spain may use the services of a foreigner who does not possess a valid work permit.

A visa must be applied for at the Spanish Embassy of one's home country. An application for a work permit may also be made at the Spanish Embassy of one's own country, although it is usually quicker to apply in Spain at the same time as applying for a residence permit. The grant of work and residence permits depends on the local employment situation, as well as on the suitability of the individual.

¶1705 Types of work permits

There are a variety of work permits available, depending on the particular requirements of the applicant, for example whether or not he works independently or for another and the length of time he intends to work in Spain. The following is a summary of the various types of work permits granted to employees and self-employed persons.

It should be noted, however, that work permits are difficult to obtain if the applicant is unskilled or wants to work in a sector of the economy experiencing a high level of unemployment. Unemployment in Spain is very high, and unless it can be adequately shown that a job vacancy cannot be filled by a Spaniard, in most cases a work permit will not be issued.

(1) Employees

(a) Type A permit

This type of permit is normally granted to seasonal workers for a non-renewable period of up to nine months. The permit is usually limited to a specific employer, and that employer may be asked to show that he has advertised the job in the Spanish press and at the local employment office but did not find Spaniards to fill it. The Spanish labour market situation (i.e. level of unemployment) will not be taken into account if the worker does assembly work or machinery repairs or work necessary to launch a foreign company in Spain, or if the person holds a position of trust or confidence (e.g. high executives), as defined by the Ministry of Labour and Social Security. Priority is given to applicants who are descendants of foreigners who have held Spanish nationality or applicants who reside in Spain or have resided in Spain during the last five years, and spouses of foreigners holding a Type B permit which is valid for at least a year.

The permit-holder must leave Spain within 15 days of the expiry of his permit. A fresh permit will not be granted for a period of three months after the expiry of the old one.

(b) Type B permit

This type of permit is granted to those carrying on certain professional activities within a defined geographical area, usually within a certain province. In the first place, the permit will usually be limited to a specific employer and for a term of one year, although it may be renewed as often as necessary.

Other requirements, such as advertising the job in the Spanish press and at the local employment office, are the same as for Type A permits. Priority is given, *inter alia*, to applicants who were born and who are residing in Spain, spouses of Spaniards, applicants having ancestors or descendants of Spanish nationality, applicants who have held Spanish nationality in the past, applicants from Ceuta or Melilla, and spouses or children of holders of Type C permits.

(c) Type C permit

This type of permit enables the applicant to work in any kind of activity in Spain and is valid for a renewable period of five years. The applicant must already have had a work permit for more than five years, during which time he was continuously resident in Spain, or he must have had a work permit for the previous 12 months and have been resident for eight years. The five-year continuous residency rule is reduced to two years in the case of applicants from Latin American countries and Gibraltar and the Philippines.

The permit-holder's spouse and children may be granted a Type C permit once their Type B permits expire.

(d) Group permits

If a group of workers is sent to Spain to complete a particular project, a group permit can be granted for a renewable period of up to three months instead of granting individual permits to each worker.

(2) Self-employed persons

(a) Type D permit

This type of permit is valid in a particular geographical area (usually a specified province) and for a specific activity for a period of up to one year. The applicant must show that he has obtained all necessary authorisations and licences allowing him to set up and carry on his activity in Spain.

Certain applicants will be given priority; for example, those who were born and legally reside in Spain, those who have resided in Spain for the previous five years, and those who are married to and living with a Spaniard.

(b) Type E permit

This type of permit does not impose any geographical limits and is valid for any kind of activity. It is granted for a renewable period of five years, and may be granted on the expiry of a Type D permit if the foreigner can show that he is settled in Spain, has no outstanding tax or social security liabilities, and the activity is his sole occupation.

(c) Type F permit

This type of permit is given only to workers who do not live in Spain but who live close to the border and come to Spain each day, or seasonally, to work. The permit is valid for up to three years.

¶1706 Application for permits

Application for a work permit and a residence permit should be made at the same time, since both permits are issued on the same document. Applications must be made before the employee or worker starts work and should be made to the local Provincial Bureau for Employment and Social Security (*Direcciónes Provinciales de Trabajo y Seguridad Social*). If the applicant is living abroad, he should apply to the Spanish Embassy or Consulate in his home country. Applications must be made on a special form and be accompanied by the original and two photocopies of the documents required.

(1) Employee applications

The employee himself, or an employer applying on behalf of his employee, must submit the following documents:

- the employee's passport;
- his visa or application for a visa;
- a certificate of good conduct from his home country;
- the employment contract or evidence of a formal offer of employment;
- a job description;
- a summary of the activities and characteristics of the business or trade;
- a medical certificate;
- documentation which justifies giving priority or special treatment to the applicant;
- six passport-size photographs;
- registration of the business or trade with the Social Security;
- registration in Spain with the Consulate of the employee's home country.

When the permit relates to a person who is to fill a high executive position, such as a Managing Director, a notarised public deed evidencing his position or authority, together with the company's certificate of incorporation and evidence of registration in the Commercial Registry (*Registro Mercantil*), must also be submitted.

If the applicant is to be employed in a new company, a certificate of payment of transfer tax (*Impuesto de Transmisiones Patrimoniales y Actos Jurídicos Documentados*), a certificate of verification of a foreign investment and a licence to carry on such operations must be submitted as part of the application. The applicant's tax code must also be submitted.

(2) Type C permit
The documents which must be filed on the employee's behalf are as follows:

- his passport;
- a certificate of good conduct;
- the employment contract or other evidence that he has been engaged by the employer;
- six passport-size photographs;
- evidence of registration with Social Security and at the Consulate of his home country in Spain.

Additionally, the following documents must be furnished:

(a) any previous work and residence permit, and evidence of the length of time the employee has been resident in Spain;
(b) a certificate evidencing that the employee still works in the business or that he still has an employment contract, and a declaration of his income during the past year;
(c) a certificate that the business is up-to-date in its social security payments;
(d) the employee's Social Security card;
(e) a certificate stating that the employee is entitled to a Type C permit.

(3) Self-employed persons
A person who intends to work in Spain on a self-employed basis must apply for a work permit by submitting the following to the Provincial Bureau for Employment and Social Security:

- his passport;
- his visa or application for a visa to work on a self-employed basis, unless he is already resident in Spain;
- a certificate of good conduct;
- a medical certificate;
- six passport-size photographs;
- a report on his proposed investment;
- documents certifying that all the necessary authorisations and licences have been obtained for him to set up and carry on his business;
- any documents, if any, which may make him elegible to receive priority treatment.

If the applicant is in the professions and wishes to practice in Spain, he must also submit his academic diploma or degree, which must be valid in Spain, and proof of his admission to his professional association.

(4) Collection of the permit

If the application is made at the same time as an application for a residence visa, then the work permit will be granted at the same time. The applicant will be notified by post that he can collect his work and residence permits in person, accompanied by the legal representative of the business if the application was made on his behalf.

If an application for a work permit is refused, good reason must be given. Within a period of one month after notification of the refusal, the applicant may re-apply to the Provincial Bureau of Employment and Social Security. If a permit is still refused the applicant may appeal to the courts.

¶1707 The EEC system

(1) Scope of application and general matters

An EEC work permit is valid for five years, and it extends to any kind of work and any sector in Spain. EEC citizens only need a work permit if they work for someone else. If they are self-employed, they need only apply for an EEC citizens' residence permit.

The following people may apply for an EEC work permit:

(a) EEC citizens who, on 1 January 1986, were ordinarily permanently employed in Spain, involuntarily unemployed or temporarily unable to work;
(b) EEC citizens who, after 1 January 1986, were authorised to be employed in Spain for a period of one year or more (i.e. those who have a Type B work permit) when their permit comes up for renewal;
(c) the spouse of an employee in (b) above and their minor dependent children under 21 years of age;
(d) the spouse of a self-employed person and minor dependent children under 21 years of age who are settled in Spain;
(e) EEC citizens who do not reside in Spain but cross the border to work there must obtain a special work permit which is valid for five years, but which restricts them to working in the border area.

If persons under (c) and (d) above were residing in Spain before 1 January 1986, for periods of residence, documentation evidencing their period of residence may have to be shown when applying for their EEC work permit.

(2) Procedure and documentation

Applications should be made on an official form and be accompanied by the original and two copies of the following documents:

- a passport;
- Type B work permit (if applicable);
- a copy of the contract of employment and, if appropriate, a letter evidencing that the business which is to employ them still exists;
- a medical certificate;
- a certificate of good conduct;
- a declaration of income in the previous year;
- Social Security identity card;
- documents evidencing Social Security payments have been paid to date;
- six passport-size photographs; and
- any other documents requested by the authorities.

¶1708 Driving licences

The Spanish Traffic Code (*Código de Circulación*) allows foreign nationals to drive in Spain if they are in possession of a relevant international licence or a driving licence from their home country.

If the foreign national becomes a Spanish resident after a period of one year, he must convert his foreign licence into a Spanish one. To do this he must show that his licence is still valid, that it fulfils the requirements of the Traffic Code, and that he is habitually resident in Spain.

An application to convert a licence should be made to the Provincial Headquarters of Traffic (*Jefatura Provincial de Tráfico*) on a special form, accompanied by the documentation specified on the form. If there are any doubts about the authenticity of the current licence or about the fitness of the owner, he may have to take a driving test before he can obtain a Spanish licence.

An EEC citizen can have his licence converted without the need to pass any kind of test, if he becomes a Spanish resident and provided his current licence is in force and the application is made within a period of one year of obtaining residence.

Index

All references are to paragraph numbers

D

Q

R

S